SPECIAL PRAISE FOR *Acrobaddict*

"Joey Putignano tells a harrowing story of a life
redeemed at great cost. Try as you follow his words
to picture the events—for this is a movie
and must be seen to be believed."

Twyla Tharp

* * *

"You will not read a more candid book this year. Prepare to be
frightened and taken to the depths of despair and then lifted up
triumphantly. It is never too late to hit the reset button on your
life—that is what you are about to learn from Joe Putignano. He
is equally adept at taking you through the remarkable journey
of his own terrible addiction as he is in the world of acrobatics,
descending from the Cirque du Soleil big top as a human mirror
ball—the figurative spark of change in humanity.

This raw and emotional tale is a roller coaster through the
depths of addiction, tragedy, hard work, and redemption that
truly reflects Joe's spirit and determination to stay clean in
a world where he is surrounded by temptation. It is
proof that with hard work, anything is possible."

Dr. Sanjay Gupta
CNN Chief Medical Co

* * *

"*Acrobaddict* isn't just another book about someone who has been to hell and back. Rather, it brings the reader into the emotional world of the addict and the step-by-step process toward an ever-elusive recovery. What I admire about Joe Putignano's story is the way he drives the reader down the highway of life with exits of temptation along the way. Sometimes you get off on one of those exits, but in the end you find the on-ramp to recovery."

Mark Lund
Film Producer/Director

* * *

"Joe Putignano's story of survival and hope against incredible odds is compelling. Understanding what drove him to drugs and, more incredibly, how he has successfully fought and continues to fight his demons, is the 'cautionary tale' that must be shared with everyone. I have had the pleasure of photographing Joe on several occasions, and it has always struck me how his stoicism clearly translates into all his images. His has not been an easy path, but, having witnessed his bravery and fortitude of character, it is one that I find inspiring."

Mike Ruiz
Celebrity Photographer

ACROBADDICT

ACROBADDICT

JOE PUTIGNANO

CENTRAL RECOVERY PRESS

LAS VEGAS

Central Recovery Press (CRP) is committed to publishing exceptional materials addressing addiction treatment, recovery, and behavioral healthcare topics, including original and quality books, audio/visual communications, and web-based new media. Through a diverse selection of titles, we seek to contribute a broad range of unique resources for professionals, recovering individuals and their families, and the general public.

For more information, visit www.centralrecoverypress.com.

Publisher: Central Recovery Press
             3321 N. Buffalo Drive
             Las Vegas, NV 89129

18 17 16 15 14 13   1 2 3 4 5

ISBN: 978-1-937612-51-1 (trade paper)
        978-1-937612-52-8 (e-book)

Publisher's Note: This is a memoir, a work based on fact recorded to the best of the author's memory. To protect their privacy, the names of some of the people, places, and institutions in this book have been changed.

Central Recovery Press books represent the experiences and opinions of their authors only. Every effort has been made to ensure that events, institutions, and statistics presented in our books as facts are accurate and up-to-date.

Cover design and interior design and layout by Sara Streifel, Think Creative Design

FOR ANYONE WHO HAS EVER WANTED TO DIE,
WHO HAS GIVEN UP ON THEMSELVES
AND ON THEIR DREAMS.

FOR THOSE WHO HAVE STOOD IN
THE MIRROR AND THOUGHT:
I hate myself.

FOR ALL THOSE WHO HAVE BEEN
TOUCHED BY SUFFERING, PAIN,
HEARTBREAK, AND ADDICTION . . .

THIS BOOK IS FOR YOU.

TABLE OF CONTENTS

FOREWORD

I first met Joe Putignano in the fall of 2008 at the Metropolitan Opera in New York City, where he had recently been employed as an acrobat in various opera productions. I had been invited there to stage Berlioz's *La Damnation de Faust*, the story of an aging man dissatisfied with his life as a scientist who encounters Satan's envoy, Mephisto, who offers to give him back his youth in exchange for his soul. After leading Faust through the many pleasures of debauchery and the illusions of love, Mephisto deceives him and drags him down the predictable path to Pandemonium, where he is condemned to be consumed by eternal flames. In this piece, Joe played one of the acrobatic devils unleashed from the bowels of the Earth to plague the world with lustful sins; the performers were asked to defy gravity by crawling up and down the abrupt façades of the set.

At the time, little did I know about Joe's own downward spiral or the nature of the hellish lifestyle from which he had just recently emerged. The young artist I had been introduced to seemed to be a fit and healthy athletic performer with boyish looks, apparently capable of accomplishing any physical task. But his frightened eyes told a whole other story. I noticed that after rehearsals he never joined the cast for a drink, nor did he take part in any of the post-show celebrations organized by the Met. It was only much later when I mentioned this to him that he confessed to me his past tribulations with heroin and his day-to-day struggle to stay in recovery.

For the next few months, Joe and I agreed to further discuss his struggles through a series of emails. There were, of course, occasional meetings where most of the time I sat quietly as a citizen of Thrace listening to the chilling tale of Orpheus's return from the underworld and felt that this was definitely something that deserved to be shared with others.

The following year I offered Joe a chance to take part in *Totem*, a new Cirque du Soleil touring show about evolution. This time he was asked to personify the Crystal Man, a luminous entity in the shape of a human mirror ball that opens the show, contorting as he descends from the outskirts of the universe, carrying with him the initial spark that is at the origin of all life forms on our planet. On tour, Joe quickly became the spokesperson for the show and eloquently took advantage of the new public platform to tell his own personal story, inspiring many recovering addicts and giving hope to thousands of substance abusers around the world.

In the past few years I have been a privileged witness to the developmental phases of Joe's book project, and discovered quite early in the process that he was a gifted writer and a great storyteller. He paints an informed and detailed portrait of a social disease that is the direct consequence of our dysfunctional families, our flawed educational system, and a competitive culture that urges everyone to try to be number one instead of helping one find his or her own uniqueness. I truly believe the reason that Joe's story will resonate so strongly with people everywhere is that it not only speaks to our addictive natures, but has the courage to raise important existential questions about the lack of meaning and spiritual void that have become so emblematic of our Western societies.

Robert Lepage
Creative Director
Cirque du Soleil's *Ka* and *Totem*

ACKNOWLEDGMENTS

Thank you to everyone who has supported, listened, and delivered patience to this creative process. For without you, I would not have been able to do this.

Special thanks to Jonathan Nosan, for a beautiful life lived together, for your inspirational talent, and wonderful care for my book.

Thank you Robert Lepage, whose friendship and creativity have inspired me beyond words and given me the strength to persevere.

To the legendary, iconic goddess, Twyla Tharp, for your magnificence, strength, and creative force that have changed my life.

Thank you Joseph Burgess, for standing by me through my very worst and very best times.

Thank you Dr. Sanjay Gupta, for your kindness and humility, and for allowing me to get my story out to other addicts in need of help.

Thank you Matt Sloane, for your friendship, support, and trust throughout this entire process.

Thank you Mike Ruiz, for your incredible talent, kindness, and support. Thank you Scott Marrs, for your friendship and inspirational spiritual talks.

Thank you Jeff Lund, for the friendship and spiritual support.

Thank you Matt Tanzer, for your friendship, patience, and understanding throughout some of my darkest moments.

Thank you Mark Lund, for your friendship and teaching me how to network.

Thank you to Cirque du Soleil and the "Totemites," whose support, dedication, and strength have allowed me to follow my dreams and never give up.

Thank you Nancy Schenck, Eliza Tutellier, and Arnold Gosewhich, for handling my story and words with such grace, dignity, and love. Thank you for allowing me to have my many meltdowns.

And thank you to my family: Mom, Dad, Tricia, Jenn, and Michael, for loving me when I could not love myself.

PROLOGUE

Nobody could see it, could they? The people passing by . . . could they see what was happening to me? I stood on a New York City sidewalk with my eyes shut, asleep, dead, lifeless, but not falling over as the cigarette fell from my lips. *Could they see him?* I wondered. Could they see how behind me the Devil propped me up, like a doll, like a puppet, both claws under my armpits while my head slumped forward, my lips white, skin greenish pale, and the dark circles under my eyes like tiny moons from the City of the Dead? He wouldn't let go of me. I would fall asleep, and nod out, but never fall over.

Anyone who has walked around the streets of any major city has surely witnessed this before, this amazing inhuman balance of the departed: the "junkie's nod," frozen in time, about to fall, but miraculously, we continue to stand. It's an adagio I perfected over the years. Nobody knows that while we junkies stand there, fading into the nothingness, the Devil holds us close to his lips, close to his skin smelling of burnt cinnamon and ash, as he melodically whispers in our ears, "Come to me, my love; I've got you forever and ever; I will devour your soul." It's the only voice we can hear above all the others as we stand there like a limp flower about to decay. Once you hear *his* voice, you will never have a good night's sleep, or enjoy food or any other earthly thing you once took for granted, because pleasure has a new meaning, and there is only one thing that can bring it. Even if you do manage to sleep, you will only dream of him, night after night, endlessly searching for a way out, wishing you had never known of this luxury, known of this existence, and you awaken only to repeat the nightmare again.

This dance is endless, and this is what it looks like to be locked in between the margins of life and death. Once the Devil hugs you in this way you can never return, and you only learn of his deception once it's too late. If we could at least fall to the ground, it would mean that he has released his grip, waking us up—but we never wake up. We float in slow motion, hovering over ourselves in bodies that were once beautiful and drug-free. The Devil wants to keep us alive as long as he can, devouring our hearts, destroying everything and everyone we ever loved, because this is what addiction looks like. It's a one-sided romance with death, but death only comes for day visits and never brings its finality. The Reaper has a truce with the Devil, and can only come once he has taken all the light and love from us. Here is the worst part: I love him and he loves me, and this is my happiness.

"I'm not the only kid

who grew up this way
surrounded by people who used to say
that rhyme about sticks and stones

as if broken bones

hurt more than the names we got called
and we got called them all
so we grew up believing no one
would ever fall in love with us
that we'd be lonely forever
that we'd never meet someone
to make us feel like the sun
was something they built for us
in their tool shed
so broken heart strings bled the blues
as we tried to empty ourselves

so we would feel nothing

don't tell me that hurts less than a broken bone
that an ingrown life
is something surgeons can cut away
that there's no way for it to metastasize

it does

she was eight years old
our first day of grade three
when she got called ugly
we both got moved to the back of the class
so we would stop getting bombarded by spit balls

but the school halls were a battleground
where we found ourselves outnumbered day after wretched day
we used to stay inside for recess

because outside was worse

outside we'd have to rehearse running away
or learn to stay still like statues giving no clues that we were there
in grade five they taped a sign to her desk
that read beware of dog

to this day
despite a loving husband

she doesn't think she's beautiful

because of a birthmark
that takes up a little less than half of her face
kids used to say she looks like a wrong answer
that someone tried to erase
but couldn't quite get the job done

and they'll never understand

that she's raising two kids
whose definition of beauty
begins with the word mom
because they see her heart
before they see her skin
that she's only ever always been amazing"

An excerpt of the poem *To This Day* by Shane Koyczan.
From the book *Our Deathbeds Will Be Thirsty*.

BACKFLIP

1

SACRUM

IN LATIN, *sacrum* MEANS SACRED OR HOLY. SOME RELIGIONS BELIEVE THAT THE SACRUM IS THE LAST OF THE BONES TO DECAY AFTER DEATH, AND THAT ON THE DAY OF RESURRECTION THE BODY WILL REASSEMBLE AROUND THIS HOLY BONE. IN GREEK, IT MEANS ILLUSTRIOUS, GLORIOUS, MIGHTY, OR GREAT. GALEN OF PERGAMON, A PROMINENT ROMAN PHYSICIAN, CONSIDERED THE SACRUM THE GREATEST OR MOST IMPORTANT BONE OF THE SPINE.

As the sliver of blue moon slipped behind the starlit clouds that hung in the night sky, I knew without question that I was the happiest child who ever existed. My short life of eight years had been one of wonder, curiosity, and excitement. I was in my own dimension, an explorer devouring every fragment that life shone down upon me.

At night, I heard the wind as it whispered through the dense, dark forest that guarded the back of our house. I would drift in and out of my fantasy world that was so real to me that I often forgot the reality in which I was living. My imagination was, in itself, a drug.

I owned almost every He-Man action figure ever made, and I would line them up on my bed so that I could submerge myself in their world. A war could have been going on around me and I wouldn't have noticed. A brown rug in my room stretched wall-to-wall, transforming the floor into a simmering lava pool while the air around me became cursed with demons. I would play in my room for hours, completely engrossed in the world of these creatures: alone, happy, and free.

It wasn't that I didn't like the world I lived in; I just liked my imaginary one better. The magic of imagination was much more interesting than anything I had known . . . yet.

One day I crept down to our basement to watch TV. I was convinced that the downstairs was haunted by an evil ghost, but I took the risk because my curiosity was greater than the threat. The basement was unfinished and exposed a broken ceiling full of wires hanging down from above.

A large pool table that my father and brother sometimes used occupied a corner of the room, and the TV sat on a piece of smooth wood suspended by giant chains that floated above a cobblestone fireplace. Over the pool table hung a light fixture covered with the logos of popular beers and liquors. Pictures and mirrors decorated the unfinished walls—part modern-day saloon, part demolition site. It was beautiful and mysterious, and reminded me of a dungeon. The musty smell of the cobblestone fireplace overpowered the lingering cigarette smoke exhaled from my mother's lips. I moved quietly across the floor so that I wouldn't wake the ghosts.

As I looked for something interesting to watch on TV, I flipped through the channels and stopped on a station where I saw gymnastics for the first time. *I will never forget this moment.* When I die and God asks me about my life, I'm going to tell him this memory. The TV screen seemed to grow larger; as a matter of fact, it was the only object I saw. Everything else in the room disappeared. Watching the American gymnasts Mary Lou Retton and Bart Conner was like watching real magic. They flipped against gravity like a machine—powerful, strong, and flexible. In that moment I was hooked. I stared at the TV and felt a fire spark within me. Actually, it was not a spark; it was more like an explosion. My body grew warmer with a sudden feeling of jealousy, making me want to compete against this new emotion and transform it into achievement.

The room grew quiet and I heard my soul speak for the very first time. It was so loud it amazed me that the entire universe didn't hear it. It simply said to me, "Repeat," and I knew exactly what it wanted me to do.

I looked around the room and looked for something soft. I noticed our couch, which told the story of a family that had outgrown its comfort and moved on. Its emptiness and sadness were my solitude because I found a safe haven to attempt a flip. This old couch and its cushions would become my guardian angels and protect me from injury.

My first cartwheel wasn't great, but by the fifth try, it was perfect. It felt good to me, like someone had bottled freedom and I had just taken my first drink of it. I felt that energy—strong, invasive, fluid, and alive. I would never go back to a life without that feeling, and would do whatever it took to keep it. I repeated the movements again and again, trying to expand and become something more. With every fiber of my being, I knew that movement would be my destiny.

That night I couldn't sleep, and thought about crawling out of bed to do flips on the cushions. The crescent moon slipped through the clouds and the autumn wind rustled in the trees. I lay still and awestruck, anticipating tomorrow so that I could return to my new discovery.

My brother Michael, who is seven years older than me, was my idol, and I told him what I was doing. He was a fearless soul who never seemed to experience physical pain. I had seen him punch holes in walls, resulting in bloody, swollen knuckles that he would just laugh off. He was a tough guy, and I wanted to be just like him. He had the Italian brown hair from my father, the shorter Irish height from my mother, and the fiery temperament of both. He came downstairs with me and I showed him what I had achieved. With Michael by my side I no longer feared the evil spirits that I believed inhabited our basement.

Michael immediately came up with the idea that we could jump over objects and land on the cushions. He scavenged the basement and found a few things that we could dive over—a Styrofoam cooler for my father's beer, a plastic cooler (also for my father's beer), a vacuum cleaner, and anything else that we couldn't easily break. We set up the cushions to land on, just inches away from the cold, stone hearth of the fireplace.

Being smaller, I ended up clearing the most objects. It was as if I had springs in my legs, and I intuitively knew how to use them. In my body, in my heart and soul, I knew how to part from gravity and interpret movement. I couldn't articulate it, but my body knew long before my mind did, and it felt like I was uncovering ancient hieroglyphics.

Like an addict needing his fix, I would sneak downstairs and do gymnastics. I thought I could figure it out on my own and be successful. I tried doing a backflip, but fell on my neck. I got up and tried again, and the same thing happened. I did it again and again, and I kept landing on my head. My brother and sisters would come downstairs to see if I'd hurt myself yet and yell, "You are going to break your back . . . stop doing that!" But I didn't stop; I couldn't stop! I had heaven to build, and that was how I would lay down the first brick.

I continued to go to the basement to learn the trick, and one day it happened. I did it. I landed on my feet and not on my head. The accomplishment of the cartwheel became insignificant compared to the new power of the backflip. I was no longer human, but more like Superman or one of my He-Man action figures. My blood turned into concrete determination, suffused with happiness and amazement. I couldn't wait to tell my brother and sisters, "I told you so!" and "I knew I could do it!" My body spoke louder than my soul, saying in the sharpest voice, "I want more!" I wanted more of that feeling and would do whatever it took to achieve it. I had to learn another flip, a different flip. My body was already accustomed to the achievement of the backflip, and it needed a new move to feed that feeling.

I stayed up until two o'clock in the morning waiting for my parents to come home from work to show them my backflip on the dog-eaten cushions. I pulled them downstairs, even though they were upset that I was awake at that hour of the night. I did it for them, and they were surprised at what I had learned on my own. The perfect execution of my self-taught skill marked the point of no return. I would never look back.

2

LUNGS

The lungs, part of the pulmonary system, are the essential respiration organs in all air-breathing animals. The two lungs are located in the chest on either side of the heart. Their principal function is to transport oxygen from the atmosphere into the bloodstream, and to release carbon dioxide from the bloodstream into the atmosphere.

My brother and I shared a bedroom across the hall from my parents. It was small, crammed with toys, and covered in off-white wallpaper with soldiers on it. The wallpaper was peeling, and when we were bored we peeled off even more, exposing the bare wall beneath.

We slept on large, wooden bunk beds—solid temples ascending from the Earth of a crumb-filled, matted-down brown rug. Black-and-white-striped cotton blankets covered us at night, making me feel like I was tucked inside a giant ice cream sandwich. Michael slept on top because I was afraid of falling. When it was time for bed he would lean over and make faces at me, trying to make me laugh. I always did.

Nighttime was troublesome for me because my parents often came home late. As part owners of the family's Italian restaurant, they worked all night and had to close up the building. I was a momma's boy and needed to know where she was at all times. When I laid my head on the pillow, I had horrible images that something bad was happening to her. I just knew she was somewhere out there, lost in the darkness, and I would never see her again. These thoughts were unbearable, and left me with a deep sense of loneliness, confusion, and dread.

As a child I feared death, and that fear soon became an obsession. I was terrified that the people I loved would die all at once, their bodies stolen by the darkness that bent through the light of the room, and I would be left alone. Most nights I would cry myself to sleep before my parents came home, and the exhaustion of weeping lulled me into a warm, seraphic state. The scent of my mom's perfume as she kissed me goodnight always made me feel safe. When my parents came home from the restaurant, their breath smelled of a powerful medicine, but my mother's breath was stronger, more potent, and more commanding, as if she *was* the medicine she breathed. I loved her smell—a mixture of Marlboro cigarettes and gin—which I'm convinced to this day must be the divine smell of angels. I knew I would be all right no matter what, once she was home.

It was a Friday night and my parents had to work later than usual to close the restaurant. My sister Trish, who is nine years older than me, babysat us since she was the oldest and most responsible. I had a psychic connection with her and often knew what she was thinking without her saying a word. Trish was short and carefree, and had dark brown hair with fire-red highlights. She was stronger than she realized, and always tried to do the right thing.

Trish had friends over when my parents weren't home. I never tattled on her because I liked her friends. They seemed lighthearted, lifted by the wind. Their smiles burst through their faces and their pale skin took on a reddened hue. My parents, on the other hand, would curb that feeling, always trying to trap their laughter before it rose to the surface so as not to expose who they really were.

Trish's friends were covered head-to-toe in denim, with buttons of my sister's favorite rock bands all over their jean jackets: Judas Priest, Mötley Crüe, the Cars, and Ozzy Osbourne. I thought they were badges of association with the Devil. There was a lot of hair, sprayed straight up and teased like giant cobwebs extending from their foreheads. Her boyfriends' faces were covered in greasy bangs that hid their eyes. They all looked like they had been drenched in a dark rain.

On that particular night, something strange happened to my body. The more I ran around the house and played, the harder it became to breathe. It wasn't like being out of breath, but felt more like there was no air at all. With my newfound control over flipping my body, I felt superior to sickness, and I became confused and irritated by what was happening. I played harder to break through this problem, but my breath wasn't returning.

My heart raced in fear, and I was embarrassed to tell anyone what was happening. I followed the blue-painted cigarette smoke down the hall and went into my room to hide. I lay on top of my bed knowing that if I could just physically figure out breath the same way I understood movement, then I would be all right. I sat in the darkness and commanded my body to breathe and rip the oxygen from the air . . . except I couldn't. I used all my chest muscles to pull the air inside me, but my body refused it in a giant choke. Again I tried, and physically imagined my lungs expanding, but they weren't responding. A hot stream of salty tears burnt along my cheeks— suddenly I knew I was going to die. Yet I refused to accept that thought. I looked out the window through the thick, pale glass that separated me from the outside. Between the window and screen lay a dead fly nestled under the spark of the moon's glow, lifeless, still, and decayed. I wondered if that was what we ended up looking like after we died.

My ghostly fingers pressed against the windowpane, tracing the shape of a birch tree bending in the wind. From where I lay, all that was on the other side of the glass suddenly felt forever unreachable. I didn't know if I believed in a God at that moment, but I prayed to him, watching the tree sway and seeing a glimmer of my reflection in the glass. My reflection couldn't feel a thing; it just watched as I gasped for air, sipping the tiny bits of oxygen that circled my body as I looked at the colored tulips around the tree.

In my childish thinking, I believed I could hide from what was happening to me. I went beneath the covers where I felt safe and could hide from that breath-stealing beast, but it had already found me, snarling in the shadows. We now shared the same space, and I accepted its agenda. For the first time in my life I felt mortality in the presence of a sinister and invisible force. It was conquering me, and I could do nothing about it.

I was defeated with each painful breath I tried to take. My small hands balled into fists as I physically fought to get the air inside me. Dread filled my mind, and the shadows in the room seemed to be silently waiting. I was now completely powerless, and it happened so fast. The air was no longer available for me to take. My heart raced faster and faster, like a drummer gone mad. I thought I was dying, and I was embarrassed that I no longer had the strength or ability to fight. Deep inside my skeleton, I imagined my air sacs relaxing and breathing rhythmically. But that meditation wasn't working, and I was losing the battle.

The air that I could get into my lungs felt painful and sharp, like shards of glass cutting me open on the way down through my breathing tubes. The seconds between each breath were getting longer and longer, and I was fighting every step of the way. I don't know if I made peace with death at that moment, but luckily my sister came in to check on me. She saw me in my bed choking, crying, and very sick. I don't remember what happened next because I drifted off into an abyss of unconsciousness.

I woke up in the hospital on top of an uncomfortable, crib-like bed that was wrapped entirely in a plastic bubble. The bed and walls were covered with thick moisture. A machine pushed air and medicine into the space, and it felt soothing. Slowly my breath returned, and I knew the medicine-filled air was killing the beast that had taken residence in my lungs. I lay there, exhausted from my fight, but once again feeling immortal and strong. I was still sick, but the storm was over. I watched my mother on the other side of the tent looking in at me with concern. She looked beautiful through the plastic, like a goddess. Quietly, surrendering to the air that filled my lungs, I breathed in every ounce of medicine that blew into the space. The anxiety left my spirit and I knew that everything was going to be okay.

The diagnosis was pneumonia combined with asthma. The doctors said I would have asthma for the rest of my life. At the time, that diagnosis meant nothing to me except that I would have to take a bunch of inhalers, which I liked. I learned a valuable lesson that day—if there is something wrong with me, I can take a certain type of medication and quickly feel better.

3

HEART

THE HEART IS A MUSCULAR ORGAN RESPONSIBLE FOR
PUMPING BLOOD THROUGH THE BLOOD VESSELS BY REPEATED,
RHYTHMIC CONTRACTIONS AND IS FOUND IN ALL VERTEBRATES.
IN THE EGYPTIAN *Book of the Dead*, THE HEART WAS WEIGHED
IN A BALANCE AGAINST THE FEATHER OF MA'AT, A DEITY
SYMBOLIZING TRUTH. THE HEAVINESS OF THE HEART
PROVIDED THE MEASUREMENT OF SIN. IF THE HEART
OUTWEIGHED THE FEATHER, THE POSSESSOR WOULD
NOT HAVE A FAVORABLE AFTERLIFE.

The dark hallway opened to a giant indoor tennis court full of gymnastics equipment. The apparatuses looked hazardous, beaten, and weary, reminding me of old-fashioned torture devices used in wars hundreds of years ago. These structures stood like tombstones jutting out of an archaic graveyard, sanctified and solid. The equipment had absorbed the souls of all the athletes who had performed and trained on those devices—each spirit giving the gym more character and stability, transforming the space into its own thriving organism.

I walked into my very first gymnastics class knowing I wanted to be a champion. I heard an ethereal voice that whispered, "This is your fate." The very thought of beginning my journey there made my heart race and my palms sweat, and created a hypnotic state of determination, desire, and hunger in my nine-year-old brain. My hunger was akin to that of a ravenous animal that had been starved for its entire life, and then freed from its cage to search for food. Only fear rivaled my enthusiasm, as I knew this was where I had to prove to a merciless God that I was worthy of the gift of movement.

I sat in the row of tiny blue plastic seats, anxiously watching the classes. I looked around the gymnasium at all the strange equipment, focusing on the high bar. I couldn't believe how tall it was, and I shuddered thinking about gripping the chalk-covered steel bar. It looked down upon me and whispered the tales of past gymnasts' abuse and violence. Their torment, blood, desperation, and drive still stained and smothered the bar. The two tall, red supporting posts formed an invisible gateway to a dimension of endless work, pain, and agony that I would need to endure. That gymnasium would become an orchestra that would flood my soul with music.

The class was trying "aerials," no-handed cartwheels, coached by a man who intimidated me. He was in his twenties, muscular, serious, and strict. Our class was beginning and I waved to my mother, letting her know I was all right. I wore ridiculously oversized red shorts with my two skinny, chalk-white legs protruding from the folds, and walked over to join the other kids. I had a moment of uncertainty, and looked back at my mom. When our eyes met, she looked down at the book in her lap, secretly telling me, "You don't need me now; you can do this." There were only a couple of other kids my age in the class, and they weren't very good at tumbling. We spent the entire hour rolling on the floor. It was definitely not my idea of a gymnastics class—more like a "Mommy and Me Gymnastics without My Mom" class. I knew I was going to come back, but still, I felt gypped.

I walked over to my mother, feeling underwhelmed at what I had just experienced, and she asked, "Why didn't you show the coach what you can do?"

"I don't know," I said, shrugging my bony shoulders.

She asked me if I would show her the flip I had learned on my own. I went over to the corner of the carpeted sprung floor and raised both arms next to my ears like they did in the Olympics. With a running start, I did a round-off back handspring back tuck—a no-handed backflip in a tucked position. I raised my arms again, finishing with pride and confidence, and looked over for my mother's approval. The coach, whose demeanor had scared me, went over and talked with my mom. I stood on the floor, pretending not to listen, watching the clouds of white chalk blur into the open gym space.

Everything was still. Time had stopped, and I was the only one there watching and waiting for judgment. I heard him ask where I'd learned how to do that flip, and my mom said, "By himself, in the basement. He's been down there for a month every day after school. He grabs the couch cushions and starts bouncing around." My mom had a beautiful way of making everything sound playful.

The next day I became a member of the World Gymnastics preteam, and my life would never be the same again. I was no longer a nine-year-old boy; I was to become a warrior. The team practiced more hours than a regular class, three times a week for two hours. I received my first uniform and began training routines to compete against other gymnasts. I couldn't believe I was on the gymnastics team after only a few classes. I was afraid, but knew my chance to dive into the unknown and release the movements lying deep within me had arrived.

On my first day of team practice, the gym greeted me with the same dynamic presence as the first time I had emerged from its long, shadowy hallway. It was massive, unchanged, and unaffected by times gone by. I knew this world would never change. It would always be man and apparatus, struggling to coexist, making peace and artistry, questioning and mocking physics and the potential of the human body. Like a church, a cathedral, a synagogue, or a mosque, that place held power for the believer, and what it represented would always remain the same. The equipment might change, but the heart of the place would remain like a divine kingdom for seeking athletes. It was to be our Mount Olympus, and we were the chosen gods.

A boy my age was stretching on a large foam mat, saying rude things under his breath in my direction. I was new and not about to confront him. I smiled and started stretching to avoid looking him in the eye. His name was Chris, and he was bigger than me, with an energy that screamed, "Don't piss me off, little guy; I'll squash you like a bug." I disliked him immediately. He was gawky and his skills were choppy. I felt his technique insulted the passion that raced through my veins, but there was something he had that I didn't: strength. That challenged me because I knew I would have to work twice as hard and twice as long as him to keep up.

There was another boy on the preteam who seemed to be a lot like me. He was quiet, focused, and talented. His name was Seth, and we instantly became friends. Being the same age and at the same skill level, we were placed in the same division for competition. I was happy to find a friend I could relate to, because there was something about Chris that frightened me.

The coach from the day before came over and introduced himself as Dan. I stood there in fear, already ashamed that my strength was less than that of the boy next to me. I could feel Dan had the knowledge and the map of how to get to my physical destination. My body understood his words before my mind could make sense of the movements. Thinking became the enemy. I had to believe in myself, let go of fear, and trust Dan with complete faith that he knew what I did not.

Through gymnastics, the lion born inside me broke out of its cage. I would travel to the end of time to finish what I started, without letting anything get in my way. It became my way of communicating with the God I'd heard about. He was there in the silence, between my breath and beneath my heartbeats, despite my physical pain. It entered me and went through me, peacefully but strong, and I loved it more than anything I'd ever known. It got me out of bed excited to greet each day, and it became the source of my existence. This human art of strength, flexibility, and determination spoke louder than anything else I could hear. My spirit was trying to be free, and this was how I would release it to exist without boundaries. While flying through the air, I found peace within me. I was satisfied. I was complete. I was finished. I was . . . beautiful.

4

LACRIMAL BONE

THE LACRIMAL BONE IS THE SMALLEST AND MOST FRAGILE BONE OF THE FACE. IT IS LOCATED IN THE EYE SOCKETS AND IS DERIVED FROM THE LATIN WORD FOR TEAR, *lacrima*. THE LACRIMAL BONE HOUSES THE TEAR DUCT, ALLOWING US TO CRY.

I imagined that education took place in a land where the gods came to learn about and question hypotheses. In my mind, school should be a giant garden of luminescent flowers snaking through corridors of perfectly cut hedges. Unfortunately, my middle school was nothing like my vision, and so I would slip in and out of my fantasy, trying to flee the drab classroom in which I always landed.

Our classroom was surrounded by giant letters of the alphabet with pictures of animals representing the shape of each letter. Horrible drawings decorated the walls alongside stories of our favorite family holidays, and the desks were arranged in a scattered line. I always felt like the children around me knew more than me because their parents had given them a book called *Secrets to Life and All You Need to Know to Be Happy*. It seemed they always knew how to pay sharp attention to what the teacher was saying, and their parents never forgot their lunches, snow boots, or winter gloves. No matter how much I forced myself to pay attention to the lessons, I somehow found myself back in the land of my daydreams. I always missed the given lesson and would become confused and angry with myself, which only served to force me further back into my land of enchantment.

It wasn't that I had problems with the educational system—I loved to learn. But I felt lost in a labyrinth, not knowing which path to take or which answer was correct. The only weapon I had against ignorance was the pencil, which I usually forgot and shamefully had to borrow from another student. The pencil became my key to escape into my newfound physical love. I would pretend my desk was a tumbling mat and the pencil was my body performing the greatest routine at the Olympic Games. I did that all the time, completely oblivious to the lessons on grammar, math, and science.

One of my teachers began to notice the dissociation from my schoolwork. With dirty blonde hair pulled back in a tight bun, she looked like an elf, making my whole fantasy illusion much easier. She smelled of anger and discontent, and I often felt that she singled me out because she herself had lost her own dreams, and I was a reminder of the road less traveled. I was that single, burning fire in a forest that she could not extinguish, and the flickering of my flames scorched her inner child's dream. She eventually telephoned my mother to ask her why I was so unfocused in the classroom.

I came home from school one day, and my mom sat me down and said delicately, "How much do you like doing gymnastics?" I told her without blinking, forcefully, as if it was the only thing I knew, "With all my heart!" It was clear the words came from a greater authority, and I was a puppet under its control. "I thought so," she replied. "I just wanted to ask you what I already knew." I heard her talking on the phone later that day. She said my teacher thought I should quit or slow down my training in gymnastics because it was taking the focus away from my schoolwork. My mom told the teacher that was ridiculous.

I don't think my teacher understood how difficult gymnastics was. My teammates and I had a good time at practice, but it was hard work. It takes a special kind of discipline that many children haven't yet cultivated. Even with the youthful energy a child carries, going to school all day, coming home, and then going directly to gymnastics was exhausting. My teammates and I missed out on a lot of things and sacrificed a lot for our passion.

I remember one year I received the game Zelda for our Nintendo. I never wanted to stop playing it, but the moment came when my mom would say, "Joey, come on, we have to leave for gymnastics." I loved gymnastics, never wanted to part with it, but I was playing a game. Did I have to go? Yes, I did, and so I went. Gymnastics is a bit different because it doesn't carry the same camaraderie that team sports do, since it is an individual sport. My teammates wouldn't have been let down if I didn't show up to practice because I wanted to play Zelda. Who would I have let down? Me! And I would have to live with myself. If I wanted to be great, then I would have to put down the game and train.

When I went to school the next day I was nervous that my teacher would be angry with me or embarrass me, but she didn't. She carried on as if no conversation had ever occurred. This intrigued me: an adult pretending that no conversation with my mom had happened, concealing the truth behind her false smile. She was an adult who was lying, and oddly, I somehow appreciated that. I tried harder to stay focused on the schoolwork, but the thoughts of gymnastics absorbed me and I repeatedly succumbed to their dominance and strength.

Walking down the hallways among the other children, I felt like an intruder. I was an alien from another planet, isolated and alone. I was the strongest boy in my grade, doing the most pull-ups, chin-ups, rope climbs, and sit-ups, but still no one wanted to hang out with me. A different vibe emanated from me; I was not like the others, and even though no one said a word, silently we all knew.

It wasn't just the other kids I had trouble with; my middle school gym teacher didn't like me either. Even though I was strong, he saw something in me that I think made him uncomfortable. He took my surname Putignano and turned it into "Putzy," which I hated, and I shuddered inside every time he said it.

To make matters worse, I was the shortest boy in my class and looked much younger than I was. I had a baby face that gave me an appearance of innocence. While that worked against me with my classmates, adults babied me and treated me with great care, like I was made of porcelain.

I had no friends in school until I met Tara. We were the exact same height and there was something about her that pulled me in. I was the

Earth and she was gravity. It was something primal and complex that I couldn't explain, but I needed to be near her. We were like twins, and she didn't like the other students either. Without any real effort, we developed a deep and caring friendship.

Her laughter and her smile kept me by her side throughout my childhood. I made a silent vow in my heart to love her until the end of time and take care of her no matter what. Tara was special to me, and I felt lucky to have her. Our friendship was more than a connection; it was as if we had known each other in another life. Tara and I could make each other laugh—one of the best ingredients for a friendship. We did everything together; she slept over at my house on the weekends and we hung out all the time during recess. The other kids at school noticed our impenetrable union and didn't like it. It was unusual for them to see a boy being best friends with a girl.

Sometimes after school I played baseball, soccer, and football with the neighborhood kids. I loved playing sports, but there was too much standing around between actual movement. It felt like we were always waiting for something to happen, and it drove me crazy. In those moments I would kick to a handstand or do a backflip, and of course, the ball would come toward me and I'd miss it since I was standing on my hands. Needless to say, this often made the other players angry since they were as serious about their sports as I was about gymnastics. They made fun of me and my sport, and accused it of being "girlie" because of our uniforms.

I was insanely defensive of gymnastics and would try to explain that the precision of the sport demanded tight uniforms so judges could see the lines of our body and form. Few other sports require the athlete to be so tuned into their muscles that even the slightest bending of the knee means points are taken off your score. Still, my peers didn't get that I was doing something dangerous almost every day, using my muscles and coordination in a way they'd never know to challenge the forces of physics. The happiness I garnered from gymnastics battled against the embarrassment and shame I felt from what others said to me. I loved that "girlie sport" with all my heart; I felt that I was meant to do gymnastics and I wasn't going to apologize for it to anyone.

Soon I began to believe my schoolmates' view of me. Their whispers, jokes, and comments infiltrated my muscles and bones. I was outnumbered, and it became difficult for me not to believe them. But instead of quitting the sport, I went deeper into my body and practice, shutting down to the outside world. I couldn't have stopped if I had wanted to: I was obsessed. After school, before gymnastics practice, the patch of grass that my brother mowed became my gymnasium. I would drag our old mattresses onto the lawn, lining up mattress after mattress, and tumbled on them. I learned new skills on my own to take to practice that night.

After gymnastics practice, I would set up the mattresses in the basement to work on what I had learned while my brother and father drank beer and played pool. I would practice until my body could no longer take it, until each movement was just right. I never had much in common with my brother and father, who were very much alike, but somehow through my practicing I communicated and bonded with them. Though my father seemed like he was concentrating on his game, I would occasionally see him give me a fatherly glance that said, "That's my boy." Together in that room, as they played pool, I practiced becoming a champion, and that space and time became precious for us all.

5

PHALANGES

THE SMALL BONES OF THE FINGERS AND TOES ARE
NAMED PHALANGES BECAUSE THEY RESEMBLE THE GREEK
BATTLE FORMATION CALLED A *phalanx*. IN THE PHALANX
FORMATION, SOLDIERS FORMED A TIGHT GROUP WITH
OVERLAPPING SHIELDS AND SPEARS.

I won first place in the state and regional gymnastics championship, which allowed me to take a trip to the Olympic Training Center in Colorado Springs. I was twelve years old and invited to a camp at the training center with other select gymnasts from across the country. This would be the first time I was going to be away from my family, and the idea of leaving them was both thrilling and disturbing.

Dan's coaching shone a light over my basic understanding of gymnastics, and I quickly absorbed his teachings. Our gymnastics team had grown in size to ten athletes, and the team dynamics had changed. Chris, the stronger teammate, was in a division higher than me because his skill level was more advanced. Even though he was better than me, I still kept him in the corner of my eye. Seth and I were in the same level, which was great because we were becoming good friends. I was sad Seth wasn't going to the Olympic Training Center with me, but knew if I let my guard down once, he would be going instead of me.

I loved to train in gymnastics, but I hated competing. I could never sleep the night before a competition and would continuously go through my routines in my head. I would lie there for hours, covered in a blanket of sweat, religiously and compulsively going through them, making sure to occupy every memory, every physical movement to its perfection. My heart beat like a hollow drum, faster and faster, as I repeated those actions until sunrise. Those nights led to horrendous mornings without having slept a wink. My body and mind were braided into a miasma of fear: to be perfect or die.

The mornings of gymnastics competitions were just as difficult as the nights before. I obsessively checked everything over and over again, as if it were part of my routine and I was to be judged on whether I properly packed my uniform and grips, or how I executed my daily rituals. I thought that if I didn't religiously follow that compulsion, I wouldn't perform well. I would return to my gym bag three or four times to make sure my uniform was still there.

Early in the mornings my mom and I would get into her little gray Cougar and drive to the competition. She would be half asleep and exhausted, but happy; and I would be a nervous wreck, in my robotic mode, trying to control the uncontrollable. The drive always seemed endless, yet never long enough, and somehow, like clockwork, I would fall asleep in the backseat as the hard smell of Marlboro Reds and morning coffee washed over me. I cherish that memory and knew that just for a moment, for as long as the drive lasted, I was safe. I was with my mom, protected from my quest for perfection. In that car ride, I could just be her little boy. It didn't matter where we were going. But those moments were never long enough.

I leapt from the car and rushed into the gym to greet my teammates and competitors on the blue sprung floor. That always felt awkward, because during competition we were no longer teammates or friends, and we all felt that division between us. Our playful camaraderie dissolved when we entered those battlefields, preparing to tear each other apart. We said hello to one another but had to fight the compassionate part of us that is human, holding on to our shields of armor like Titans. Quietly we stretched, warming up for the six events in men's gymnastics. Structurally, the equipment we knew from daily practice remained the same, but the atmosphere was altered at the level of competition. We had come to know each apparatus as well as our own bodies, but on competition days the merciless equipment became unapproachable and unyielding.

The judges, coaches, and parents who watched from the backbreaking bleachers never saw the underlying levels of stress and rivalry. To them it looked like we were "playing" gymnastics, but to us athletes, our humanity came down to those fine moments, forcing us to ask ourselves, "What are we made of?" The gymnastics apparatus appeared to have its own agenda and demanded respect by throwing us off, causing injuries, and displaying how man was inferior to those solid structures. However, we came prepared with years of practice, numb from the self-made beatings, and we hung on, combating with all of our love and hate.

After our warm-up, we got dressed in our gymnastics uniforms, marched out to a familiar Olympic melody, and stood tall for the national anthem. The national anthem always startled me because it started the competition, like the gun fired for runners. During the anthem, I prayed for the ability to do my best and to remain injury-free. I prayed for perfection. Once the song ended, it was time to be judged and scrutinized for what I loved to do. "O'er the land of the free and the home of the brave." BANG! Would we ever be the same after that song?

Competition was serious, and we had six rotations in Olympic order: floor exercise, pommel horse, still rings, vault, parallel bars, and high bar. While the athlete before me performed, I engaged in yet another ritual of preparation—I spat on the white palms of my hands to allow the chalk to be absorbed and then kicked the floor, pushing my socks between my big toes, like Japanese "tabi." I dreaded the moment when the athlete ahead of me came close to finishing. My mouth got dry, the warm color in my face receded, and the gym's atmosphere became a dizzying carnival of madness and illusion. Fear paralyzed my system even though I appeared to be prepared, as a most unusual condition occurred: the dead bells. I heard this deafening buzzing in my ears until I could hear nothing else. If that was my body's way of coping with fear, then it was useless. It actually felt like I was having a silent seizure. This phantom sound resembled the noise one hears the day after a loud rock concert. I would think to myself, *I can't go out there and compete; I can barely stand up straight right now; get me out of here.* My stomach knotted and my breath collapsed in my throat. Somehow, within seconds, I would have to salute the judges and begin my routine.

The first skill that broke the stillness was the most difficult. I chalked my hands as I obsessed about the details, and raised my arms for the moment that should magically transform trepidation into self-assurance, suggesting to the judges, "I'm ready to do this. Watch me!"

We trained daily to condition ourselves to unconsciously perform the first skill under pressure. Once I engaged with the movements, my surroundings faded away. I had rehearsed my routine in practice hundreds of times, but during competition the sensation of the skills became Herculean. Floating in the sky, I was an imperfect cloud judged by God, filled to capacity but unable to rain. I couldn't hear anything, not my heartbeat or my breath, just a deafening silence.

In a trance, my body automatically executed my routine. I had no idea if I was performing the way I had trained or if I was making mistakes. A tangible emptiness replaced my energy while the tension mounted, but I continued to battle through each movement, knowing it would be over at some point. Then, within a breath, it was finished. The landing of my feet on the mat made a luscious sound of satisfaction, crashing like a giant ocean wave battering the shore, replacing the stillness. I stood tall and proud, saluted the judges, and then walked off, my heart hammering against my rib cage.

As I walked away, the moment hit me like a thunderbolt. That special and sacred feeling could only be summoned during competition. I couldn't produce that emotion at practice or at home no matter what skill I acquired. It was like a unique drug. I would get a rush and my stomach would turn to fire. It was the ultimate high. In a competition, that feeling of being a windblown acorn in a hurricane would repeat itself six times during each event. It was a feeling of complete dread followed by a feeling of elation—I am nothing; I am everything. I am nothing; I am everything.

I left for Colorado Springs on a morning flight with some other members of the regional team. The colossal mountains surrounding the Olympic Training Center created a barrier of protection—encircling that sacred temple hidden deep in the valley. Pikes Peak was the mountain towering over the center, and the snow-capped rocks reflected the sun's fractured light. From where we stood, the peak sparkled and glistened like a white magical blanket covering the Earth. This was Mount Olympus, where the gods came down to watch the mortals compete for their fleeting lives.

As we walked closer to the residence, I could see the five-colored Olympic rings in a huge, grassy field, symbolizing greatness and triumph. Being at that place was beyond my wildest dreams. I knew I belonged there, and the Olympic rings standing outside challenged my future. Would it end here? Would this be the final accomplishment, or would I go beyond this level? We went to our rooms, which we shared with four other gymnasts, unpacked, and met where the Olympic gymnastics team trained. It was an honor to practice on the same equipment that was used by the Olympic team.

As we assembled on the huge blue mat, I realized how many astonishing athletes there were from other states and regions. I studied them and thought, *What if that guy over there is better than me?* I looked to the next one as panic ran through my core and shook my skeleton. I immediately began to sweat while we lined up like ants on a hill.

We went through two grueling hours of testing, which meant that after we executed a skill, we were then grouped according to ability. Gymnastics is ruthless because one is constantly being judged, watched, pulled apart, criticized, and studied so that one can achieve perfection. The judges and coaches acted like political leaders deciding our country's future. Would we be worthy to progress to the next stage?

My coach, Dan, instilled an athletic mentality in us to never act conceited or snotty toward other athletes, regardless of whether they were better or worse than us. I absorbed those words and lived by them. It bestowed an honor to the sport much like in martial arts, and I tried to be grateful for my gift of movement. Instead of inspiring me, the diversity of skills I saw performed was deflating. I was consumed with envy and petrified I wouldn't be able to achieve the same skills.

At the camp I was grouped with six other little daredevils like me. The other athletes were just as dedicated as I was, and for some reason that fact really bothered me. I got to feel that I wasn't athletically special and not the only person imbued with supernatural powers. That understanding was profoundly humbling, and I knew I was going to have to train harder and longer than any other athlete in the world. I was positive other gymnasts didn't have my plan. I knew they didn't want to be an Olympian as badly as I did. But of course, I was wrong. They were as hungry and devoted as I was. We were all starving for a piece of glory, and we would tear each other apart to get it. To the human eye, we were little kids doing gymnastics; but in reality we were bloodthirsty, razor-sharp-clawed demons, ready to win. The blood loss from others would be our victory. We all shared the same desire, obsession, and lust.

I decided to make friends with them and to learn everything I could and bring it back with me to Massachusetts. I learned many new skills at the training center, but I was homesick and I missed my sister Jenn, even though we didn't get along. She was three years older than me. I admired her wildly creative presence and deep-blue eyes, which seemed to be made of starlight, water, and diamonds. I left a piece of my soul under those mountains in Colorado. When I returned to World Gymnastics I continued to practice, but knew there were others who were training like me, tiny warriors sharpening their swords, carving their weapons, fighting with themselves to become the best, strongest, and fastest. There was nothing I could do about it—and it killed me a thousand times over.

6

ULNA NERVE

THE ULNA NERVE IS DIRECTLY CONNECTED TO THE LITTLE FINGER AND PASSES NEAR THE ELBOW. BECAUSE IT IS NOT PROTECTED BY MUSCLE OR BONE, INJURY IS COMMON. IT IS ONE OF THE THREE MAIN NERVES IN THE ARM AND THE LARGEST UNPROTECTED NERVE IN THE BODY. THE ULNA NERVE TRAVELS ALONG THE INSIDE OF THE ELBOW UNDER A BONY PROTRUSION KNOWN AS THE "FUNNY BONE." SOMETIMES WHEN THIS AREA IS BUMPED, IT CAN CAUSE A SHOCK-LIKE FEELING.

When I was thirteen, my father began to disappear from the family. I didn't notice this because he often worked late and my focus on gymnastics kept me in an impenetrable world, with only my dreams and goals surrounding me. I knew my parents fought, but I didn't know to what extent.

During those years, my entire family worked at the restaurant, Giovanni's Avon Towne House. My father and his two brothers had inherited it after our grandfather's death—an event that created a giant chasm within my family. What I remember most about my grandfather was a teddy bear he had given me named Oatmeal. Oatmeal was covered in soft white fur with a plaid bow tie and plaid paw pads. As with most gifts we get from people we cannot remember, we somehow take those people's essence and infuse it into the thing they left behind. Oatmeal was my grandfather.

Unlike my parents, my grandfather seemed to be acutely cognizant of everything around him. His focus frightened me because it was alien to my family's ways. His death broke the links in the iron-chained fence of my extended family, and the peace we had obtained began to corrode, forever changing the family dynamics.

My brother Michael worked in the kitchen as a prep cook, supervised by my father; my mother was the hostess and manager of the waitstaff; my sister Trish was a bartender; my sister Jenn was a bus girl; and my cousins and aunts were waitresses.

My mother and father worked the same nights and saw each other more than they wanted to. I wanted to work with them, but I was too young. My family gave more importance to working a job than to education or sports. They had an "Old World" work ethic, and if someone didn't work more than forty hours a week, they were considered lazy. I was petrified of being called lazy, and did anything to avoid being labeled as such.

Growing up in that business made for an interesting childhood. We had to celebrate our holidays on other days. Holidays were the busiest times, and even though we came together as a family to work, we weren't actually *together*. The success of the restaurant brought us everything we ever asked for as kids. We weren't rich, but we had enough money to live comfortably. The difficult side to this was that everything revolved around the restaurant. All of our family conversations were about other employees, and arguments that started at home continued into the restaurant, and those started at the restaurant continued into the home. The building was not just constructed from wood and stone; intertwined into the structure was the mortar of my family's flesh and blood. It held us together, and it eventually destroyed us.

I had gymnastics practice every day after school from 5:30 to 8:30 p.m., and because the place where I trained was closer to the restaurant than to our home, my mom would take me back to work with her because she couldn't leave her duties long enough to drive me home. Practice finished during the restaurant's busiest hour.

I loved going back to the restaurant because I felt like I was hanging out with the adults and sat at the end of the giant, island-shaped bar doing my homework. My father would cook me something in the kitchen and my sister Trish would pour me a Coke using the bar's soda gun.

While other kids my age were getting ready for their next day of school, I was at the center of another world. To me, this was a much better experience than attending school, and being the owner's son made me feel like a celebrity. I realized I had more respect at the bar than I did at school, and I was treated with extreme kindness by all the waitresses. Patrons sitting at the bar appeared to be friendly too, smoking and laughing and consuming fancy-looking drinks that sparkled from their perfectly round glasses.

I would bring my schoolwork to the restaurant, but it was difficult for me to concentrate. It hurt to grip my pen because my chalk-stained hands had deep calluses and ripped skin from the high bar, and no matter how many times I washed them, the chalk dust came back. I would stare at the textbook in front of me, trying to absorb the words, but I couldn't—the world of the bar was too alluring.

My exhausted father came out of the kitchen looking unapproachable and tired. At the bar, my sister automatically poured him an ice-cold beer. The color of the beer made it look like urine and the foam at the top appeared sweet but sinister, although I knew it wasn't sugary because I could smell the drink from his breath when he talked to me. My father changed when he held his beer, and that transformation was immediate. The color in his cheeks deepened and glowed like a firefly in August. The unapproachable man became approachable, and his beer-induced mood was different at the bar than at home or in the restaurant's kitchen. It was his moment of relaxation, the peace people equate to sitting on the beach when the waves come crashing in, washing away their cares into the sea. I liked seeing him there with his beer in his hands as he stared contentedly at the television screen, drowning in the noise of happy people.

I sat at the bar and tried to do my homework against the noise of a realm in which a child did not belong. It was impossible to concentrate, and, given the option, I didn't want to. After the rush hour ended, my mother had her drink at the bar with her friends. In that moment, my mother looked happy, but uncomfortable. She was caught between two places, waiting for my father who was sitting down the way and whose eyes never left his beer. But after her first drink, she changed. The more she drank, the more she became part of the bar, morphing into a gorgeous glimmer in the darkness. She lit her cigarette and the blue smoke danced around her bleached-blonde hair as the alcohol strengthened her, guiding her from girl to woman, from confusion to hope. That thing she seemed to be waiting for only moments before had arrived. Her beauty became blurred as she crossed over from her sober self to her drunk self. I sat there between two statues: my mother and father brewing a feud like a thundercloud over my head. I was ready to go home. I was exhausted and needed to sleep. The illusion of this lifestyle didn't last. At first it all looked so glamorous, but each passing hour brought more darkness and despair. Glamour had a curfew.

The distance between my parents became obvious, and even though they stood only a few feet apart, with customers and waitresses finishing their shifts with a drink, they were already in different places. My mom still loved him; her smile contained all the honesty and purity that love could ever offer. But my father was consumed in a darkness he perceived as the light of freedom, and his judgment was too clouded to be anything but selfish. I hated him for that, because it was obvious that he was moving away from the family he created. Ashamed to display us, his unfinished pieces of work, he decided to start his life over elsewhere.

As I waited for my mom to finish her drink so we could go home, the hours pushed toward midnight, and the closer it got to midnight, the more belligerent the customers became—stuttering like zombies, entranced in a ritual to erase their thoughts, their memories, and all that made them human. This place allowed people to slip in between the lines of the lives they were living, forming a liquid society of solitary pain. Every hope, prayer, resentment, and relationship was tied to the drink in their hands. They drank to rewrite their histories and futures. I began to hate alcohol. I hated what it did to people and the way it changed them from normal and nice to angry and mean. I knew that I would never touch a drop, that I would keep those memories alive, clanging in my head like huge, iron church bells at a funeral. Sitting next to those drunks almost every night, with dopey, slobbering smiles on their numb faces, I received the strongest antialcohol message of any kid in the world.

Michael would come out of the kitchen during his shift, just to get away from the mayhem and heat. He'd lean up against the bar where I was sitting and observe the place for exactly what it was. Then he would look at me and laugh as he made a wisecrack about some poor, ugly drunk. He was the hardest worker I knew, and would go back into the kitchen to do the brunt of the work that nobody else would do. He didn't seem to mind, and he did it well. I loved his presence because he brought humor to the demented world I was visiting.

After my mother's repeated good-byes to her friends, we'd get into her car. She was always quiet, and I knew she was thinking of my father, who still stood at the end of the bar entertaining his own phantoms. Her eyes squinted in the darkness as she concentrated on getting us home. The empty highway was a perfect accompaniment to the silence we listened to, but I could hear her thoughts, and her rage altered her perfume, adding a mystery to her determined smile and denial.

What happens to a home when the people living in it leave? What happens to the family left behind? Do they live with the old memories, unable to move forward? The house's reassurances slowly vanished and the memories once shared became dust on the furniture. My older sister Trish moved out, my brother stayed at the house of the girl du jour he was sleeping with, and my sister Jenn was often out with her new best friend, going to the movies or the mall. The isolation and quietness were my mother's and mine to share, to live with, and to endure like a single burning candle that has the responsibility to heat a palace. My father was never coming home, and that was no longer a thought in our minds, just an unspoken truth never voiced.

How could I ask my mother where my father had gone? Wasn't it written on her broken heart, on her clothing, on her pride? Her dark-brown eyes sparked with rage and resentment, burning the memories of his body and face, searing his flesh, and sweeping the ashes of his laughter from her mind.

My mother, whose profound intuition for nature transcended anyone's I had ever known, was betrayed by love, a missed shot from a broken bow. She was a woman lying by an icy riverbed with her head on the frozen grass, listening for the universe to give her direction. From her secret garden of ingrown thoughts, she watched the TV screen and pretended that moment didn't exist, along with all the others forever locked in the solid waters. Her eyes filled with heavy tears that fell like ice drops from snowy branches. I couldn't look at her, because to see her weep would make me cry, and all children are powerless over their mother's tears. It was too late to get into this conversation again because the day had already been a lost war, and I had school in the morning. I turned to her, because I had to, and began to cry as we lost ourselves in our sadness. Together we cried—she cried for him and I cried for her, and the thunderclouds of her emotions sent lightning down my spine.

This cycle at night became a normal event in our lives. The raw emotions thickened like a dense fog blotting out the light. Her endless tears could have filled up oceans, and the delicate golden ribbon that strung her wounded heart together unraveled. Even though I knew the answer, I always asked her what was wrong, but she never spoke about it. I would hear her crying in the living room as I went to bed, and it killed me. I became a hostage to the music played by the broken instrument that had replaced her heart. I wanted to fix it, but I couldn't. All that was once beautiful had gone. Together we perfected misery.

I would see my father at the bar each evening and wanted to ask him, "Where have you been? When are you coming home?" But I never did; I couldn't utter those words, and instead observed all of the alcoholics as I reassured myself of how much I hated the substance that seemed to be the lifeblood of my family.

Countless long, uncomfortable nights led us to finally move on from the thought that my father would ever return home. We didn't talk about it. To speak the words would mean it was true, and it would have shattered the illusions and pretense in which we lived. My mom sank deeper into herself, and I began to believe her lies. I believed her fake smile in the same way I convinced myself plastic flowers were real. They looked like flowers, so they must be flowers. I believed she would be okay, but she would never be the same again, and neither would we.

7

LARYNGEAL PROMINENCE

COMMONLY KNOWN AS THE ADAM'S APPLE, IT IS THE
PROTRUSION FORMED BY THE ANGLE OF THE THYROID CARTILAGE
SURROUNDING THE LARYNX. DURING MEDIEVAL TIMES A MYTH
AROSE ABOUT THE ADAM'S APPLE, ACCORDING TO WHICH THE
FORBIDDEN FRUIT BECAME LODGED IN ADAM'S THROAT AFTER
HE TOOK A BITE OF IT. THE ADAM'S APPLE IS USUALLY
MORE VISIBLE IN MEN THAN IN WOMEN.

My asthma came seeping back into my lungs with the changing of
the seasons, autumn to winter being the most challenging. Every day
I lost my breath. I was always trying to catch it, and that feeling
of mortality and death crept in alongside the perfect, vibrant fall
colors. Those are the colors prior to death's arrival, before the hands
of winter reap all that is living. The deepest colors always come
with death.

In the months of September, October, and November I would end up
in the emergency room for a treatment with a nebulizer. The nebulizer
allowed me to breathe better, but I was ashamed of using it because
of its pipe-like structure that resembled a hookah. In my mind I
was an athlete, and drugs were the substances created for the weak
and desperate. In addition to the nebulizer treatment, I was given
injections of prednisone, a steroid that decreased the inflammation
in my lungs. That medication is not the same as the much-abused
testosterone and muscle-building anabolic steroids, but I was scared
my teammates wouldn't know the difference.

I became fascinated by the hospital and quickly began to pick up the medical terminology for my ailments. I had visited the emergency room so many times for my asthma that I began to feel like an intern. There was something romantic about a person who could prescribe medication. Those doctors were powerful to me, and I was attracted to the patient-doctor pattern—illness, diagnosis, medication. In a peculiar way, I felt I belonged there.

The doctors had changed my medications many times, and it was difficult to know which prescription made me feel better; all of them left me feeling hyper and edgy. During the numerous X-rays taken of my lungs, the doctors discovered an abnormality in my rib cage. This was more evidence that I was born different. I was born with an extra rib, a deformity that could not be seen by the human eye and was basically purposeless. My mom, who always tried to turn my awkward discomfort into ease, was a witness to the doctor's discovery. Excitedly, she recalled the story she had been told as a child in church, about how God had taken one of Adam's ribs with which to create Eve. She had read that Adam had been given an extra rib, like me.

As a boy, I didn't attend church because it conflicted with gymnastics competitions that were held on Sundays. I found the sport to be a much grander religion, with a more promising outcome than any story supposedly written by God and told by men. My mom's story made me feel better, and even though this extra rib didn't hurt me in any way, I would have given it back to be "normal."

A new asthma medication started giving me horrible anxiety, and I constantly believed something bad was going to happen. Panic and despair replaced my inability to breathe, and I would lie in bed wide awake. It wasn't just a few hours of thinking of the many horrors and wonders the world held; no, this insomnia kept me awake until morning. The daylight announced a horribly arduous day ahead without any peace at all. A sleepless night left me feeling like my entire body was filled with rusty nails, heavy and dull, and my daily tasks at school followed by gymnastics practice seemed impossible to complete.

In the quiet of night I would sit in my room, staring at the walls, terrified for no obvious reason. I could never pinpoint what was behind those feelings, but it brought up an overwhelming desire to create something beautiful. At first, the feeling urged me to produce something original, to make some form of art or create something from nothing. I knew if I did not begin to create, I would live forever in frustration.

The form of creativity that eventually drew me in was writing. During my fits of sleeplessness I would write to keep the panic at bay, and the more I wrote, the more I had the desire to do so. I called my stories and my desire to write "ghosts," and they moaned and lingered, stabbing me until their tales were written exactly as they tormented me to. Ghost-writing was the only way to freedom. Strangely, when I finished with one story, another one appeared, and sometimes two or three entered at the same time. I would sit on my bed, pen in hand, scribbling and writing, thinking beyond my imagined limits and discovering pieces of myself.

After endless attempts to fall asleep, I willingly surrendered to my imagination and began to summon the ghosts to my side. They were always in control of the stories, and I became a conduit to their voices and invisible forms, transforming nothingness into matter. I had been stabbed in the heart by a merciless muse that demanded my attention. I loved them because of the creativity they gave me, allowing me to be the vessel for their words and lives, but I also hated them because they kept me awake at night.

My mother was my biggest fan, and she was the only one besides my English teacher with whom I shared my stories. To me, they weren't just stories; they were words born out of my own flesh, blood, sadness, and euphoria.

During that time, I was free to do whatever I wanted without being questioned by the people around me. However, when I turned thirteen, my freedom started to get curtailed by the unspoken rules for a boy my age. I had a desire to act, dance, and perform. I couldn't help myself, but I realized the other boys around me, who used to do those things, had stopped, unwilling to cross a line in the sand that was invisible to me. I didn't have that age-related restraint with which they seemed to have been born.

Tara was still my best friend, and I was under constant scrutiny by my peers as to why I had a girl for such a close friend. The glue that held us together was our ability to laugh, but the larger reason why I hung around her was simply that I loved her. When I wasn't around Tara I felt a terrible loneliness. We were the same height, four feet eleven inches—the shortest students in our class.

Tara was turning into a beautiful young woman, and I secretly knew I was the ball and chain she was dutifully dragging behind her. She was a cheerleader and had many friends; I shied away from the other kids. All of my free time was spent practicing gymnastics, while most kids were doing their homework, hanging out, or watching sitcoms. I had nothing in common with them. I couldn't make new friends the way Tara did.

So there I was, short for my age and best friends with a girl. To make matters worse, my classmates called gymnastics a "girlie" sport. I felt betrayed by the kids my age. I even felt rebellious against the wonderful spirit that gave me my gift, asking it, "Why couldn't you have made me a football player or basketball player instead of a gymnast?" I could not understand why people thought gymnastics was a girl's sport, because pound for pound, I was stronger than anyone at my school, including everyone who teased me.

I was an easy target for ridicule. In addition to being short, I had a squeaky voice that didn't deepen when the other boys' voices did. I would often go home to my mother crying, "I'm always gonna be short and I will never get taller!" She was short too, and would empathize by telling me, "Good things come in small packages." I adopted that phrase as my comeback for everything.

I became so self-conscious about my voice that I would sometimes mumble or talk in a low whisper, which made it difficult for people to understand what I was saying. I stopped making eye contact with other kids, letting the words tumble out of my mouth. Concerned about the tone of my voice, I even asked my doctor if there was something wrong with my throat. But he assured me that there was nothing wrong with my voice, that it was unique. The word "unique" stung like a thousand bees. This single, Latin-based word would keep me up at night, wondering why I had to be "the one" gifted with a voice so different from the other boys'.

I didn't know what to do because I wanted to talk, but knew as the sound wave left my throat that it would become a rusty wheel against the air—a disgrace that threatened the perfect silence of nature. Did the birds mock me when they heard me speak? It was during those long nights of over-obsessing about my voice that the idea of suicide began to form in my mind. I would think about taking my own life because living with my voice, my falsetto of death, seemed unbearable.

I felt cornered by the sounds coming from the larynx of my own body, and I had no idea how I would get through an entire life sounding like that. Should I become mute? Should I hide my voice in my throat, tucked away beneath the skin and muscle? Could I somehow change my voice? I didn't know the answer, nor did I want to think about it, but the daily teasing began to strangle me, and the person I should have been in the process of becoming began to hide deep within my skin.

Although my spoken voice fell flat, I believed that my written voice would withstand the ages and leave a deeper impact than any physical voice I had been given by the creator of humans. It was then that I realized Pandora's box was not evil; rather, it contained her voice box, and by opening it she was able to speak her own thoughts as a strong woman. She angered the world around her and was condemned for it, and so was I.

8

SKULL

THE HUMAN SKULL IS A COMPLEX STRUCTURE THAT HOUSES THE BRAIN. WITHIN THE BRAIN IS A SPECIFIC REGION RESPONSIBLE FOR RECOGNIZING FACES. IT IS SO ATTUNED TO FINDING THEM THAT IT CAN IDENTIFY FACES IN RANDOM PATTERNS, IN SYMBOLS, IN FOOD, AND IN NATURE. THE HUMAN BRAIN CANNOT SEPARATE THE IMAGE OF THE HUMAN SKULL FROM THE FAMILIAR HUMAN FACE. BECAUSE OF THIS, BOTH THE DEATH AND PAST LIFE OF THE SKULL ARE SYMBOLIZED, AND HUMAN SKULLS HAVE A GREATER VISUAL APPEAL THAN ANY OTHER HUMAN BONES IN THE SKELETON. THE SKULL FASCINATES EVEN AS IT REPELS.

A menacing shadow had been following me for two weeks, and I couldn't shake it. It quietly lurked until I was desperately vulnerable. That shadow was Death, and I had been marked. I could feel the chill of its breath in the autumn breeze with its intoxicating, clove-like scent.

I had become a regular at the hospital due to my asthma. Even though I couldn't breathe properly, I continued to show up for Saturday afternoon gymnastics practice. Endorphins released by exercising usually helped me breathe easier, but that natural chemical relief was no longer occurring. At the end of practice we raced each other up a giant hill. Running made my lungs vulnerable and frail, but I couldn't tell my coach because I didn't want to appear weak. He would have allowed me to rest, but I wouldn't—I'd be giving up on myself. I wasn't going to sit back and watch my teammates' strength increase.

Chris was usually the fastest, but on one glorious Saturday I won the race three times in a row. At home after practice my breathing quickly disintegrated into a tight, wheezing gasp, making me sound like I had swallowed a whistle. I took my blue inhaler, showered, and watched my mom get ready for work.

Once my mom left, I searched the channels on TV for a good horror movie. As the daylight faded, my breathing began to decline quicker than ever. Usually attacks took time to increase in strength, but this was a sudden tidal wave roiling over my body. The dark shadow I feared sat next to me, holding my hand. It was not dark in color, but more an absence of light, and it chilled my skin. Its frigid hands touched my chest, feeling my heart beat, trying to memorize the sound so it could crack the code and stop it.

When my attacks got that bad, I would close the bathroom door, run a hot shower, and sit by the steam to loosen the thick phlegm's black grip around my lungs. I would sit there for hours with the shower door cracked open, tilt my head back, and suck in the white mist. The steam and repeated shots of my inhaler weren't making a difference that night. Each minute the tightness worsened, and I could feel my airway closing.

As my breath slowly waned, I saw the appearance of Death for the first time. I couldn't tell if it was male or female, but it was exquisite, commanding, radiant, tranquil, and genuine. We sat face-to-face at a dinner table, and I looked deep into its bottomless eye sockets. Death, handsome, gorgeous, and composed, was dressed in a suit, and I wore a hospital gown. The room was empty except for us, but there was background chatter, as though we were dining in a crowded, fancy restaurant. A piano played in the background, a familiar song I couldn't recall. I put my hand to my mouth and noticed it was gone. I tried to feel the outlines of my lips and teeth, but they had vanished, and all that remained was a smooth, gruesome patch of skin. I began to panic.

I looked down at the silverware that sparkled like stars in the sky, and the tablecloth resembled a giant galaxy. Death gestured with its hands, as if to say, "Bon appétit," but there was nothing to eat on my side of the table. I looked across to see a large, sterling silver lid covering a platter. Death's bony fingers reached down to grab the handle, and it said pleasantly, "You know how badly you've wanted me to come." Its voice was ecstasy echoing through my life. It spoke graciously. "There are so many people imprisoned by their bodies, and I am the peace that lets them escape it. I know you've been waiting for me. I know about the teasing, the sleepless nights, the terrorizing dream you have of being an Olympian. I can make it all go away; I can help you become a star in the sky and you will eternally shine your light down on your family."

Just then its bony fingers pulled back the silver lid, exposing a grisly set of raw lungs—my lungs. They were sitting on a bloody plate and still breathing, like two captured fish about to die. I looked down at my hospital gown and touched my chest, and there was a huge, open hole where my lungs used to be. I was empty, and if I stood naked, one could see right through me. Death grabbed the shiny silverware and began cutting into my lungs, slowly and evenly, and I felt the gnawing pain beneath my skin even though they were no longer in my body. I wanted to scream, to yell in pain, but I had no mouth, breath, or voice. Blood oozed out of my lungs as Death mindlessly cut into each slice, raised the piece to its mouth, and began to chew. I felt a sensation more agonizing than the cutting. I felt Death consuming my lungs, and the torture was unbearable. My blood dripped from the corners of its mouth, and still, Death looked attractive. It leaned forward and kissed me on the forehead. I wiped the stain of the bloody kiss off my skin. Its seduction was paralyzing, and for a moment I had no pain. I felt free, sacred, and complete.

I woke up on the couch with sweat stinging my eyes and fear closing my throat. All the agony on Earth was concentrated in the center of my chest. My small, clasped hands turned to fists, fighting and drawing breath from beneath the Earth. I gasped and struggled, but nothing happened. Eventually that intense pain would become unbearable as Death waited patiently for me to beg. It wasn't going to take my life unless I willingly gave it away. However, along with that discomfort came the greatest desire to hold on and fight to keep breathing with every fiber of my being. I should have called an ambulance, but I waited for my mom to come home. The hours fell into the night and the sun would come up again, releasing her from the underworld. She would help me breathe again, ridding Death from my body, but morning was far away and I was losing the battle.

I couldn't hold on much longer. As I went in and out of consciousness, Death spoke to me, whispering its quiet intentions. It told me I could lie down and surrender as it naturally plucked me from the Earth the way I thoughtlessly picked flowers. It told me the transformation would be quick and all my struggles would be over. I wanted to give in; I wanted to lie down and relinquish, but I couldn't. To this day I don't know what kept me going. My life force refused to hear the solemn sounds of Death, and fought every second for survival. This was proof that the body, of its own accord, wants to live; but Death wasn't leaving without a fight, tempting me with heaven and its sweet, watery bliss—a place where I could go to avoid all conflict that preceded that moment.

As my spirit began to dim, the lights from my mother's car rolled across the ceiling like a chariot of horses from the stars. I immediately ran to the door, and when she saw me, she knew I was in bad shape. She seemed angry, not with me or herself, but with my asthma and how frequently I kept getting sick. She couldn't understand why the hospital kept discharging me when I kept having attacks. I wasn't embarrassed, as my pride had left and all that remained was my fight for breath. All things mundane and usual were drowned out by the seriousness of my sickness. My mom put me in the car and drove me to my primary care physician. When we got in the examination room he took one look at me and called an ambulance.

I don't remember what happened next, but when I woke up I was in a room surrounded by machines and nurses. The nurse at my right had a warm smile for me, but had a large needle in her hand; she said she was going to draw blood. I wasn't afraid of needles, but she was going to draw blood from an artery near my wrist for a blood gas test, an extremely painful procedure where the blood is taken from the radial artery to check the oxygen levels. It felt like a hot poker plunged into my bloodstream. There were multiple injections of medications, oxygen tubes up my nose, and a heparin lock. Still, I couldn't breathe and wasn't in a safe zone yet, as the constrictions in my lungs continued.

A week went by, but it felt like a month. Separately, my parents came to visit, and my mom brought my teddy bear Oatmeal to keep me company. I was still very weak. For an athlete, being sick or injured is one of the worst things that can happen. We work so hard to be strong and healthy that when we are not at our optimum level we feel "less than." Even though I was dreadfully sick, I still had the compulsion to exercise. I knew the other athletes on the team weren't taking this week off. I kept thinking, *What if they learn a harder trick while I'm stuck in this hospital bed?* Just thinking about it made my breathing worse, but I had to figure out a way to exercise in bed. Several tests continued to check my lung functions, and the results weren't good. Every other day I was wheeled down to a room to breathe into a huge fish tank-like machine to check my lung capacity. The oxygen levels in my blood were still below average, and the tests showed lung damage and scar tissue from my asthma.

Another week went by and I was still lying in a hospital bed. The eggshell-white walls and hospital gowns began to drive me crazy. I attempted to do some leg lifts, but got caught by a nurse who yelled at me, saying I was sick in a hospital bed and shouldn't exercise. I believed exercise would heal me quicker, so I continued the leg lifts after she left the room.

Tara brought me all my missed schoolwork and I did as much as I could, but it was difficult to concentrate. Instead I lay in bed watching daytime TV. Yet another week went by, and I slowly began to recover. The doctors tapered off my nebulizer treatments and promised I could go home in a few days. I was on a chemist's cocktail of powerful medications when they finally released me from the hospital.

As soon as I got home, I returned to gymnastics. Every move was a struggle; I was extremely out of shape, and I thought my body would never get back to the condition I had previously achieved. To rekindle the fire, I tried to remember the warrior I once was. I thought about all my hard work over the years, trying to reconnect to the boy inside me, the boy who would never quit or give up, and the spark reignited—something telepathically demanded me to keep going. I doubled my workouts and conditioned my body as often as I could. My physical return was much slower than I anticipated, but my soul wouldn't allow me to quit the fight.

After I was back in competition shape, I thought about Death. I thought about its beauty and power, and knew that beyond the stars and beyond the clouds, it was there, waiting for the end of our fleeting lives.

9

HAIR AND NAILS

TODAY WE KNOW THAT FOLLICLES AT THE BASE OF HUMAN
HAIRS, FINGERNAILS, AND TOENAILS CONTAIN CELLULAR
MATERIAL RICH IN DNA, WHICH CAN BE USED TO DETERMINE
THE IDENTITY OF AN INDIVIDUAL. PERHAPS IT'S NO COINCIDENCE
THAT ANCIENT VOODOO DOLLS WERE PREPARED USING BITS OF
HUMAN HAIR AND NAILS, BECAUSE THEY WERE BELIEVED
TO COMPRISE ELEMENTS OF A PERSON'S IDENTITY. THE DOLLS
WERE OFTEN USED IN VOODOO RITUALS DESIGNED TO
CONTROL, REWARD, OR PUNISH INDIVIDUALS.

I was finally in high school, and naively believed it would be a new start for me with other kids my age. It was a regional school that combined two towns: Norton and Easton. Our small-town group of Easton students did not know the Norton students, and so none of them knew our past. I believed we all secretly wanted to hide our former selves. The girls who were chubby and made fun of, the boys who had peed their pants in second grade, and those caught picking their noses—all wanted their stories to die in the past along with our preteen years and last year's clothing styles.

This was not a school of higher learning, but an alliance of fallen souls. It was an experiment in socialism and power play executed on a group of same-aged beings desperately trying to find themselves in a culture of unforgiving greed and dominance. Those of us from the Easton schools wanted a new start more than anything—geeks and losers getting a chance to become popular and cool.

Every day I woke up at 6:00 a.m., moments after the sun rose, and prepared for war. We marched into the school building like bloodthirsty zombies out to get tortured—not by our teachers, but by each other—as we tore one another apart, flesh from bone. As the blood and goodness bled out, nothing remained but anguish and despair. The teenage mind and social system is an atom bomb wrapped in denim and designer clothes, drenched in perfume and cologne, and steered by an intellect that thinks it knows everything.

I decided not to tell the new students about my gymnastics. I was already filled with self-hatred that simmered daily to a boil, and I couldn't stand to add to that. I couldn't allow the teasing to grow, and I had to strategically reinvent myself. I strived to conceal the passion and love for the art that gave purpose to my life. I tried other sports to fit in, but they just didn't feel right. I was good at soccer, but my deep romance with movement wouldn't let me go. Like two star-crossed lovers, gymnastics and I were going to die together.

The new kids in school from Norton were more socially advanced than us in every way. We were the good kids suddenly introduced to a pool of new people who smoked weed, drank beer, and had sex. It seemed like heaven and hell were colliding. Sure, we were teenagers, but I think we were more like angels and demons creating a social nightmare while having to learn irrelevant and untenable things for a future that was permanently held above our heads. As much as we tried to study and become good students, curses and evil intentions won over our minds, and the difference between right and wrong became impossible to tell. In our teenage years we were completely powerless over all of that, but I was determined not to fall victim to peer pressure. I had firsthand experiences at home of the destructive and insidious nature of drinking and smoking, and I knew those temptations would pull me away from my Olympic dreams.

High school is an exaggerated microcosm of the world in which we live, and despite my attempts at disguising myself, I could not hide who I was. Everyone knew I was a gymnast. The sides between towns crossed, and the pasts we secretly swore to keep were told. The ridicule I heard made it excruciating to love what I did. The teasing got worse than it had been in middle and junior high school, and everyone at my new school seemed to believe gymnastics was not a real sport. I didn't bother fighting that perception, and instead drew closer to the invisible world I had created for myself, a thin line between fantasy and reality.

Tara defended me like a Valkyrie against the tormenting monsters, but when teenagers believe something, they cling to it as if all of creation depends upon it. Faith and ignorance are the complete workings of a teenage mind. In addition to that, kids whispered "fag" as I walked past them in the hallways. Hearing that word set me on fire, and all the rage in the world burned through my body. It was the one word that immediately shattered all that I was into tiny, meaningless fragments. It was the one word that took my masculinity and vaporized it. I couldn't understand their attacks, since I was physically stronger than most kids in my class. How could they call me that? To me, the word *fag* represented femininity, weakness, frailty, and I had none of those things. Yes, I was short, with a squeaky voice, but this was my first year of high school and most of the other guys my age hadn't completely matured physically either.

How could they call me "fag" when I felt attracted to girls? I heard the voices in exactly the same pitch and volume in which they were spoken. I got nauseated every time "fag" wormed its way into my ear, and the person I thought I was began to evaporate. The thought of ending my life popped up again. I wanted to rid myself of the torment and teasing. That thought flickered, sharp and smooth, impossible to imagine for real, but still I found it wildly entertaining. Something stubborn inside me carried that idea away, something pure and sacred. If life got bad enough, death would still be an option, but movement owned me and it wouldn't let me go until it had used my body as its vessel.

I began missing school, skipping Mondays or Fridays, because I needed an extra-long weekend. I increasingly felt sick, and my breathing began to worsen. I was often exhausted to the bone and had a constant runny nose. I was a freshman with three more years of torture ahead, unable to sleep at night because I was manic and desperate. My imagination kept me awake, believing there was something great out there, something magnificent that would change my life forever. I prayed to the moon for answers and waited for the howling winds to take my pain away. But they never did.

10

MUSCLE

MUSCLE IS A BAND OF FIBROUS TISSUE THAT HAS THE
ABILITY TO CONTRACT AND MOVE AN ORGANISM'S BODY.
THERE ARE THREE TYPES OF MUSCLE TISSUE: SKELETAL,
SMOOTH, AND CARDIAC. MUCH OF THE BODY'S ENERGY
CONSUMPTION IS THROUGH MUSCULAR ACTIVITY. A DISPLAY
OF STRENGTH IS A RESULT OF THREE OVERLAPPING FACTORS:
PHYSIOLOGICAL, NEUROLOGICAL, AND MECHANICAL.

Gymnastics is dangerous and can easily lead to serious injury and
even death if not carried out properly. We visualize the challenging
and hazardous skills before performing them. As athletes, we need
to internalize the movement, programming its code into our every
muscle fiber. The complex challenge comes after the visualization
when we let go of fear and trust our bodies to mimic exactly what
we envisioned in our minds, relying on the deities of artistry to meet
us halfway and to ensure that our bodies are placed in the correct
positions. In order to succumb entirely to this physical confidence, we
have to shut down the thinking part of our minds and allow the body
to take control. Occasionally the mind awakens, instantly warning
the muscles, "This is dangerous! Stop!" When that happens, the body
seizes in midair, disengages from all movement, and crashes down
to the ground. That was part of our training, and most gymnasts
frequently fall. Our reliance on the unknown is critical, but there is a
fine line to our physical limitations, and the importance is in knowing
the boundaries. Too much faith can make gymnasts believe they can

fly like Icarus. And when gymnasts do not heed the warnings of their coach, they plummet, like Icarus, to their demise.

There is a transition from confidence into what I call *knowing*. To *know* something is a total absorption of faith into the mind and its vehicle, the body. Once something is understood and conquered in this way, it creates a force we use to perform. This *knowing* is a perfect harmony between the mind and the body: We *know* we can't fly, so we don't attempt it. Those who attempted flight had disharmony between their body and mind. That power takes years of practice to summon, and isn't always accessible. Sometimes I would call on the force and nothing would happen. Then there were times when I performed a baffling skill without harmony, but I landed perfectly on my feet and had no idea how it happened. I would launch myself into the air with intention and become entirely lost to centrifugal force and gravity, not knowing which direction was up or down, but somehow I would safely land on the mat.

Getting to the Olympics was all I could think about and all I wanted. I never saw anything beyond that goal. To say I was obsessed is an understatement. I continued to excel in the sport while tightly holding onto my Olympic dream as if my life depended on it—and to me it did. Everyone around me knew this—the neighbors, the kids at school, my teachers, and even my doctors. I knew that if I didn't fulfill that dream I would be a failure, every day, for the rest of my life.

The old wallpaper in my bedroom had been torn down, and the walls were redecorated with my competition ribbons and medals. I had more first-place medals than any other ones, and they were strung all over the walls, telling the story of a determined boy who had endured the pain and agony of a sport he loved so much. My room was also covered in pictures of my heroes from gymnastics magazines, alongside a few posters of Freddy Krueger.

I returned to the Olympic Training Center for another training camp, and this trip was different from the first one. The young troops of warriors were more fervent and tenacious than before. Their skills were sharper, cutting with precision, and that worried me. It appeared they handled the stress of gymnastics better than I did. Again, I was amazed at how many other outstanding athletes there were throughout our country, other soldiers like myself who would undertake anything for an opportunity to live out their passion and obsession.

My coach, Dan, was my hero and began to take on the role of a father—a Daedalus to my Icarus—as many coaches do with young athletes. I was becoming the warrior he had trained me to be. He taught me about aspects of myself that I never knew existed. He taught me to surrender to this unique power and helped me uncover a profound resilience and to have complete trust in my abilities. I knew he was responsible for my success in the sport, and I looked up to him. Dan taught me the value of being a good person. He showed me how to win and how to be respectful when I did. He was the greatest adult I knew, and together we would succeed in achieving my goals.

The relationship between coach and athlete is immensely important. The coach must unearth the strongest part of the individual without crushing it and convince the human body that it can achieve anything the mind asks of it. The coach must persuade the athlete that he or she is invincible in the face of obstacles and to be pure of heart while conquering them. Finding these skills in a coach was difficult, because even though there are great ones, there are also many bad ones.

I was not prepared for what was about to happen. On a random winter day in the gym, Dan sat us all down by the pommel horse for a discussion. I sat on top of the apparatus, in my need for the most attention, and he told us he had some bad news. My body stopped moving and I listened closely to his words. He said apologetically, "I have been coaching you guys for a long time now, and it is very hard for me to tell you this, but I got offered a new job coaching out West." He paused for a moment, and I waited for him to say he was joking, but then he continued. "So I'll be leaving here in a few weeks."

After realizing that Dan was serious, I suddenly felt self-conscious about my choice of seating. I wished I hadn't sat on the horse, higher than everyone else, because my eyes filled with tears, but there was no way I was going to cry in public. I felt sick and nauseated. I looked down at Seth, who began to cry, apparently unaware that young warriors are never supposed to let their guard down. I saw the tears in his eyes and felt his emotions, but I refused to let a single drop fall. I pulled the tears back into my eyes, letting my anger swallow them up.

As the meaning of Dan's announcement sunk in, I became enraged. I was surprised the leather pommel horse I was sitting on didn't catch fire from the intense heat coming off my body. Dan couldn't leave us. I needed him! For the rest of practice that afternoon, all of Dan's warriors were hushed and solemn, and I felt like I'd just been told my best friend had died.

When I got home from practice and told my mom, I started to cry. She told me she had already been informed of Dan's decision and hadn't wanted to tell me. She attempted to soften the blow by trying to convince me that the new job in California was a much better opportunity for him. She said the pay would be better and he would have more career-building opportunities. But I didn't care about any of that. It was about me and my loss, not Dan's good fortune.

Part of me died that night, and I was consumed by an overwhelming sadness. My whole world was demolished, and lightning struck, igniting a massive blaze and setting fire to my Mount Olympus. Zeus would never reign again, and I would never be an Olympian. I felt ripped off, angry, and betrayed. Dan was the only positive influence I'd had in my life, and I could not imagine living without him.

I grew obstinate and self-obsessed, unwilling to see how that move would benefit Dan's life. In my rage, a small piece of darkness was born within me. Life continued, but I couldn't see past the situation. The sun still rose in the morning, my mother continued to love my absent father, and life sped along the way it always had. I no longer felt support at home, and everything seemed to turn into an emotional war. All I kept thinking was *How could Dan leave me behind?*

That week at practice I thought if I worked harder, he would stay; that if I somehow became Olympic material he would change his mind. But it was already decided. Each day brought his departure closer, and the bright future I used to dream about became a threatening enemy. I felt weak because I couldn't stop what the future would bring, and frail because I had become so affected by another human being. During practice I held my emotions in my chalky palms, commanding them to flow through me. I would use my wrath to push myself through difficult skills.

Finally, the day I had feared the most arrived, and Dan left. I did my best to ignore what was happening and convinced myself he would come back. I just continued in the same direction, athletically preparing myself for the future. Over time, I would write letters to Dan describing my progress. I never gave up hope that he would return.

In place of Dan we got a new coach who was older, and I instantly despised him. I attempted to place myself on the same level as him. I allowed him to coach me, but he wasn't able to guide my artistry the way Dan had. His descriptions of how to perform a skill were unfamiliar to me, and, like a plant without sunlight, my gymnastics skills began to wither. I didn't have confidence in his coaching abilities, and I began to hold back. This was odd to him because he knew of my history and abilities, and had watched me compete since I had started. He couldn't understand why I was suddenly frightened when I executed simple skills. His teaching methods were the exact opposite of Dan's; he used fear instead of explanation. Throughout my competing life, I often watched other coaches screaming at their gymnasts to get them to perform terrifying elements, but that approach never seemed to have a healthy outcome. I didn't need any additional panic in my sport—it was frightening enough on its own. I hated my new coach and resented his presence.

Aggravation replaced the feeling of freedom I had come to rely on at the gym. Chris, the stronger teammate I didn't get along with, went to another gym. Though I was happy I didn't see him every day, I still had to compete against him, which made him more of an enemy. Seth, my best friend at the gym, quit gymnastics. I was devastated when he left.

I missed Dan. I wished his new job would not work out and that he would have to return to coach us. Distraught, I even checked out another gym, but quickly returned, yearning for the comfort of the familiar apparatuses I had started out with. Even though the equipment is the same in every gym, those particular pieces had become my allies. Feeling defeated, I went back to the new coach with all my shattered aspirations, but I never gave him the trust I had placed in Dan, and kept my power locked inside. It was not his to have, and he would have to beat it out of me to take it. In the end, I only sabotaged my own abilities.

I was still a competent competitor, but never the gymnast I could have been. My concentration had been broken, and the drive I once knew had dispersed. I stayed at the old gym for another year, slowly gaining confidence, but never accepting the new regime's approach to athleticism.

One day I returned to the gym I had previously scouted out, and realized I had never given Olympia Gymnastics a chance. The coach, Antonio, was also friends with Dan, and they both had attended the same college. His voice was deep and voluminous, a baritone-like commanding sound, and his enthusiasm and temper shifted quickly from exhilaration to outrage. He coached champions and athletes I admired, but he reminded me of my father in his stubborn Italian ways. I think that familiar characteristic blocked our attempts at a solid relationship. But his team had many great aspiring, talented gymnasts, and I found a new family of friends who pushed each other to become better athletes.

Gymnastics was still my sanctuary as the energy at home became more and more gloomy and hopeless. My mother drifted further away from the woman she had been, and I, too, grew in a different direction, no longer able to abide by her rules. I discovered a powerful new vocabulary and outlook, born of hatred, melancholy, anger, and anguish.

Something was beginning to devour me, infecting every part of my life, and my insomnia only made it worse. Everything became black, like an eclipse blotting out the sun, and in a strange way I found myself drawn to it. I began to isolate in my room and daydream about death. I would try writing as a way to reconnect with my humanity, but my choice of adjectives only drew me closer to that darkness, forging a peculiar intimacy with it. The more agony I experienced, the more nightmarish my outpourings of literature became. My suffering had a purpose, and I became the translation for pain.

My mother was lost in her own sadness and couldn't see the wrath within me. We both allowed the silence to grow, slowly building an impenetrable wall between mother and son. My safe space was writing alone in my bedroom, and hers was drinking alone in the living room. Neither of us could see what was approaching. I gradually realized what had been at the core of Dan's influence on me. He was *not* a father figure to me—rather, I was in love with him. Granted, it was a teenager's crush, but it is often those that translate into undying love—and therefore, undying heartbreak.

"he

was a broken branch
grafted onto a different family tree

adopted

but not because his parents opted for a different destiny
he was three when he became a mixed drink
of one part left alone
and two parts tragedy
started therapy in 8th grade
had a personality made up of tests and pills
lived like the uphills were mountains
and the downhills were cliffs
four fifths suicidal
a tidal wave of anti depressants
and an adolescence of being called popper
one part because of the pills

and ninety nine parts because of the cruelty

he tried to kill himself in grade ten
when a kid who still had his mom and dad
had the audacity to tell him "get over it" as if depression
is something that can be remedied
by any of the contents found in a first aid kit

to this day
he is a stick of TNT lit from both ends
could describe to you in detail the way the sky bends
in the moments before it's about to fall
and despite an army of friends
who all call him an inspiration
he remains a conversation piece between people

who can't understand

sometimes becoming drug free
has less to do with addiction
and more to do with sanity

we weren't the only kids who grew up this way
to this day
kids are still being called names
the classics were
hey stupid
hey spaz
seems like each school has an arsenal of names
getting updated every year
and if a kid breaks in a school
and no one around chooses to hear
do they make a sound?

are they just the background noise
of a soundtrack stuck on repeat
when people say things like
kids can be cruel?
every school was a big top circus tent
and the pecking order went
from acrobats to lion tamers
from clowns to carnies
all of these were miles ahead of who we were
we were freaks
lobster claw boys and bearded ladies

oddities
juggling depression and loneliness playing solitaire spin the bottle
trying to kiss the wounded parts of ourselves and heal
but at night
while the others slept

we kept walking the tightrope
it was practice
and yeah
some of us fell"

An excerpt of the poem *To This Day* by Shane Koyczan.
From the book *Our Deathbeds Will Be Thirsty*.

ELBOW STAND

11

TEETH

ONE OF THE MOST COMMON DREAMS IS LOSING ONE'S
TEETH, WHICH REPRESENTS EMBARRASSMENT, FEAR, SHAME,
ABANDONMENT, AND FEELINGS OF POWERLESSNESS. A PARALLEL
WAKING EXPERIENCE CAN BE FOUND IN THE PHRASE *losing face*.

I hated everything about alcohol—the smell, the way it changed people, and how insidiously it crept into my life. I had watched as it slowly destroyed the relationships in my family, like a cancer carving its way through our bodies.

My brother drank a lot, and would come into our room reeking of beer. I never understood how people smelled like alcohol; if I drank a gallon of milk, did I smell like a cow? He came into the room with bright, demonic eyes, excited, dizzy, energetic, and drunk. His drinking worried me, and I feared something terrible would happen. One night that fear turned into reality when he got into an awful accident. He wrapped his car around a tree so badly that its metal frame twisted around his body, locking him into a steel grave. He was rescued by the Jaws of Life and brought to the intensive care unit. When I heard the news, I was filled with fear. Was he going to be all right? Was he going to die? After a long time in the hospital and a few surgeries, he recovered, but the accident didn't change his behavior. Like many of us, he continued to believe he was immortal.

My mom also drank a lot, but it affected her differently than my brother. She didn't get the same energy as him, and seemed to be sliding down a hole, taking all light down with her into Hades' lair of endless repetition. Her life cycled around finishing the drink and filling it back up for that defined "fulfillment."

I hated alcohol.

I was determined never to drink, because I had seen and lived through the destruction it caused and, bottom line, it would ruin my gymnastics. I had seen older kids start drinking and watched how alcohol slowly destroyed the athlete they could have become. I was not going to let that happen to me. I was afraid of losing my physical control that I had worked so hard to achieve.

In my sophomore year, everyone in school started experimenting with alcohol and pot, including my closest friend Tara. She came over to my house on weekends with her friends to drink. I had the house to myself until two in the morning since my mom was always at work, so it became the "drinking house." I had learned from my sisters to clean the house so it looked better than it did before Mom left, and she would never suspect a thing. Our family adage, "If no one saw it, then it didn't occur," was in full effect. I watched my friends get drunk, laugh, and dance, and then cleaned up after them.

After months of being the perfect human specimen, always on the outside of my friends' world and always eating properly, working out, caring for everyone, and cleaning up after them, I decided to have a beer with them. I drank it as fast as I could because it tasted so awful. Everyone told me the first one always tasted bad, but the second one would taste better. I didn't feel anything after the first beer, but as I drank the second one a small wave of calm and pleasure washed over me. I felt a little taller, and the rest of the second beer did indeed taste better. I felt myself gaining confidence that allowed me to drink even more. Small waves of pleasure intensified, and I felt the huge, hollow well of my soul slowly fill up with warmth and happiness.

Tara was thrilled that I finally drank with her, crossing into the enchanted place teenagers go, the place I had sworn against—the place I had denied myself through control and fear. I continued drinking and thought, *What took me so long?* If I had known it felt that good, I would have started years ago. Each bitter gulp helped dissolve the tremendous burden of trying to be a perfect champion, draining my mind of its circling problems and presenting the answers in simple laughter. This was better than medicine, and provided exactly the effect I needed: a burst of light to penetrate my dark world. All this time spent alone in my head, cursing myself, hating myself, beating myself up, being ridiculed, and fighting for my breath to reach Olympia built up into this moment of relief—and in that moment, it was all sort of . . . funny. Finally, I didn't care.

After my fourth beer, we went swimming in our kidney-shaped pool. The pool water glistened in the darkness, perfectly cool and numbing against our skin. We could not contain our laughter, and we didn't dare; laughter would seek its revenge if we denied its release. The giant pine trees watched behind us, and I knew with every fiber of my being that *this* was the cure for what ailed me. The night belonged to us, as did almost every weekend that followed.

All I could think about during school was the weekend. I knew everything would be okay as soon as I could drink that second beer. It gave my mind and body a short vacation. My mother never suspected anything, and I never admitted to drinking. All the people I resented, the drunken slobs at the bar, and my father, well, I realized they were on to something. I still believed drinking was a weakness, so how weak did that make me? How could I be angry at my mother for something I was doing myself? I had discovered its wonder, realizing I needed it as much as she did. I never drank in front of my brother; that was a boundary I was unwilling to cross. He knew me as his little brother, and I didn't want him to see me enjoying the family cure and curse.

Every weekend that I could drink, I drank, mostly with Tara. I drank a couple of times with some guys on the gymnastics team. I found out quickly that I was able to drink a large amount without experiencing any side effects in the morning. I was always the first one to crack open a beer and the last one to put it down, and never understood why my friends would stop, brush their teeth, and then get ready for bed. Why weren't they drinking like me, until the sun rose?

That year I bought my first car, a gray Toyota Celica, from Trish. I loved it, and would follow my brother to parties with kids his age outside of our town. I had gymnastics practice on Saturday mornings, and when I drank on Friday nights my practices suffered because I finally started to experience side effects. I woke with my mouth dry as the desert, stomach wrenching, head spinning, and sweating from the alcohol. Sometimes I was still slightly drunk as I hopped into my little gray car and drove to practice, showing up late. My coach immediately knew what was going on, seeing how dramatically I had changed from the year before. I wore my carelessness as a new layer of flesh, proud of the trouble growing underneath.

My coach took me into his office, which was rare for him to do with any athlete. He told me how talented I was, and that if he had half the talent I did, he wouldn't piss it away like I was doing. I stood there with my arrogance, confusion, fear, and anger, wanting to break down in tears and scream to him, "Save me. I'm in pain. I'm dying. I can't breathe. I want to die. Please help me." But I didn't. I quietly swallowed his words and felt a deep shame. What would Dan think of me right now? It didn't matter; Dan had left me here, and this was the result. I knew that I needed to slow down my drinking on the night before a practice, and I had to work harder to control the situation.

I was trying to balance a difficult schedule: going to school, gymnastics practice, working, and drinking with my friends. When I worked at my parents' restaurant, I ran heavy racks of bar glasses through crowds of drunken people to make sure the turnover of drinks was fast enough for the bartenders to serve. I had to collect them and wash them quickly to maintain the cycle. It was hard work, and the money was good. Working there made me feel important and gave me a sense of satisfaction and belonging, all while allowing me to pay for my car.

When I wasn't working, I partied every opportunity I had. My brother and I decided to have a huge keg party one summer. I had just finished reading *The Great Gatsby* and wanted it to have the same opulent feel as the parties in the book. We bought giant tiki torches and dug small trenches around the pool, decorating the yard in a Hawaiian luau style. Our house was perfect for a party—a large, open backyard guarded by giant pine trees; a romantic, crystal-clear pool that reflected the moon; and a large basement room where I slept. We charged five dollars a cup to cover the costs of the decorations and beer.

On the night of the party everyone from school was there. I felt a deep sense of camaraderie that I had never felt before. I had been the loner, the hermit, and always compared myself to everyone else. I was convinced they all had better lives and felt sorry for me, but that night we were all friends, drinking over the moments that normally divided us. We celebrated youth together, under the same moon I had cursed and hated for never saving me in the past, and now I could declare to it, "I don't need you anymore . . . you weren't enough for me anyway."

We made so much money from the party that we decided to have another one at the end of August. But when the time came, the weather was different, and the air was heavy as Death spread over the summer and the sun burned its rays across our dying grass. A large harvest moon rose over the horizon, turning peach, then purple, and finally black, surrounded by tiny twinkling stars. The crowds of kids came fast. Word had spread about our first party, and people came in from other towns. Parked cars lined our road, and people started jumping the fence instead of going through the gate where we were collecting money. So many people were coming so fast, rowdy and ready to party. I knew I couldn't drink because the party was already out of control and I couldn't stop it. The calm sea of people in our backyard had turned into a tsunami.

I stood there, puzzled, and watched my own party blast into chaos. My brother grabbed cue sticks from the pool table and stepped on them, snapping them in half to use as weapons, because it was obvious a fight was going to break out somewhere. It looked like he was going to stake a vampire. I knew the cops were coming because our phone was ringing off the hook. We couldn't control it as the smell of pot and cigarettes rose up in a cloud from our backyard. I went into my mother's room and locked the door behind me to remove myself from the situation, and at that moment the cops arrived. Our whole town's law enforcement was at our front door. Kids went running everywhere. I was glad the cops came, afraid the party would destroy everything we owned. The cops arrested several people who had pot on them. A few hours after everyone left, Michael and I took the remaining kegs and drank them as fast as we could.

The next morning the entire backyard was trashed, with vomit in the bushes and empty beer cups everywhere. My mom was so proud of her beautiful backyard, and we had trashed it. She was very upset with me. I had no smart-ass comeback for what had happened. I felt guilt coupled with a teenage hangover, and knew I needed to clean up my act. My summer of drinking was interfering with my gymnastics, so I decided to cool out for a bit. I was going to drink less and calm down for my junior year.

On my last drinking night before the new school year began, I decided to smoke pot. I had watched my friends smoke, and they always laughed at the most ridiculous things. Since I believe laughter is a great and powerful natural medicine, I thought smoking pot would be a good idea. My friends told me the high from pot was more mellow than drinking, and I wouldn't have a hangover the next day. That sounded like exactly what I needed.

I took my first puff from a loosely rolled joint. The smoke stung my throat, and I instantly coughed like a rookie. It tasted good on my lips and smelled natural and damp. I took another puff and held it in my lungs the same way I did with my asthma inhaler, holding the air deep down so my body would absorb the medication, and then I exhaled the thick smoke like a proud dragon. For the first time, I understood what the word *high* meant—I was somewhere in the air with my feet on the ground. Perceptions of my surroundings changed slightly, and I started to feel like a character in one of my own stories. Unlike alcohol, which revved me up, pot brought a quiet sense of peace and restfulness, and made me want more.

We replaced alcohol with pot and sometimes mixed the two. I didn't think it interfered with my Saturday morning practices, and was able to continue training hard without that horrible hangover. By now my parents knew I drank, but they never suspected I was smoking pot. I still had my clean-cut, all-American look—innocent baby face and puppy-dog eyes that could convince anyone I wasn't doing drugs like the other "stoners"—but I had firmly sunk my teeth into it.

12

SKIN

SCARIFICATION IS THE SCRATCHING, CUTTING, OR ETCHING OF DESIGNS, PICTURES, OR WORDS INTO THE SKIN. NOSE PIERCING WAS FIRST DONE 4,000 YEARS AGO IN THE MIDDLE EAST. THE FIRST TONGUE PIERCING WAS SEEN IN AZTEC, MAYAN, KWAKIUTL, AND TLINGLIT TRIBES AS AN ANCIENT BLOOD-DRAWING RITUAL TO PREPARE FOR THE ARRIVAL OF THE GODS. ROMAN WARRIORS PIERCED THEIR NIPPLES TO SHOW STRENGTH, COURAGE, AND BRAVERY, AND BRITISH AND AMERICAN SAILORS WERE KNOWN TO PIERCE THEIRS AS A RITE OF PASSAGE FOR TRAVELING BEYOND A SIGNIFICANT LATITUDE AND LONGITUDE.

The nineties alternative music revolution swept the nation, and I became its greatest fan. Like generations of teenagers before us, we declared our purpose to the world through the notes of the songs we worshipped and the styles and attitudes our music dictated. True to the new grunge, we were unkempt and careless, and looked like we had just rolled out of bed.

I saw the first sign of body modifications' rise in a man with his nose and tongue pierced at Lollapalooza, the summer's largest musical festival. I immediately wanted it, drawn to the juxtaposition of hard steel on soft skin. It looked painful and powerful—a spike though the center of a tongue represented physical and mental anguish, as if the wearer were saying, "I had my tongue nailed to say 'Fuck you and fuck off!'" The idea of expressing myself without using words that betrayed my horrible voice was hugely appealing to me.

The only body piercing place I knew wouldn't pierce anyone under eighteen years of age, and I was only seventeen. So I decided to pierce my nose on my own, believing I wouldn't get in trouble as long as I hid it from my parents.

That night I got drunk and removed a thumbtack from a poster on my wall. I marked the spot on my nose, cleaned the dull spike with rubbing alcohol, and slowly pressed it through the skin of my nose. The thick nasal cartilage made it difficult to penetrate all the layers of anatomy, and it hurt more than I had imagined. Every time I attempted to puncture that sensitive target, my eyes watered in blinding tears, but I wasn't going to let physical pain stand in the way of my identity. A grueling hour of rigorous pushing passed by, but the skin fought against me. It wasn't working.

I stood squinting at the mirror through watery vision as blood leaked from the hole. I twisted the thumbtack, and tried to wiggle it through the flesh. Finally, after four hours, it popped through to the other side. I was filled with relief and exhilaration! I was thrilled with the prize of having a green thumbtack sticking out of my nose. Now came the difficult part—I needed to remove the thumbtack and replace it with a steel hoop. I figured this was low-level surgery, and nothing was going to stop me. I poured a mixture of rubbing alcohol and hydrogen peroxide on the bloody area as a fizzy, stinging, painful wash. After I removed the thumbtack I couldn't find the punctured hole, and a maroon-colored river rushed down my face. Sheer determination guided me in threading a hoop through the hole I had created, and I looked in the mirror, thrilled with the result of my work. This was my first physical tribute to teenage angst. As I admired my new prized possession, I thought, *Well, I like it, but . . . this isn't enough,* and immediately thought about other places to pierce.

I went to wash the blood from my face and forgot about the protruding steel and slammed my hands into my raw nose. It felt like getting punched in the face. Sleeping was impossible, as I'd roll over and wake up in stinging pain, but my identity was worth a few sleepless nights.

The only other body part I could pierce without my parents knowing was my navel. Like a surgeon, I sterilized the area and marked the location to dissect the skin. The pain was worse than it was with the nose, and I realized this tool wasn't sharp enough to penetrate all the epidermal layers. I searched all the sharp objects in my house that could tear through a stomach and decided on a safety pin. It had enough metal surface for my thumb to securely apply pressure. My stomach quivered as the sharp pin stuck into my flesh. The nerves of my skin sent signals to my brain begging me to stop, but I didn't care; my pain receptors didn't understand the things cool kids had to do. I took a deep breath and pushed the pin, slowly drilling into the dermis. A dark maroon pool filled the entrance around the safety pin and blood trickled down, reminding me of a watercolor painting I had made as a child. I was happy to have hit blood.

My navel looked gruesome, but I continued to push into the pain like I was popping a balloon. I knew the blood meant the operation was halfway done, and I had to see it through. I held my breath and could feel tissue tearing underneath my skin. Was the laceration so intense because I was severing the mystical umbilical cord? Would that operation finally separate the son from the mother? My fingers shook as I tried to finish the job, and it seemed like the needle would never completely puncture through to the other side. The safety pin wasn't sharp enough either, but it was all I had.

I tried to convince myself I was a machine. I used steady pressure to complete my composition and, many agonizing hours later, tore through to the other side. The temple of my body now possessed a solid spike through its core, and I adored it. I had threaded a safety pin through my stomach and had arrived at perfection. That was my sacrifice to the gods, my own flesh and blood. Like Michelangelo, who carved away from the limestone the bits that weren't David, I was removing the pieces of flesh that weren't Joseph.

My navel brought the same repercussions as my nose—gymnastics, jeans, and sleep were agonizing—but I was willing to pay the price because pain defined and symbolized me. Piercing became my new obsession. If I had been a year older, I would have covered myself in glorious steel. I was in love with steel hoops, fascinated with the way a perfect circle with no beginning or end could go through one's body. I loved the shine of surgical steel and the message it carried: strong, heavy, and abrupt. Once my flesh would turn to dust, those endless circles would be the only remains in my casket. Even after the Earth would burn or freeze or crumble, my steel piercings would forever remain.

I looked in the mirror beyond my eyes, deep into the person I wanted to become. I was building armor protection and scars to tell others, "Stay away, I'm dangerous." I had dyed my hair jet-black. My pale face under my tarlike hair transformed me into a corpse with a silver hoop through its nose. I couldn't have been happier. For the first time I was satisfied with my outside appearance, because it started to match the pain of my insides. This was what high school had done to me—as others began their journey into a beautiful and hope-filled world, I grew into a "pretty hate machine."

I started getting attention everywhere I went. People stared at me and looked either horrified and afraid or fascinated and attracted. It didn't matter, because I believed I was making a point. I was angry; I was in hell; and now you had to see it. My pain was my fashion, the music was my inspiration, and my body became my masterpiece.

At school I gained confidence from my dark exterior's "I hate you" attitude, and it was true—I did hate them. I despised them for calling me fag, and hated them for hating me. I resented them because I felt nothing but animosity toward them. For the first time I was communicating, and people heard me. My black demon stalked the halls of education. "Fag" turned into "freak," and I embraced my new label.

My gymnastics coach was not happy about the change. Gymnastics had a certain look to it—preppy, clean-cut, and muscular—and I looked like I had been dancing all night in a mosh pit. Body piercing was a deduction in competition, but I wasn't willing to change myself for a score. I felt we should be judged on our movement and skill, not on what we looked like. I wanted this rule changed and felt responsible as a role model for the next army of alternative gymnasts.

I believed in my heart that my coach knew I was suffering. I believed he wanted to take me in, but didn't know how to confront my parents. Again, he pulled me into his office, trying to talk some sense into me. One-on-one without gymnastics to hide behind made it brutally uncomfortable. He told me that I had more talent in my little pinky than most of the other guys on the team, and I was letting it all go. I had no idea how to keep my spirit alive with everything that was happening at school. I was angry and wanted to spill my guts on his office floor, but couldn't bear telling him the truth about what I was truly feeling and what the kids were calling me. I was a warrior for the art of gymnastics, and that meant I had to be strong. I left his office wishing I could still find a shred of innocence in me, but it was too late. I had made the deal and crossed over. And new flesh was already growing over the good boy I used to be.

Next I wanted a tattoo, but I was still underage. I heard it was possible to create your own tattoo with a needle, India ink, and desire. I thought if I created something on my own skin, I would cherish it for life. I had to choose a place on my body where my parents wouldn't be able to appreciate my artwork. I decided my foot would be best, since I could cover it with my socks. My artistic symbol was a black widow, which represented my emotions—dark, angry, and lethal. It was also something I could draw without making too many mistakes.

I cleaned my foot with rubbing alcohol and drew the spider with a pen. I sterilized the needle by burning it with my lighter, dunked it into the India ink, and started to slowly carve the design into my foot. The idea was to remove the skin and let the ink absorb into the flesh. After seven days the wound would heal and the ink would become part of my body as newly designed skin. I slowly dragged the needle through my skin, tearing, ripping, and pulling the pieces of flesh out that blocked my design. As with all my new hobbies, it bled a lot and I could no longer see the pattern. I had to take breaks along the way because of the intensity of the pain, but after a few hours, I finally finished. I couldn't show it to anyone since my artistic creation would no doubt get back to my mother, but I had to show *someone* my accomplishment. I thought Michael would appreciate the lengths I had gone to in scarring my body, but when he saw my foot he looked nauseated. I was still bleeding, and he just asked, "What the fuck is that?" He seemed angry with me and looked at me as if I had become a stranger.

Two days later my mother called home from work. She was outraged and cursing, saying, "If you have a tattoo on your foot I will murder you. When I get home from work there better not be anything there! I've had enough . . . with your clothes, nose ring, and that hair! You're a disgrace!" I told her it was fake and that I didn't have anything on my foot.

I hung up the phone and looked down at the sore wound of my prison tattoo, thinking of ways to remove it. It had been only a few days, so I thought maybe it was possible to scrub off the inky scab. I knew my mother would kick me out of the house if she saw the tattoo. I scrubbed intensely for twenty minutes, but after I rinsed the suds away a horribly drawn black widow spider stared back at me; it wasn't coming out. I ran to the kitchen and got a Brillo pad. The bleeding increased as I scrubbed it raw with the steel wool, scratching the design out of my skin. As the sanguine-colored suds drained away, I saw that the ink was gone, along with my skin. The wound bled more than during the making of the tattoo, but I was thankful I'd somehow managed to kill the spider. I applied some Neosporin and wrapped my foot in bandages. When my mother came home I unraveled the bandages, exposing a raw, bloody wound, and said, "See! There's no tattoo!" She looked disgusted, didn't say a word, and stormed off. I was relieved there was no argument, but her silence always cut deeper than her rants.

∞∞∞∞∞∞∞∞∞

I could no longer work at the restaurant with my new look; the only job for freaks like me was at a music store. I worked at Sam Goody Music Land in the local mall, which gave me listening access to all the music I dreamed of. This was the perfect job, and my boss even had connections to a great piercing place in Providence, Rhode Island. My friend Randi—a daffodil holding a machine gun, with bleached-blonde hair and a hoop through her nose—and I drove there with no thought of the consequences, and decided to get our tongues pierced.

My mother had a new rule: If I were to get my tongue pierced, she would kick me out and I would have to live with my father. I didn't think she was serious, and knew she would never see the piercing unless I deliberately showed her. Randi and I shared the same anger with the world and saw the piercing as a necessary solidification of our identities. Still, we were both nervous to get it done.

I went first. Trance music played in the background and beautiful, stainless-steel body jewelry was on display in glass cases all around. This was nirvana. I picked a long barbell for my tongue and headed into another room. The piercer looked exactly like the entity I wanted to become—covered in piercings and tattoos that blurred the boundaries of his skin. I couldn't see where his flesh started or ended, and the line dividing his art and life's creation became one unified body of work, transforming him into something new through ink and steel—becoming his own God and creator. He looked beautiful and mean. Those weren't just decorations, they were tribal scars, and I was eager for my next initiation.

The room looked like a doctor's office, immaculately sterile and clean. Small gargoyle statues hovered on shelves above the piercing chair. Would those little silent demons watching my baptism allow me to pass? The piercer clamped my tongue with something that looked like hotdog tongs and said calmly, "Don't move it and take a deep breath out." Then a quick, sharp pain shot through the center of my tongue. He removed the huge needle and inserted the precious metal through the center. I was instantly high and filled with euphoria. I knew I would be back for more.

Randi and I were thrilled on the drive home. Sucking on ice cubes to keep the swelling down, we kept sticking our tongues out in the rearview mirror, making sure they were still there. I knew when I arrived home I wanted more, and I returned a week later for my septum, a bullring through the center of my nose. This was much more painful, but easier to hide since I could wear a curved barbell and just flip it up into my nose. Nobody would know it was there unless they did a nasal inspection—angel by day, demon by night.

The tension between my mother and me grew to monstrous proportions. It was constant screaming, and during one of our shouting matches my mouth opened wide and she saw the steel ball on my tongue—a precious silver pearl resting on the belly of an oyster. She looked mortified and betrayed. It was either take it out or move out. With perfect teenage conviction, I told her, "Over my dead body!" and started packing. We had driven each other to the point of rancor and she was angry with the results, unable to look at me—her homemade suburban Frankenstein.

∞∞∞∞∞∞∞∞∞

Enraged, I threw all of my stuff into the trunk of my car and left my mother's house, thinking, *I'll never come back here. I hate you. This is all your fault.* I sped away in pure hatred. I thought of how I had sat by her side as she cried over my father, and now she kicked me out for a pierced tongue. I had the perfect justification for even deeper self-destruction.

My father didn't know what to do with me. He could tell I was a ticking bomb, but had no clue as to what wires to cut so I wouldn't detonate. Deep within my eyes rested the question he feared most: "Did I do this to my son?" He didn't like the tongue and septum piercings either, but was afraid to pick a fight with me. He saw where I was headed and feared that maybe his leaving my mother had contributed to my induction into darkness. I could read his thoughts as he looked at me. "My son. What happened to my beautiful son, the amazing gymnast and good kid? Why is he doing this to himself?" I couldn't explain my transformation to my father. All I knew was that the ugliness made me feel alive, and the reaction on people's faces gave me joy. I thought my piercings made me look tough and mean. That was my armor, my protection against the world. I would reject everyone before they could reject me, and I would never again have to go through the pain of being denied or unaccepted. I was different, and felt comfortable with my metamorphosis into a thing people feared.

The ocean by my father's house was magic, and I believed it could heal my pain. I would stare at the sea for hours, watching the waves roll back and forth, crashing to the shore. My anger became nothing in those moments, and I breathed in a sense of peace.

A summertime New England beach is luxurious, but New England winters can be harsh and unforgiving. It was an hour's drive from my father's house to my high school, and my little gray car didn't have heat. I didn't have enough money to fix it since all of my cash went into body piercing and gas. I passed through each town with a sheet of ice on the windshield and would sometimes stick my head out the window to better see where I was going. The ocean air was freezing, and I didn't have gloves so I wore socks on my hands. I couldn't imagine what that must have looked like to the morning commuters: a boy covered in steel driving a block of ice with socks on his hands.

I was happier living at my dad's house, and his girlfriend tried to ease my pain with her kindness, but the drives to school and gymnastics were killing me. I was beyond exhausted, and would fall asleep at the wheel. I don't know how I didn't crash my car. I think on those long nights something powerful and caring took hold of the wheel. I started smoking cigarettes to keep me awake in case my angels didn't show up. Before I finished a cigarette, I would take two inhalations of my asthma medication because of how badly the smoke hurt my lungs. I drove those long hours into the night with smoke in my lungs, anger in my heart, and the sea by my side.

13

LIGAMENTS AND TENDONS

LURKING WITHIN A VICTIM'S OWN GENETIC CODE,
A VILLAINOUS DISEASE CALLED *fibrodysplasia ossificans
progressiva* IS ABLE TO CONVERT MUSCLES, TENDONS,
LIGAMENTS, AND OTHER CONNECTIVE TISSUE INTO BONE,
FUSING INTO A TYPE OF EXOSKELETON THAT CAN
TRANSFORM A HUMAN BEING INTO A LIVING STATUE.

As I watched my past roll out to sea, a falling star dropped into the empty space over the horizon. The ocean reflected the night sky like a huge liquid mirror. I sat on the soft sand and knew deep within my bones that my dream had not yet turned to stone, that behind my fury and hysteria, I still had the desire to compete. Together with the sea and the moon, I decided to continue to try my best in gymnastics.

Despite all my body modifications, I was in the best shape of my life. I trained every day—stretching, lifting, and performing routines better than ever. My grades and SAT scores, on the other hand, were not doing as well. I needed to bulk up my senior year average in order to continue my education and gymnastics. I needed to get noticed by college-level coaches, which made my senior year a very important one.

Once I would get into a good college, I hoped to turn my education around. I had stopped drinking and smoking pot, and increased the intensity of each workout. I had accepted that my Olympic dream would not happen; the best I could aim for now was to compete at a good college. Although I admitted this truth to myself, I still hadn't accepted that I had fallen so far behind. To be an Olympian remained my secret aspiration, even if it was submerged in a sea of regret.

The Junior Olympic National Championship was being held in Oakland, and I wanted to go for more than one reason. California, in my mind, was a wonderful land of palm trees and hope, the complete opposite of the dreary seasons of New England. I secretly planned to run away after the competition and stay in California to start my life over again.

Although I felt like I was spiritually drowning, the warrior in me made a pact to rise up from the ocean floor for one more fight. I strategized and obsessed and focused on the perfect execution of skills, solidifying every bent knee and pointed toe. Gymnastics competition is a science of safety and numbers. We had to do our routines hundreds of times exactly the same way, error-free, but more importantly, we had to be perfect on the day of the competition. What we did in practice ultimately didn't count. I ran through my routines in my mind every night against the throes of insomnia. Those routines were my flesh and blood, my children, and I mentally and physically knew every inch of them. Even sleep allowed me no rest, as my muscles twitched and my body perspired, executing harrowing skills instead of having sweet dreams.

Gymnasts all over the country were preparing for their state championships. We were strong, dedicated athletes used to extraordinary amounts of pain. Every day we woke up with incredible amounts of soreness. We murdered our bodies, and the apparatuses we used gave us horrible beatings. It's an odd relationship between the gymnast and the structures we flip on, swing around, and hang from. Anyone with a love or respect for his or her body would not endure the slow re-formation, or the bone-bashing and joint-jarring challenges gymnasts place upon themselves in their obsession to achieve greatness. But the deep love and bizarre devotion kept us flipping on fire as our ligaments, joints, and muscles ripped and stretched. Years of pursuing this agonizing relationship had hardened our bodies and conditioned our minds to transcend normal pain.

Each apparatus was unique as it doled out its own punishment. Our knees and ankles were destroyed after endless punching of the floor, sending crunching pangs of agony through our bones. We pointed our toes and tightened our legs to extremes. The pommel horse never appeared dangerous, but it was a hard, leather-covered beast, and hitting it wrong was like getting punched by a prizefighter. The leather covering the horse sometimes ripped the top layer of our skin, like the bite of its namesake. Swinging from the still rings stretched our shoulders to their fullest point of flexibility, until it felt like our ligaments and tendons would pull out of their sockets.

The worst discomfort for me was the high bar. It took years of training to strengthen the muscles in my forearms to hang from the bar, and then the constant friction between the steel bar, chalk, and leather grip tore the skin off my palms. We called these deep, bloody, flesh tears "rips." Even with multiple rips, we still had to perform. A drop of water on the torn flesh stung like rubbing alcohol poured on a wound. Rips made everything unbearable—showering, opening doors, holding a pen. When we slept, the raw meat of our hands pulsed in pain, like skin on fire, as if pain found its birth in our open wounds.

But, for us gymnasts, this was our love and we wouldn't have it any other way. We begged for the glory to battle against gravity through the extreme movements of man. Our obsession, desire, loyalty, and discipline overshadowed any treacherous notions of quitting this beautiful sport. We were protected and possessed by the unspoken power of gymnastics. We wanted to be warriors, and in many ways, we were. If we weren't going to be great, what would we do? What kind of future would we have after years of dedication to the sport? Our bodies were broken and whipped into the human machine gymnastics demanded.

For the true gymnast, physical pain becomes as natural as the tortured breathing I experience during an acute asthma attack. We get used to it, hate it, love it, sleep with it, and absorb it into our beings. But if we tired of the agony, or hated the never-ending endurance testing, or couldn't wait for the war to be over, it was never spoken. Those things go beyond the sport of gymnastics, and every athlete feels a deep passion to push through the affliction of injury. I often wondered if my desire to win was worth the mutilation and destruction of my body.

I won the state competition, and it meant everything to me because Coach Dan was there to see me take the first-place medal. I was still embarrassed competing in front of him, because I knew in my heart I could have done better. I knew I could have been a true champion, and now I was only a suggestion of that, a mere shadow of what I could have been.

The next level was regional competitions, consisting of all New England states. Chris and I were constantly neck and neck, and I was afraid he would win this one. He was much stronger than me, and resembled a body builder more than a gymnast. He also worked harder, but I felt I had more passion and had sacrificed more. I think my coach was eager to watch the story unfold, to see which one of us would win at that level.

During warm-up for our third event, Chris injured his ankle coming off the vault. He had to withdraw from the competition, ensuring we would never know who the better gymnast was. I won that regional championship, but it never felt like it was a true fight, both because Chris could not compete against me and because I had held back on some skills I would have tried in an effort to highlight my strengths. This made me hate the fact that I won. Although I knew my choice to play it safe was how you played "the game," I wasn't in it for the game as much as for the pleasure of the beatings. I chose to take the gold rather than to go all out and potentially screw up.

The regional win meant that I was now qualified to enter the Junior Olympic National Competition in Oakland. We would be gone for one week, with one day free to tour California. On our way to Oakland I revisited my daydream of not getting on the return flight and running away. The palm trees gave me refuge from my thoughts, and it was good to see a different environment. I thought that if I could just get away from my home, then maybe I would have a fighting chance at life.

We spent our "free" day seeing California before getting ready for our competition against the country's top gymnasts. Practicing in their midst was pure intimidation, and our entire team felt the pressure. They all appeared confident, mature, and ready to deliver, while we all quietly fell to pieces. I don't know if we were tired from the trip or just overwhelmed by the reality of the competition, but as a group, we did not want to compete. Yet we had no choice. We had to perform; we had worked too hard to pull out now. I realized that I had peaked too early in the season, and let myself be devoured like a small fish in a shark tank. I was all over the place during the first two events, and my performance was awful as I changed routines on the fly instead of going for solid skills I knew.

In my normal state of competing, I became deaf to sound. My mind would become a place of absolute quiet as I located the warrior within, but now, for the first time, I heard the chaos around me, and the champion never stepped forth. I couldn't summon him. I drowned in the noise of the crowd, the sounds of other gymnasts as they met their marks, and the canned music in the background. My warrior got lost in that sea of sound.

To make matters worse, I fumbled my best event, the floor exercise. On my last tumbling pass I walked into the skill, giving up on the difficult movement and doing something basic. I don't know why I did that, and as I left the floor I heard my dreams shatter. I couldn't look my coach or teammates in the eye. I was so disappointed in myself, knowing how important that competition was to me . . . and to them. I had to perform exceptionally well there to show collegiate coaches that I was a good gymnast and a tough competitor, but I blew it. It was devastating.

If I didn't have a motivation to kill myself before, I had just found one. I was nothing. Empty and completely confused by the sport I loved, betrayed by the grace and gift of gymnastics, I wanted to cry, but didn't. Like a statue, I just sat there, solid and expressionless. In that moment, I surrendered my sword. I dropped the blade that was perfectly carved by years of training. I gave my power back to the heavens, saying, "I don't want this fucking gift anymore; take it

back, because I cannot handle the responsibility and demands of it."
I couldn't endure another minute of this agony, and even though I
had no idea what I would do with my life, I knew that I could not
remain a gymnast.

I was filled with self-hatred, and, as my animosity burrowed deeper
into my bones, I had to find the warrior in my soul so I could kill
him. I knew if I could exorcise this longing to be a champion from my
body, it would take the obsession and desire with it. If it left, maybe
I would have some peace; maybe I would get a whole night's sleep
without the fear of not performing to perfection. I had had enough.

I gave my power back to the moon and the sun, and forfeited all
the golden prayers I had ever sent into the sky. In that moment, in
a random stadium in California, an absolute darkness took over the
space where my warrior champion had been. The passion I had felt so
deeply for gymnastics died. The darkness and I became one, with the
Spirit of Movement as our witness. My teammates and competitors
watched me walk away from an entire life's work, as my day turned
into night. The moon would be my sun, and I felt the darkness
blacken my eyes. I watched the rest of the competition unfold and
smiled as the newfound dark peacefulness warmed my soul.

14

EYES

MYDRIASIS IS AN EXCESSIVE DILATION OF THE PUPIL DUE TO TRAUMA, DISEASE, OR DRUG USE. NORMALLY THE PUPIL DILATES IN THE DARK AND CONSTRICTS IN THE LIGHT TO IMPROVE VISION AT NIGHT AND PROTECT THE RETINA FROM SUNLIGHT DAMAGE DURING THE DAY. A MYDRIATIC PUPIL REMAINS EXCESSIVELY LARGE EVEN IN A BRIGHT ENVIRONMENT AND IS SOMETIMES REFERRED TO AS A BLOWN PUPIL. PUPILS MAY ALSO DILATE DURING TIMES OF FEAR TO SEE EVERYTHING MORE CLEARLY, ALLOWING FOR A BETTER EMERGENCY RESPONSE.

I didn't get support from my parents when it was time for me to choose a college. They were deeply involved in the restaurant and their own lives. I repeatedly asked them for help, but they seemed confused by the concept of picking out a school. They didn't go to college and didn't understand the application, registration, and financial-aid process. Despite my relinquished warrior, I still had a small desire to compete in collegiate gymnastics. I thought that competing in college could be fun, and if I could keep the seriousness of the sport at bay, or rather my need to be perfect, then perhaps it could be my ticket in.

Coach Dan was a Staunton College alumnus and two of my teammates were going there in the fall, so I applied there. But my SAT scores were too low, and when I received my rejection letter I got drunk and punched holes in my bedroom walls. I hadn't applied to any other colleges and had no idea what to do. I had attended a gymnastics camp at Staunton when I was younger and knew the head coach, Paul. He was good friends with Coach Dan and had watched me compete for years. He called and said he wanted me on the team. And if I really wanted to get in, I should enroll at a junior college and transfer, showing Staunton that I could handle serious college work.

City Community College was the joke of our high school, considered the college for losers and burnouts. But if I didn't go, there would be no way to get into Staunton. I finally surrendered and enrolled at the College for Rejects. My parents' restaurant business had been faltering for some time, and they were hardly bringing in any income. Without family financial help, I had to depend on state financial aid and student loans.

I worked full-time teaching gymnastics to kids to pay for my car and school. I tried to inspire them to love the sport, but it was the most emotionally challenging time of my life. I had no time to train myself, and training for gymnastics was all I knew. Even though my Olympic dream had sunk, I still couldn't live without the movement, without flipping and being upside down, but heaven took away my wings and I was now a civilian like everyone else. To teach gymnastics and not train was agonizing—I felt like a wingless bird watching others do what I loved through my directions. I gave them the map and design to fly, and I hated it. I resented them and myself.

During that time I pierced every possible part of my body and dyed my hair a new color every week. I looked poisonous and deadly, and I wished my stare could turn people to stone. I didn't make any friends at City. Smiling would ruin the dangerous and tough exterior that my years of agony had allowed me to develop. My scowl was the glory I wanted to show the world, the flesh of hate and pain. As I walked around the campus, going from class to class, the words "freak" and "weirdo" floated past my ears like an ice-cold breeze. Hearing those words made me smile inside.

I tried to find consolation by the ocean, to keep my soul on the planet by watching the moon's powerful reflection shimmering off the water. I always ended up feeling like a human shell on the wet sand. I don't know what kept me alive. I stopped drinking and smoking pot again because I didn't have anyone to do it with and was doing better in school as a result. The whole time I kept two paths of choice in front of me—suicide or success. I believed either choice was better than my pathetic existence.

I embraced the moments Tara would come home from college for vacation. I wrote her often, trying to stay involved in her life. At the end of her first semester, she returned home for winter break. I picked her up in my still heatless car, and then we sat in front of her house. She had the same charm and laughter that I had fallen victim to years ago, but something seemed different that night. Tara, the one human being who could get me to do anything, pulled a piece of tinfoil with the tiniest piece of paper in it from her pocket. It was two little specks of paper. I thought to myself, *What is that? It can't be a drug, it's too small.*

Before I could ask, she said, "It's acid. You have to do this."

That was all the permission I needed, and I put it on my tongue. I had never done acid before and considered it one of those drugs that I probably should never take. We had all learned in health class about the bad trips that could destroy the brain forever, leading to a life spent in mental institutions. I didn't know what to expect and didn't think something so small could be that powerful. We drove to our friend Dana's house as the paper dissolved.

Dana was watching TV and didn't know we had taken acid. We decided to keep it a secret and pretended to look really stoned from pot. The effects of the acid still hadn't hit and I began to doubt it would work, so we started smoking pot and drinking beer. I watched the shadows in the corners of Dana's room, trying to see if I could feel something inside me change, but nothing happened.

Then my concentration was broken by something that was said on TV and it tickled me into a fit of uncontrollable, volcanic laugher. It was laughter so strong that it rattled the deepest places of my body. I became the translation of laughter, its muse and catalyst, and there was no stopping it. I glanced over to see if Tara had heard the same thing and saw her contorted into a fetal position, shaking and laughing so hard she couldn't breathe. Dana laughed, but the laughter didn't consume her the way it did us. When I looked at Dana she seemed to slip into a different time than we were in, and I could only see Tara, who shone so brightly I couldn't stop looking at her.

I was plugged into an electrical outlet with a beautiful, Earthlike rhythm coursing through my veins, not wanting to sit still, yet only sitting felt comfortable. Dana still didn't know we had taken acid, and I had a difficult time acting like someone who had only drunk and smoked pot. If the effects got any stronger, it would be impossible to hide, and it did get stronger.

The room changed, and colors I'd never seen before splintered into the shadows as patterns transformed my thoughts into abstract designs. I felt whole as I became the final piece in the puzzle. I felt connected to each breath, my own and Tara's, and had a profound awareness of the great artist of creation. I started tasting individual colors, falling into a vortex of rainbows. Every object in the room had developed a depth and meaning beyond the three-dimensional world. I had never seen life from this perspective, and felt a deep sense of caring for the Earth we lived on. I cradled the world in my hands, like the strong grip of a tree, and sensed a connection to its roots. Did I really just drop acid, or was I transported into a sacred room in heaven and given the secrets to life?

It was now clear that the three of us weren't on the same plane, and Dana asked what we had taken. Without the confining, concealing, and burdensome restraints of my past life, I exploded with a new freedom. "Acid!" Dana was getting mad, and we had to go somewhere else because we knew her anger would ruin the opening of our heaven-sent gift.

We opened the front door and stepped into the fresh winter air. A chill of ice kissed our warm skin as we took a deep hit of frozen, crisp oxygen into our lungs. Our cells drank in the perfectly delicious night haze; we swallowed the night sky, and digested the great constellations. We laughed until the stars fell from our bodies, the kind of laughter only a child understands, that vanishes at adolescence and never returns. Tara's black pools of dilated pupils mirrored my own, and we melded into each other's thoughts.

We got into the giant machine of my car, and though I was able to drive, I couldn't remember how to change gears. The stick shift felt the same way Dana looked—mechanical and not part of our newfound universe. I tried leaving her driveway, but had to dodge massive colors of fabric draped in space. I couldn't tell what was or wasn't real as I led that metal monster along the yellow line dividing the street in half. The car wasn't real; we weren't real; only our laughter existed and blinded us from seeing the road ahead that led to our destinies.

Shadow-sketched concrete trees and pencil-drawn branches lined the road, as a dry rain sprinkled fire and ash on the windshield. We arrived at the void where dreams are created, the place every child knows, under the orange cloud where rainbows bend, and we drove right through it. A stop sign sparkled in its divine statement. I was living the video game I had always dreamed of. Everything became a mystery, and driving was impossible, but I did it. Cars that passed by became huge beams of light traveling on rubber wheels, nearly colliding but irrelevant since they were mechanical instruments without our life force. And all the while Tara spoke in whispers, creating a soundscape with the power of three humans harmonizing.

We parked the car and sat near a glow of light that felt sacred and safe, laughing, smoking, and listening to music under the galaxy. Deeper and deeper into each other's souls we went; no two humans had ever been more spiritually close. We blossomed from fuzzy caterpillars into butterflies, with wings stretched out and our true selves exposed as we pledged our endless friendship. For the first time, we both understood that life is not meaningless. I felt so awakened, and never wanted to sleep again.

As the sweet sounds of morning came closer, our laughter slowly began to weaken. Even laughter needs sleep. It was the most amazing time of my life. I had changed. I was no longer the same individual as before, and that tiny piece of paper contained a religious spiritual essence, which converted my Catholic vengeful God into a power of goodness and love that only wanted harmony and peace for each life form on our planet. I understood that the Earth itself, as a planet, was a living, breathing being. That experience awakened in me a desire for knowledge. I thanked Tara for the life-altering journey and dropped her off at her house, where it had all begun.

I drove back to my father's house with the residual effects of acid bouncing around in my vision. Nature had never looked so alive as it whispered final farewells along the way. I got home and took a hot bath and cried. I cried for my past, for the boy I was, and for the man I would become. My tears were the baptism of my new body and soul.

15

RADIAL AND ULNA BONES

THE CRUCIFIXION USUALLY DEPICTS CHRIST ON THE CROSS
WITH NAILS THROUGH THE PALMS OF HIS HANDS. MANY
SCIENTISTS AND DOCTORS DISAGREE WITH THIS,
BELIEVING THE NAILS WERE DRIVEN BETWEEN THE SMALL
RADIAL AND ULNA BONES OF THE WRISTS. NAILS THROUGH
THE PALMS WOULD BE INCAPABLE OF SUPPORTING THE WEIGHT
OF A HUMAN BODY AND WOULD TEAR BETWEEN THE FINGERS.

What is faith? I had faith in my ability to do gymnastics, but beyond
that it was water dripping through my fingers. I could not hold onto
it, and I only felt it for brief moments. It was the day before Good
Friday, a day that always confused me. What was so good about
Jesus getting crucified?

I was raised Catholic, but never made my First Communion and went
to church only on rare occasions. Secretly, I was scared of entering
churches: the huge arches rising into the sky, stained-glass windows
depicting bloodshed, loss, and resurrection, and a man hanging on
a giant cross as the centerpiece. One could not look away from that
human, though what we were told of his life wasn't very human at
all. I knew people didn't rise from the dead. I just couldn't wrap my
brain around that belief. Considering the same macabre feelings I
loved while watching horror movies, you would expect me to love
church with its stories and supernatural elements that choirs sang
about so angelically. Their voices stretching over the pews reminded
me of the ending of *The Exorcist* or *Rosemary's Baby*. What were we
as humans trying to say to each other about religion? It wasn't that I

didn't believe in something; it was just that I wasn't exactly sure what it was. Religion seemed to result in hatred, animosity, and war rather than increasing peace, love, and light. Could that be faith?

Catholicism also posed a great threat to my eternal soul. What if the kids at school who called me a fag were right? What if I was gay? Would I go to hell because of the way I was born? While I didn't know the answer to this, I knew that the chapter that said a man cannot lie with another man also said that a man may stone a liar to death. So maybe I could join the stoners to balance out my lying. While I tried to keep an open mind to the belief in some higher order, I could not find faith in that religion.

Instead, I decided to do something different. I was fearless in gymnastics, but not in my everyday life, where I still sought acceptance. Aside from my piercings, I didn't make many changes outside of gymnastics. A new temptation hung from a branch, and I decided to take a bite of that apple.

I made one friend at City, Piper from my history class. I was instantly charmed by her threatening pose, slanted smile, and hip lingo. We shared the same style of big, baggy jeans that dragged on the ground and steel hoops through our eyebrows and lips. We were from the same tribe. She lived in Southie and invited me to a rave in Boston with her and her friends the night before Easter. Raves weren't that popular yet and were kept quiet and underground. I didn't know what she was talking about. She explained with bewitching enthusiasm that it was a party with loud dance music. The spell was cast.

She told me that I had to try this new drug with an enticing name: ecstasy. For some reason it scared me. In Boston and other parts of the East Coast it was called "E," while the rest of the country called it "X." I loved my acid experience, but something in a pill seemed deadly. After weeks of listening to her beautiful, intoxicating voice, I decided to see what it was all about.

I told Randi, my tattoo and piercing partner, about the rave and she said that she wanted to come. We got into my car and headed toward Boston and got off at the Southie exit.

Southie was like a giant party, with kids all over the place. It was an amazing drug hotspot, with too many dangerous teenagers to arrest them all, and a lot of the cops taking part in the same activities as the kids. This area was like an underground secret covered in broken bottles, deceit, and graffiti, and it shone brightly to me. The Pied Piper summoned me here and I was one desperate rat, willing to follow her song to my death, regardless of the shit I had to walk through. I thought to myself while approaching Piper's large Victorian house overlooking a playground full of teenagers, *I will become one of them—the criminal, the dangerous one who lurks behind the shadows and wrestles with the darkness of his soul because then, and only then, nobody will tease him because they'll fear him.*

A thick air of pot smoke led the way to Piper's room upstairs, which was crowded with the neighborhood kids and weed. How could she smoke so much pot in her house without her parents flipping out? The kids were in a circle passing around three blunts (cigars full of weed), and we joined the circle like it was a pagan ritual that needed our blood. They were all heavily pierced like Piper, Randi, and me and wore the same brand-name baggy jeans. I met everyone with a deep fear in my heart and smiled in as manly a manner as I could muster, trying to create a version of myself different from the one God had made.

An hour later we piled into an SUV and headed to the rave. The rain pounded against the windshield as I listened to the kids tell stories of robberies and drugs I'd never heard of. I thought of my mother. I thought of her smile and warmth. I thought of her heartbreak if she saw me in a car full of criminals I barely knew.

We emerged from the car into a scene of thousands of kids looking like us walking up large stairs to a giant stadium. The rain had stopped and the stars came out to witness our fall into the abyss, through the cracks of right and wrong, into a place so deep that light never entered. The line was long, and the cold winter air forced us into a huddle.

A deep thudding sound from inside the building shook our bodies. Before life there was this sound, a pulse from the deities that ruled this planet, and only this sound remained as their legacy—an eternal heartbeat that now shook our bones.

Admission cost thirty dollars, which was all the money I had. We walked through the entry into a large room filled with cops, security, and weapon detectors. Stoned and paranoid about mixing with the police, I shuddered in my skin, thinking they would arrest me for smelling like pot. They patted me down and I passed through without a problem. One of the kids had drugs on him and got stopped. They took the drugs and let him into the party. The sound of the music grew in intensity as we approached the doors, and it became impossible to hear one another.

The room exploded with energy and madness. It wasn't just dance music. It was a massive entity made up of kids who danced to the same rhythm and became a part of the sound. The sound bypassed my brain and attacked my heart. It was so loud I felt my blood bubble. We looked down from the balcony at thousands of kids dancing as lights, mirror ball beams, fog, and lasers penetrated the spaces between us. It was one of the most amazing things I had ever seen; the music morphed the beats and bass bounced off our bodies.

I felt terrified and anxious. I didn't want to participate or dance. The place was a drug in itself, and I definitely didn't need anything else. I wanted to stand and watch from behind my protective window of isolation. This window broke when Piper came bursting through, grinning from ear to ear with her bright eyes peering through mine.

She smiled, grabbed my hand, and said, "Take this, it's a present."

I took the pill into my already-sweaty hand and asked, "What is it?"

She spoke with perfect mystery. "It's called 'white cloud.' It's 'E'!"

"Piper, I really don't need it—" She cut me off and said forcefully, "I just paid twenty-five dollars for this. Happy Easter, you better take it."

Afraid of getting caught with it in my pocket, I bit half of it, and the bitter taste in my mouth was terrible. She demanded that I eat the whole thing, but finally allowed me to first see what happened with the half. It reminded me of the long line of people at church receiving the wafers and wine that represented Jesus's flesh and blood. I'd never made communion so never joined that line. I always remained an outsider, watching and wondering in guilt, uncomfortable in the pews, contemplating my eternal damnation. But that night, I took my First Communion.

I left to find Randi, who had taken a tab of acid earlier. I found her dancing in a storm of people, but if I wasn't competing I had no self-esteem, so dancing was out of the question. I rehearsed my routines a million times; otherwise, I didn't know how to move. It made me happy just to watch Randi dance. She smiled at me and kept moving.

Then the music changed, like it skipped a beat, and the room started to roll over onto itself. It wasn't a slow change; it was quick and drastic, and I lost my balance instantly. On acid I had been in full control of my body, but now my muscles were mixed into this sensation and it was terrible. The lights got brighter and more intense, and then Randi's beautiful face melted. The confusion happened so fast that there was no way to slow it down, and within seconds the most intense fear I had ever experienced ran through me like a blazing fire. It was too much. I couldn't stop it. I couldn't talk. I couldn't move. How long had it been? The music fell into one big, awful sound, and then something inside me exploded. All of a sudden I felt good, then a little better, and then I felt fucking great. It all happened so fast, like falling off a giant cliff. It felt so good that I reached into my pocket and quickly chewed up the bitter other half.

I began to move with the music, back and forth, and then it happened. Heaven crashed into the Earth and spilled all of God's peace and love over us. The music turned into angel wings beating in synchronicity as harmonies created the most pleasant hymns inside me. I not only felt the music, I *was* the music. I was warm. I was cold. I was love. I was . . . love. I looked around the room at all the other dancing beings in perfect sync with the music, and I loved them—all of them. These dangerous creatures like tiny delicate moonlit moths became my brothers and sisters, and I could see their souls, pure as sunlight, beaming out of their bodies. Without speaking a single word to each other, we all felt it and we all knew it, and in that moment we advanced as a telepathic race transmitting the pleasure and sensations of harmony, unity, and empathy. I wanted to hug each of them and assure them everything was going to be all right.

Dancing became my religion; I was no longer human, I was something angelic, and "E" was my new God. Never in my entire life had I felt that good, and the best part was that I could breathe. All those horrible hours in the hospital fighting for air to fill my lungs, and suddenly the cure was this little white pill. I'd never breathed so effortlessly, and I inhaled life deeply. I felt it. I felt everything—the formation of stars, the evolution of beings, delicate dew petals, and my own heart as I fell into euphoria and magic. *This drug is the cure for asthma*, I thought. Feelings of elation and affinity washed over me, and each angelic beat vibrated my transforming body.

A million painted butterflies took all the fear, anger, and anxiety from my body and elevated me into the sound, leaving me with pure happiness. In that moment I found complete satisfaction. I no longer had to be the world's best gymnast, and for the first time in my life I experienced relief and resolution.

No longer a geek on the dance floor, I was suddenly in the center of a break-dance circle doing backflips, and everyone went crazy. I left the circle feeling higher than ever and went upstairs to a different room, floating on a cloud. We were the new angels, creating our own heaven. Two giant TV screens displayed orgasmic visual sensations of fractal images that were intense and blinding. I wanted to die in that feeling, to have it take me in and absorb my soul.

Watching the screen, smoking cigarette after cigarette, and rocking back and forth while grabbing my knees, I heard the same mantra in my head over and over—"Everything is gonna be all right, everything is gonna be okay"—and for the very first time, I believed it. I believed it so much that it brought tears to my eyes. I couldn't stop rocking back and forth. It felt so good, the sway, the motion, the sound. I saw Piper and hugged her as if she had just saved my life. In a way, she had.

She was in the same state of mind, and her hug made all the hair on my body stand up. I continued holding onto her and said over and over, "Thank you, I love you, thank you, I love you," and she knew exactly what I meant. Touching her flesh sent an electric sexual tempest through my skin, and we hugged each other tight.

This was so different from what I'd felt when I took acid. It was greater; it was tasting God's tears; it was drinking my friends' souls, wearing their love and rolling in the oneness that created us all. I had stumbled upon Eden, and there was no greater love and peace than that moment. I was blessed. I was alive. I was a great fire burning bright.

I kept dancing, following the music's orders, directing my body and spirit. I was breath and love. A man walked by who I wanted to get to know on a different level—on a physical and sexual level beyond what I had previously known. I wanted to get to know him sensually and intimately, something I hadn't yet admitted to myself or the world around me. I was like a wolf seeing his pack for the first time. I finally knew where I belonged. But for that night I would go silently alone into the moonlight, letting that knowledge burn inside me. To my new friends, I was straight like them, but now that didn't matter. I had fallen in love with "E," and it erased ever having been teased, ever having been made fun of, or ever having been called a faggot. In that moment, I accepted who I was.

I continued dancing until the sun's rays burst through the cracks. I didn't want that feeling to stop or to ever see or know the prehistoric world again. I tried holding onto the feeling as if it were water in my hands, pleading with the liquid, "Please, don't leave me . . . you can't go . . . I need you . . . don't go," but the more time passed, the more the water trickled through my fingers.

The effects of the drug slowly faded, and I left the building a different being than when I had entered. I had changed. I was better, brighter, and more intelligent. As we walked into the morning it felt like we were victoriously leaving a sacred war and entering into a new chapter of history. I thought of the first hippies in the sixties who were part of a movement before it was actually a movement. Kids passed flyers out for the next raves, and I took each one, collecting the pages of my new testament.

The residual effects of ecstasy rolled through my body, and I felt a small sense of shame, remembering it was Easter morning. I wondered if Jesus really did rise from the dead on that day. Good Catholic families were putting on their best Easter clothes and going to church to honor Christ's resurrection, and on that day I honored myself: my body, his body, our bodies reborn.

Later that week an article ran in the newspaper about the rave I'd gone to, telling of how it was endangering the youth of Boston and was a gateway to a destructive lifestyle. My parents knew I had gone, but they didn't say anything. They knew I drank a bit, but believed I would never take drugs since as an athlete I took great care of my body. There was a picture of Piper in the paper. I cut it out, put in on my wall, and crowned the first saint of my new sanctuary.

16

ANATOMICAL SNUFF BOX

A TRIANGULAR DEPRESSION ON THE DORSAL, RADIAL ASPECT
OF THE HAND THAT FRAMES A FLOOR CREATED BY THE
SCAPHOID AND TRAPEZIUM BONES, THIS SURFACE CAN BE USED
FOR PLACING AND SNIFFING POWDERED TOBACCO, COCAINE,
CRYSTAL, OR ANY OTHER SUBSTANCE THAT CAN BE SNIFFED.

My mother drove me to the Staunton College campus for my first day of orientation. I brought all of my belongings in several large, black trash bags. Even though we were barely on speaking terms, she tried to be kind and supportive and gave me a twenty-dollar bill. I laughed at the absurdity of this since I had no money for textbooks, toiletries, or dorm necessities. My parents had no idea what a college student needed, and I felt like a poor vagabond. But I was out, and would never return home to live with my parents again. There was too much pain and resentment between us.

My dorm room was covered in white paint, with a jail-cell, cinder-block motif. It resembled an ivory mausoleum. After my mother dropped off my things and left, I lit a Marlboro and watched the smoke fill the small space. Minutes later there was a large bang on my door and I opened it to see two campus police officers. They aggressively walked into my room and started searching through all my things because they smelled marijuana. Sadly, I didn't even have any. I couldn't believe that the first social interaction on my first day of *real* college was with the campus police. I guessed I had succeeded in my criminal-look aspiration.

As I walked through the dorm hallways, I noticed everyone looked the same—clean-cut, all-American, and sporty. Meanwhile, I appeared to have clawed myself out from the depths of hell. I had acquired even more body piercings and sported a bright-red Mohawk with large spikes stabbing the air. I clung to the hope that college kids would be mature and open-minded.

The campus was beautiful, as if they'd taken an apple orchard, added some grand buildings to it, and called it a university. It was a perfect New England autumn day as leaves changed to deep, dark, vibrant colors in harmony with a baby-blue sky. I laughed to myself, *This was my dream college.* Surrounded by that picturesque scene, I acknowledged the accomplishment of simply being there, and prayed for personal change like the change in the trees around me. I vowed to get serious about my education. I swore that I would not drink alcohol or smoke pot. I already knew how tripping and taking ecstasy would impede my education. The trees sighed in the gentle breeze and agreed with my spiritual decision.

I was happy to start back into gymnastics again, especially since people weren't lining up to be my friend. I hadn't trained for a year. Our gym was set in the back of a large athletic hall and it was covered with plaques and pictures of former Staunton College athletes who had placed in the top six in NCAA competitions. Near the entrance to the gymnastics area was Dan's picture, a plaque, and several of his all-American awards. I loved that he was there, looking over me and protecting me. Maybe I could fight my way back and find my champion again.

The first day of practice went smoother than I expected, and I was amazed at how much I could still do. My muscle memory kicked in, and I knew I would be ready to compete in a few months. Even though I looked freakish, broken, and like an unorganized mess, my teammates were friendly and didn't judge my exterior. They saw the strong gymnast within. I had to remove my piercings to avoid deductions during competition, but didn't need to cover my tattoos or change my hair.

I got a job delivering pizza on campus, and one night at the shop I met two people who would become friends for life—Cloud and Darren. Cloud dressed in gothic-like doll clothes, smelled like patchouli mixed with pot, and wore mystery around her body that illuminated her spirit. She had curious, big blue eyes, pierced lip, a pouty smile, and a shy face hidden under dreadlocks. Darren was the kind of guy you didn't want to see in a dark alley. He was tall and stocky like a football player, with tattoos and piercings. Despite his punishing look he had a friendly smile, and we shared a secret glance that said, "I want to know you better," which made me both excited and afraid.

Cloud lived upstairs in the same dormitory as me, and immediately after meeting her I broke my "no smoking weed" vow. She reminded me of friends back home, and her company was comforting. We both hated the people at school and clung together like conjoined twins united through our freakishness.

Darren was a senior and lived off campus. A large shadow hovered over his apartment in the city of Holyoke, past broken train tracks under a burned-out streetlight. It was the last house on the block. I loved leaving campus to go visit him. I was intrigued by Darren. He had a very quiet demeanor. He looked at me differently, and I couldn't figure out his interest. He was able to see past the person I was trying to be, and saw the man I was. I was sure he was straight, but more open-minded than the other students, and my sexual confusion didn't faze him. Cloud and I smoked weed at his place almost every night.

One night Darren took out a small glass vial of white powder, pushed the magazines aside on the glass table, and poured it onto the table. Instantly Cloud's eyes lit up like fireworks and she yelled, "Oh my God, can I have some? I've been looking since I got here!" Darren said proudly, "Yeah, that's why I'm putting it on the table."

I had never seen coke before and was scared of it. Once again, I thought of my mother.

Cloud held her dreads back as she leaned over the table, careful not to mess the white, powdery lines that were bigger than I imagined.

Darren handed her a plastic straw from his pocket and she sniffed the powder up loudly and passionately. She dabbed the small residue that didn't make it into her nose with her finger and wiped it on her teeth and gums. She gave a huge smile, like a proud little girl who had just finished making a macaroni necklace for her parents. Darren leaned down and performed the same procedure.

Stoned out of my mind, all I heard for the next four hours were the annoying sounds of people sniffing, snorting, and talking absolute insanity. We were on two different planes, and I couldn't connect. I was not going to touch it, afraid I would kill myself by combining a speed substance with my asthma medicines. I thought about all the horror stories I'd heard in health class about doing coke, which made me laugh since all the lessons about the drugs I had already taken had clearly failed. Still, I was not going to do coke.

Cloud and I constantly hung out at Darren's apartment, but I made it a rule not to smoke pot until after practice. It would be way too dangerous to do gymnastics stoned; even I knew that. Training was Monday through Friday from four to seven and then I went home, ate, showered, and went to Darren's and got stoned. Cloud and I would leave his apartment completely wrecked out of our minds, watching the moon as we snuck back to our pretty, safe campus. I thanked the heavens for connecting me to my new friends.

Darren and I secretly got together, which made me feel a little better about my sexuality. I still didn't think I was gay, but being with Darren felt natural. He looked so tough, mean, and dangerous that I never thought he was gay either. Maybe we were just getting high, and knocking down and exploring our boundaries. For the first time someone was attracted to me for who I was, but I absolutely had to keep our liaison a secret. I didn't think I could deal with more ridicule from others. In truth, Darren could have been a serial killer and I would have still been attracted to him and looked up to him, because no one had ever treated me as kindly as he did. I had never experienced that kind of friendship, closeness, and sense of being respected with any person before, besides with Tara. He and the pot erased the negative feelings I had toward myself as we laughed and fell into our illusory world.

I slowly broke all the rules I had made to keep up both my grades and gymnastics skills. I became another fixture on Darren's street, alongside the broken lights, the crackheads, and the dirty lies. The three of us were inseparable, and the nights were ours. Darren started dealing coke, mushrooms, and pot. I wasn't part of it, but thought it was cool and gave him an even more attractive, broken, and elusive quality. He was a soul so strong he risked going to jail for his beliefs, which eventually he did. His arrest for possession made us all rethink our roles in that story, but our dedication, friendship, and desire to laugh kept us together through those challenges.

Tons of coke surrounded me for months, and I still hadn't tried it; however, it was inescapable, and by the second semester of my freshman year I had tried it three times. I was going to a gymnastics party that had heavy drinkers, but no drugs. I did a line of coke and jumped into the shower. The steam from the hot water mixed with the cocaine and it hit my brain the way it was intended to. I immediately felt powerful, sexy, and brilliant—filled with an intense energy vibrating through my bloodstream. I was Zeus, ruler of all gods, and all the other elements orbited around my body. I had complete control of my body and felt like perfection, as though made of porcelain, or of perfect smooth glass created from a powerful lightning bolt striking the white sands of a beach. After I finished my shower I needed another line to keep the feeling going. I couldn't let it slip through my hands. If one line felt that good, then two would feel even better.

I had the best time ever with the gymnastics team that night. I snuck a couple more lines in the bathroom, played pool, and got shit-faced. It was fun, but I couldn't sleep from all the coke. My throat and nose were sore, and my heartbeat sped up as the sun rose. I tried to enjoy the last remnants of the feeling, but it gave way to pure anxiety. A new monster was born in me that night. Cocaine electrified me, and once again, I was excited and terrified.

Despite my ongoing destructive path, my gymnastics improved. I worked hard and valued my time in practice. But each day that I passed Dan's picture on the wall of all-Americans, I stopped and wondered, *What would Dan think if he saw me doing what I was doing to myself? Would he approve? Did he do the same thing when he was in college?* I tried to connect the memory from his picture to the little boy who knew him, a little boy so determined to achieve his dreams that he would have battled the galaxies. I was more of a man when I was nine years old than I was now. I tried to find the strength of that young boy, the champion and warrior, but it was too far away. Even a photograph of the man I admired most and considered my only role model couldn't knock me off my broken path. I had gone past the event horizon and was crossing over into the void.

17

LIVER

THE LIVER IS THE LARGEST ORGAN INSIDE THE HUMAN BODY AND WEIGHS ABOUT THREE POUNDS. IT IS ALSO AMONG THE MOST IMPORTANT ORGANS, AS IT WORKS WITH THE GALLBLADDER AND PANCREAS TO HELP DIGEST, ABSORB, AND PROCESS FOOD. THE LIVER BREAKS DOWN TOXIC SUBSTANCES AND METABOLIZES DRUGS. THE LIVER IS NECESSARY FOR SURVIVAL; THERE IS CURRENTLY NO WAY TO COMPENSATE FOR THE ABSENCE OF LIVER FUNCTION.

Summer arrived, my freshman year was finished, and I was headed back home. Darren graduated and moved off campus, deeper into the gloom of the city, looking for a better job than answering the campus pizza phone. I moved back in with my mother and got shifts waiting tables at the restaurant. She was happy for me. It appeared I was doing well, back in gymnastics and working hard at college.

I found some new "friends" who shared my new interests in Southie. From there we drove to Axis, a club in downtown Boston. We did lines of coke while listening to hip-hop and rap music in a parking garage, and then we would go inside the club for more of the same. The new thing was prescription pills such as Valium, Klonopin, and Xanax. All I knew of Valium was that it helped with falling asleep, and I didn't get where the high was in sleeping. My new friends explained that they were benzodiazepines that brought euphoria, relaxation, and a sensation beyond drunk, a sensation known as "pilled out." The next lesson in that crash course was how to get pilled out. It was simple: take ten pills.

I chewed up all ten, washed them down with a beer, and waited for the unknown to arrive. First I experienced a huge sense of relief and relaxation, like with ecstasy, and felt like somehow everything would be okay. It hit me harder than alcohol, filling all those spaces alcohol missed. Suddenly those pills blotted everything emotional out of me. The muscles in my body relaxed, making it difficult to walk. In my entire life I had never felt that calm—awake but dreaming, in euphoria, everything slowed down to a state of perpetual peace and tranquility, under a giant palm tree on a deserted island soaking in the sun's gentle rays. There was a complete sense of safety with the world around me, and I didn't care what I said or did because I knew nothing bad would happen.

I knew the Southie kids would have kicked my ass if they knew I was gay, but the Valium made me careless and care less. Every other moment in life I'd been afraid to talk to people, even though I wanted to, but in that moment I talked to everyone and anyone. My words slurred and my sentences fell into one another, but the burden of life washed away in a halcyon wave, leaving a calm grin on my face. This was a miracle drug. Why didn't someone prescribe this for me in high school? Maybe I could have coped with the people around me. Maybe I would have slept at night.

Valium was much cheaper and lasted longer than ecstasy. If I ate a handful of them and drank a lot, I could still be pilled out the next day, extending my high into tomorrow. But the greatest effect was blacking out. I would have complete amnesia, with no recollection of the hour, day, or string of days previously lived. Intended to combat serious stress, anxiety, and post-traumatic stress disorders, Valium helps patients forget their troubles, and that was exactly what I needed. It made me unafraid of the world I was afraid of.

It was one of the greatest summers I ever had. Waiting on tables was easy and gave me enough money to get blasted. Every night was the same: go home from work, open a beer, chug it in the shower, have two more on the drive to Southie, arrive at Axis, and take a handful of pills with a few lines of coke to straighten my head. Gradually, I found the more pilled out and drunk I was, the less I needed coke to stay up. Raves were on the weekends, and I started sniffing crystal meth. On the bleachers at the party, I saw people checking their pulses like self-appointed doctors and learned that if my heart thumped faster than the dance music, I was in trouble. I became one of them, always checking my heart against the music and wondering how far I could crank the speed without stopping my internal beat.

One summer night of too many pills, security kicked me out of the club for walking crooked and slamming into walls. The Valium really messed me up. I needed to get some coke or speed to wake me up and override the drowsiness. We all left and packed into my mother's car to try to find some. My friends saw I couldn't stand up straight and tried to keep me from driving, but high or not, I was convinced that as a gymnast I could control every muscle and movement. I had tested and proven that ability through random drunken handstands or tumbling while on angel dust. The more messed up I got, the more I believed I was just operating a giant physical machine, and I was usually right.

I also believed I could beat an overdose through the years of physical training, able to stay alive and handle bodily demands beyond what simple civilians could take; but that night the pills were winning. I pulled out of the parking slot, slammed into a parked car, pulled out in the other direction, and hit another one. We were in the parking garage with no witnesses, so I gunned it again toward the exit and ran into a car passing by. I didn't hit them hard, so I kept driving, too high to stop, and forgot about it until a summons arrived in the mail. They had seen the license plate and, of course, when my mother asked me about it, I barely remembered a thing. I had scratched the side of the other person's car; no one was injured, and the case was dismissed. That sort of thing continued all summer long. Whenever I took a pill I knew trouble would follow, and I loved it.

When the pills ran dry, and they often did, I snorted coke in my room until the sun came up. I cried about everything: commercials on TV, old memories of gymnastics, songs on the radio, or certain words;

it didn't matter what it was. I would crash down so low, I couldn't tolerate the depth of my sadness. I was so confused. Every time I told myself, "I'm never gonna do that again," I would do it again and again.

Darren came to visit me and could see that I had changed dramatically within just a few weeks. I considered myself an expert on prescription pills, and even bought a nurse's pill manual that helped me to identify each pill and its effect. Prescription bottles with yellow warning labels were my favorites. Any label that warned not to drink alcohol or operate heavy machinery was the best. My new favorite hobby was going to friends' houses and looking through their medicine cabinets.

On a particularly bad night of recklessness, Darren and I bought enough Xanax to kill a small family, and we ate as many as we could. Cops woke me up from my blackout as I drove the wrong way down a one-way street. They thought we had stolen the car, and after checking the plates realized we hadn't, and let us go. I had twenty hits of acid and a couple of bags of cocaine on me. I could barely stand up, and we laughed the whole way back to my mother's house. When we arrived home, she asked where I had been for the last few days and why I wasn't ready for work. I told her, "Mom, what are you talking about? It's Tuesday." She slammed the door on her way out to work and said, "It's fucking Thursday." I had no idea where I had been for the past two days. I went to work that night, but my father saw that I couldn't walk a straight line and told me to get my ass home.

I was barely treading water, but I didn't care; I was having too much fun and didn't want to stop. It was anti-gymnastics, the complete opposite of discipline, loyalty, and strength, and I loved it. My mother noticed how my behavior was changing. I fell asleep at the dinner table, slept fifteen hours at a time, and sometimes two days in a row, from taking so many Valium, Xanax, and Klonopin.

After a huge pill binge and while I was dead asleep, she came barging into my room and screamed at me to pack my bags and get out of her house or she'd call the police. In a rage, I called Darren and asked if he would come pick me up. He always cleaned up my messes and got me out of bad situations. Our plan was for me to stay at his place for a few weeks until my sophomore semester started, and then I would head back to my dormitory. I hung up the phone and, in complete pill-detox anger, trashed my room and everything in it. Whenever I came down from pills I would be filled with an inhuman urge to destroy things, and the only way I could release that monster inside me was through demolition.

During the two-and-a-half-hour drive to Holyoke, Darren and I began eating all the Valium I was supposed to sell. I didn't have any money, and needed to sell those pills to have some cash for school. I had no money for food; I had bought the dorm meal plan, which didn't start for two weeks. We would be screwed for food if we didn't sell those pills, but once I started eating them I couldn't stop, and the more pilled out I became, the more I ate. We arrived at Darren's new broken-down apartment as slurring, falling-down, staggering messes, barely making it out of the car. I had no idea how we survived the Massachusetts Turnpike.

He warned me about his new place—it was as poor, run-down, and broken as we were. The first thing I did was ask a man walking by where we could buy some coke; the pills were making me too sleepy and I needed an upper to enjoy them. The guy shot us a look of steel, told me to fuck off, and kept walking. In an absolute state of calm, we walked down another street and asked someone else. All boundaries were removed by the pills, and things that one should never do, like asking strangers for cocaine, felt perfectly normal.

The neighborhood was perfect for us because others were partaking in the same activities, and after several attempts we found a man who could take us to nirvana. We got into this guy's car and he drove us to the place. Suddenly cops came bolting out from behind us, sirens wailing, and pulled us over. They got us out and forced us to put our hands on the roof of the car. A cop kept kicking my feet, trying to spread them apart, but I just kept laughing. I was so relaxed in my stupor that I continued to talk as he thrust me against the car door. From my pocket he pulled out an empty bag that at one point contained my pills. Apparently the man driving had been arrested a number of times and the cops knew him, but with no drugs on us we were free to go. The guy shrugged it off, left us in the car, ran down a dark, shadowed street, and then came back.

We were supposed to share the coke we bought with him; however, it wasn't coke, it was crack, and I had no desire to smoke crack. Holyoke was full of crackheads, and I saw what smoking rock did to them. I was pissed, but still I needed the high. I asked if we could crush it up and sniff it, and the man looked at me as if I were crazy, like it would be an abomination to crush the buttery rock. Crack seemed like a dirty drug, and a gateway to Loserville. I briefly thought about the consequences, but I couldn't turn down a high.

I pulled the thick smoke into my lungs and held it as long as I could. A surge erupted from Mayan temples, from mythological Atlantis, and all the cosmic divine places came together to create a new power centered in the middle of my brain. In a single breath I became everything—the sun, moon, and all the elements of life, more gorgeous than every spring's blossom. An endless power was mine. But the feeling didn't last long, and I needed another hit to keep it going.

I don't know how the night ended, and I don't know how I survived. Pilled out, I wandered Holyoke's rough streets alone after Darren and I got into a huge fight. I felt terrible from all the drugs I had taken and resented and hated him for not saving me from myself. I gave my power to Darren and wanted him to get me high and fix me, take me from me, and remove all my pain and discomfort. When he couldn't do those things for me, I blamed him, throwing harsh words of hate and frustration at him.

I woke up from my blackout unable to remember leaving my mother's house or how I got over to Darren's new apartment. I reached into my jeans pocket for another pill, but they were all gone. I couldn't believe it, and could feel the anxiety mounting. I checked my wallet and there was no money. Darren had a jar of loose change, and we lived for two weeks on twenty-five-cent ice cream sandwiches.

I called my sister, along with everyone else I knew, and admitted my problem. They were relieved, and I swore never to touch drugs again.

I was hungry, scared, and broken. I went to the emergency room a few times complaining of pain, trying to get pills. If I got pills, then I wouldn't be hungry. I knew I was at a horrible place and had to stop. This was a new form of pain and one with which I could not continue living. I wanted to get help. I knew I needed help. I went back to Darren's place and sat in that decrepit one-bedroom apartment on a dirty mattress and said a single prayer: "God, please help me!"

18

TONGUE

"THE MOUTH OF THE GODLY PERSON GIVES WISE ADVICE,
BUT THE TONGUE THAT DECEIVES WILL BE CUT OFF"
(PROVERBS 10:31). EVEN TODAY IN CERTAIN CULTURES,
THE REMOVAL OR ALTERATION OF THE TONGUE IS USED
AS A METHOD OF PUNISHMENT OR TORTURE.

My sophomore year began in September of 1997, and my perfect rave world became infected with immature college students and other kids jumping on the bandwagon to take their first hit of ecstasy. The pure vibe, originality, and passion we had brought to the scene were ruined. We dressed in bright hip-hop Ralph Lauren and Polo Sport; Men in Black and Puff Daddy dominated; and I continued my death spiral with cocaine. Cloud didn't return to Staunton College, and I was devastated. She decided to transfer to a design school near her home in Oregon. It was up to Darren and me to find some new friends who enjoyed the same recreational habits as us.

I tried to move beyond the negative memories of my summer of destruction, forget the bridges I had blown to pieces, and only remember the wonderful highs. I kicked off my sophomore year with no intentions of going to any classes or even buying a textbook. I set my sights on partying.

One night, Darren got a large amount of cocaine, more than we had ever seen, and decided to cut it and then sell it. Cutting the cocaine allowed us to add powder to it to increase the quantity, which gave us more coke to sell. We dumped all of it onto a mirror like they do in the movies, wrote our names in the white powder, and sniffed until morning. After that night, I began to think I could no longer exist without it.

During a long, sleepless weekend of doing coke all night and seeing daylight only twice, I came crashing down. My body was numb and my heart raced as I stared out my window at students drinking coffee, walking to class, and talking to each other. I hid from the light in my cave and tried to snort my way to salvation. The sight of humans being human brought small breakdowns; however, those breakdowns were rare, since the drugs elevated my emotions to points beyond my ability to reason. I was high, guarded, untouchable, safe, loved, and beautiful, but as the drugs wore off all of those feelings weakened and cracked, and then reality gushed in, flooding my spirit with anxiety and depression of biblical proportions.

I used more coke to erase those feelings, which just left a giant emptiness in my heart. I prayed to a God I no longer believed in, and begged him to remove my emotions and pain and return me to that place to which cocaine first took me. Darren didn't have meltdowns. Sure, he felt like shit after a sleepless weekend of doing coke and pills, but he didn't self-destruct like me, and I hated him for that. Maybe I wasn't using the right combination of pills and coke. Maybe I just needed to drink a little more on top of all that I took. After experiencing so many of my breakdowns, Darren suggested that I talk to a counselor at school.

That same day, in desperation, I made an appointment with a student counselor. I liked the sound of her voice on the phone. She sounded welcoming and trustworthy, but I was afraid I'd get kicked out of school if I told her exactly what I had been doing. The week before my appointment I had done so much coke that I thought I was going into cardiac arrest. My pulse beat faster than the dance music we were listening to, and I tried to conceal my fear with a smile. I made my way to the dorm bathroom and splashed cold water on my face. The coke was too strong, and I did too much. Sweat poured from my forehead and my skin looked pale and greenish. A friend from the gymnastics team walked in while I stood at the sink, trying to find my vision in the mirror. He looked terrified and asked, "Joey, are you okay?"

"Seriously?" I looked at him with pure conviction and said, "I feel awesome."

I met with the school counselor a few days later and liked what she had to say. She was taller than me, with long, blonde hair that sat perfectly on her shoulders. She was clearly educated in her field, and pulled me in with her good bedside manner. I felt I could trust her and believed she would honor the confidence between counselor and patient. I revealed my drug use, the raves, and many things a student should probably not expose to a college therapist—after all, this was a university, not a mental institution. I wanted and expected her to take away my pain and exorcise my emotional mania. But I wasn't going to stop using drugs.

After weeks of therapy I noticed the only things really changing were the dying leaves on increasingly bare trees. My counselor suggested that I start attending twelve-step meetings, which I thought was a ludicrous suggestion. She told me about gay meetings, which made me even more embarrassed and doubly ashamed. I was not an addict and didn't need to go to twelve-step meetings. I was only nineteen; how could I be an addict?

Through all this I still trained and competed on the gymnastics team, though my skills were fading into a cocaine haze. I still took competitions seriously, indulging in the beautiful dreamscapes gymnastics provided. There was still one rule I hadn't broken: I never used drugs the night before a competition. The most important meet was coming up, the NCAA, and Staunton was hosting the competition. Colleges throughout the country would be coming to compete at our school.

The night before, I prepared my grip bag obsessively with the same bizarre ritual I had engaged in as a young boy. This was my only connection to him, the only tie to that child warrior and my past. Without acting out this obsession my memories would crumble, leaving me alone with my reflection in the mirror—a depressed college student with a severe cocaine problem. While I rechecked my bag there was a loud knock on my door. It was Ginny, a girl I sometimes smoked weed with and generally found annoying. Her badly dreadlocked black hair looked like it was fighting itself as her youthful eyes desperately screamed, "Love me! Love me! I am nothing without your approval!" That voiceless plea made us kindred spirits.

She danced into my room with ease and asked what I was doing. Already irritated, I told her, and then she chimed, "Well, you will never believe what I got tonight." My ears perked up, and instantly she turned into my best friend. I loved her, asked what she had, and she smiled. "I have mushrooms!" Mushrooms were a rarity on our campus. Acid and coke were easy, but mushrooms were like winning the lottery.

"Awesome. Can we take them tomorrow after my competition?"

"No way," she replied. "I want to trip now!"

I knew what it was like to want to trip, and didn't even bother trying to convince her otherwise. She would take them with someone else if I didn't step up. It just wasn't negotiable. "All right, let's do it."

It was still early in the night. Maybe it would wear off before morning, and I could get an hour or two of sleep and be okay for the competition. I checked my uniform one more time, making sure it didn't grow legs and walk out of my gym bag. She opened the clear plastic sandwich baggie with pieces of dried mushrooms inside. She gave me the bigger pieces and divided the broken ones equally between us. I immediately chewed them up and drank some water. They tasted bad, but not as bad as ecstasy. I continued to prepare for my competition, and tried to control the upcoming trip. Ginny looked at me like I was crazy, but most people had been doing that lately.

A half-hour later I was lost in my clothes, folding laundry, when the mushrooms hit. I couldn't remember how to fold a shirt. Did the left go to the right, the right to the left? What if I did it wrong? I instantly burst out laughing and fell in love with the shirt covering my hands.

It was now a part of me, forever, and I put it on over the shirt I was already wearing. We became best friends, and we would never leave each other. When I was on acid I connected with the peace and oneness of all things, but on mushrooms I gained the ability to speak to those things without making a sound. Even synthetic objects took on a pure nature, and everything sparkled with magnificent glory. Ginny and I walked together through a beautiful, enchanting dream down the hallways of our dorm, seeing everything for the very first time. Everything had its own life force; this was *real* magic.

I forgot about my competition as we fell deeper into the spiritual realm of ourselves and our surroundings. The auditory hallucinations were as powerful as the visual ones, and the Earth's core whispered, "Walk to me, find me." Every time I laughed, it embraced me. I could not contain this cosmic laughter, and all the colors that made up our lives were released in sound. Then, I saw sound. I ran to my CD player and put on as many different bands as I could think of and sat on the floor between the speakers. Glorious chords pulled me from myself, and in that moment I knew there was an afterlife, that when we die we'll leave our bodies on Earth and become a vapor cloud, breathing with the universe. Each note became its own separate being as the music intensified. I saw the birth of sound, the first bell that was rung and the first explosion of laughter. The thickness of sound swallowed me whole, deeper and deeper, until I was no longer alive, but only perpetual vibration. It was mentally orgasmic.

Morning came fast, as it always seemed to when I was having a good time, and I was still tripping hard. All the love and appreciation for sound and music had to go, since I was competing in six events in a few hours; however, I couldn't even see in front of me without a whirlwind of color blinding my eyes. How was I going to do this? How could I stand with composure on the floor exercise without bursting out in laugher? I had to get un-high and get there quickly. I called Darren, hoping he would come up with a solution.

In the past when I was tripping hard I would do some coke and it usually brought me down. Darren came over with a few leftover lines from his own partying that night. I did the lines, but they didn't help.

Now I was tripping with a thirst for more speed. We crushed up some Ritalin and started making big, long, yellow lines. I sniffed them, hoping it would eradicate the mushrooms' effects, but it just sped up my hallucinatory dreamland. The situation had lost its humor. I would need a good explanation for my coach and teammates. I knew I couldn't compete in that condition.

I needed to figure it out, and in my beautiful hallucinatory state I found a moment of honesty. This honesty seemed to glow from within. I said to Darren, "I'm just gonna tell coach the truth." He burst out laughing, but I knew I had to. In the blizzard of my mistakes I saw that coming clean would bring me peace. It seemed like the best solution. I continued sniffing Ritalin until it was time to go into the huge stadium.

Wanting to be alert and responsive, I did as much speed as possible before talking to the coach. Everything sparkled. The sounds of my sneakers made me giggle, and I was afraid that when I admitted to my coach that I was tripping, I'd break down in a fit of laughter. My fear grew as I got closer to his office door. I knocked and heard regret bounce off my fists. He said in a kind voice, "Come in." I opened the door, and he looked comfortable in his office chair. His wife and son were sitting in chairs around his desk. I couldn't believe I was in this situation. I was soaring through the clouds, and here in front of me were good, normal people having a nice Sunday morning together. I was about to drop a bomb.

Shame and regret washed through my veins as I remembered how he had helped me get into this school, how he had recommended me, and how he had given me money so that I could continue attending college. How could I tell him the truth? I was a grinning mess in dirty jeans, full of prescription and psychoactive drugs. I don't know how it happened, but a voice came from my center and said, "Coach, I need to talk to you . . . alone . . . if you have a moment." He looked perplexed, but still had a gleam in his eye as he said to his family, "I'll see you guys in a bit. I just have to talk to Joe."

I had four seconds to figure out if I was really going to ring that bell. I tried to speak my truth, but the Ritalin started dripping down my nasal cavity, into the back of my throat, and onto to my tongue. Gagging on my chemistry experiment, I needed to spit.

"Coach, I'm tripping!"

"What? You tripped? Are you okay?"

"No, Coach. I'm *tripping*!"

He looked confused, so I blurted, "Mushrooms, acid, I'm tripping."

All the beautiful sounds froze in his stare as I was no longer able to suppress the growing monster glob in my throat. I spat a huge loogie of yellow pills onto his trash, already filled to the top with paper. He saw the blob of yellow spit, which had an uncanny resemblance to bile, and I said, "It's just speed, Coach." Oh god, here I go. I've really done it now. *Just keep talking, Joe, just keep fucking talking.*

It was the only truth, the only thing actually real about me that I had announced out loud in a very long time. In a small, quiet moment of grace I said with subtle conviction, "I think . . . I think . . . I have a drug problem." I wasn't even sure if I believed it, but I was already circling in a drain I never intended to fall into.

His anger turned to compassion, and he talked to me for a long time and asked what I wanted to do about it. I told him I needed help and needed to come clean with everything. I thought to myself, *Maybe I do have a drug problem.* I was struggling to live without cocaine, and the small bouts of not using crippled me. I hated being in my skin, and had to be medicated or high to feel normal. I didn't know how I would be able to live without drugs.

After we talked for a while, he told me to put on my uniform and go cheer for the team. I don't think he understood what I meant by tripping—there was no way on Earth I could see my teammates' faces. I was still high as a kite and needed to stay aloft. "Coach, I've been up all night. I really need to go home and sleep," I said right before my tongue forked. "I'm also going to tell my parents I have a drug problem." He commended me for my lie-laden honesty.

I went back to my room, finished the Ritalin, and then had the most tormented sleep of my life. Trying to sleep while tripping and speeding invited all the demons I had just released to come stab and tear my mind.

The next day a call from my counselor woke me up. She wanted me to come in and talk. I went to her office, destroyed by the weekend, and we talked about giving rehab a shot. She said my school insurance would cover the cost, and I could take the remainder of the semester off for medical leave and return in the spring to retake all the classes I was failing. It seemed like the smartest thing to do—even if I didn't want to stop using drugs, it would erase my bad grades and give me a bit of a clean slate. She told me to give it a try, and I could leave the place if I didn't like it. I had to be there fourteen days. It was a Monday morning, and I would leave the next day. I surrendered, called Darren, and told him we had to party hard that night.

I packed clothes for a few nights' stay, and as I left my room for a pre-rehab fuckup at Darren's place, the entire girls' gymnastics team came in with a huge card that said, "Good Luck, Joe." I was completely disgusted by that gesture. It felt like a horrible Hallmark movie. All I could think about was that first line of coke with Darren, and here were these people, hugging me and telling me everything would be fine. I wanted to douse the place in gasoline and burn us all alive. They repeatedly extolled my bravery. It was all I could do to conceal my laughter by staring at the floor. They finally left, and I ran to Darren's in desperate pursuit of my high.

I treasured my first line like a lover's tender kiss. The first line of that night will be forever burned in my memory, for better or worse. After I snorted the "opening credit," I loved to light a cigarette and suck an Altoid mint, calling this combination my "steak dinner." I believed this reference gave me dignity and class.

After we did coke all night, Darren drove me to rehab. I arrived with my nose burning and my lungs on fire from all the cigarettes I had smoked. I didn't expect a five-star hotel, but it was a lot dirtier than I imagined, with a damp, moldy feeling. Someone immediately came and took my bags, opening them and going through all my stuff, searching for drugs, cologne, mouthwash, or any other creative thing an addict might use to get high, but I didn't try to smuggle anything in. I went upstairs for my intake and told a nurse about every drug I had ever taken. I went to my room, kept my clothes in the bag because I didn't plan on staying that long, and took out my teddy bear, Oatmeal. He had gone everywhere with me. He had been at the Olympic Training Center, and now he was in rehab. Things weren't looking up for that bear. He used to have beautiful, soft fur, but it had become matted and stuck together because I had put him in the washing machine. After that he started looking more like real oatmeal, left out in the sun, caked together and hard. He was missing his nose and an eye.

He sat on my bed staring at me, reminding me of my childhood. I had to look away, unable to talk about my situation with him. The room was dark, and I was exhausted. All I wanted to do was sleep. It was hard to function after partying all night, and now I was crashing. I needed medication, pills, anything, but all I got was solitude, goose bumps, and a runny nose. The room had five additional beds, but for now I was the only person who occupied one. I was terrified someone else might come in. In an hour I had to go downstairs and meet the group.

I called my college counselor to let her know I had arrived. I told her I wanted to leave, and she strongly recommended I stay for the entire fourteen days. I told her I couldn't miss Thanksgiving with my family and began to cry. Her kind exterior changed, and she put up a strong, tough-love front. I hung up the phone and felt powerless in that hellhole of a rehab, and hated her for putting me there.

It was difficult to stay put in that place. All I could think about was calling Darren to come rescue me, but when I did speak with him, I felt calmer. After a couple of days I realized the rehab wasn't all that bad, except that I did get a roommate—a forty-year-old ex-con alcoholic and drug addict who was on his third time through rehab. I prayed that wouldn't become me. I made a friend who called me "baby." She was a sweet sixty-year-old woman addicted to crack. I wished she could have stayed, but she left to go to a halfway house.

On the fourth day I got into a fight with my rehab counselor, who told me if I didn't open my eyes I was going to come back in here as a heroin addict. He handed me a copy of AA's Big Book. I thought I was being clever as I wrote a quote in it from a movie I liked about how some birds aren't meant to be caged. I slipped the book under his door, and then called Darren to come get me. He knew I wasn't supposed to leave, but I said, "Just be here," and hung up the phone. We headed back to school.

∞∞∞∞∞∞∞∞∞

The phone woke me up. It sounded angry and desperate. I answered sleepily, and it was my college counselor. She wanted to see me immediately in the dean's office. Without time to shower or brush my teeth, I ran out to meet them. When I walked through the door, I almost threw up. Both of my parents were sitting in the office. It felt like a bruising slap in the face. My father hadn't even seen my school, and there he was, looking estranged, disappointed, and afraid. My mother looked concerned, but managed to hold it together. Their relationship was still oceans apart. I sat down. I wore the sleep of last night on my skin.

The dean started talking and said if I did not finish some sort of rehabilitation, I could not return. And because I left rehab before my stay was completed, the school insurance wouldn't cover my next stint. If I didn't go, I wouldn't receive my gymnastics grant money and would be kicked out of school. I was enraged. It was my decision to go, and it was my decision to leave. I wasn't caught with any drugs on campus, but that didn't matter. My counselor flipped through her book and found an intensive outpatient program. It was all day every day for two months, and it was my responsibility to get there. It was decided that I would start a week after Thanksgiving, and I knew I needed to complete that one.

My parents left, and I didn't say good-bye. I blamed them for all of this. Darren and I made a new pact, a list we would stick with to help us change our lives. At the top of the list was "No drugs!" Then came exercise, then schoolwork; at the bottom was "Be happy!" We knew we could do it. I invited Darren home for Thanksgiving to honor our new clean and sober beginning, a good holiday with a fresh start.

Well, needless to say, my fresh start didn't last very long. I fell asleep on the table during my family's Thanksgiving dinner. I had a xanny bar (the 2 mg dose of Xanax) as an appetizer, Klonopin for my entrée, and a delectable desert of Percocet. My family knew I was loaded, and my mom kicked me out of the house . . . again.

Darren and I drove back to Holyoke and got an eight ball. I tried to stop doing coke, but I found it hopeless. Darren's birthday was coming up, so we ended up going back to Boston for more Klonopin. We didn't have any money (as usual), so I lied to all of my friends and told them I would use their money to buy mushrooms. I stole their money and pawned my favorite pewter sculptures of warriors and skeletons in battle that my mother had bought me when I was a child.

I bought three bags of crystal meth, twenty-five Klonopin, and four pills of ecstasy. I took the ecstasy on the drive back from Boston, along with a few other pills. I ended up being pilled out for a couple of days, and then I needed to buy coke to stay awake. For Darren's birthday I scammed someone else and got ten OxyContin. The effects of those pills felt awesome. I decided during my drugged-out state that I would actually do my best once I started in that new recovery program. I couldn't believe that I was a drug addict.

19

NEUROTRANSMITTERS

SEROTONIN, A NEUROTRANSMITTER, IS A NATURAL
CHEMICAL MADE IN THE BRAIN AND SMALL INTESTINES.
IT IS RESPONSIBLE FOR FEELINGS OF WELL-BEING. SEROTONIN
DEFICIENCIES CAN BE TREATED WITH SEROTONIN-SELECTIVE
REUPTAKE INHIBITORS (SSRI) SUCH AS PROZAC. THESE
ANTIDEPRESSANTS ATTEMPT TO PRESERVE THE SEROTONIN
ALREADY IN THE BRAIN RATHER THAN HELP PRODUCE MORE.

It was winter break between my fall and spring semesters, and I was in the second week of the intensive outpatient program. A light snow covered the city of Holyoke and dusted away the gloom and corruption. I felt hopeful. Two weeks without using, and physically I felt better than I had in a long time. I began to see the terrible things I had done and was ready for a change. I knew my future depended on passing every Wednesday's drug test and on my ability to follow directions, and knew to ask for help.

The program was intense, with group therapy, individual counselors, and a psychiatrist who helped me address my anxiety, depression, and insomnia—problems that had plagued me my whole life. The group's great faith and shared similarities led me to start enjoying the required twelve-step meetings. The psychiatrist had diagnosed me as manic-depressive and said my depression had a name and it was *not* "drug addict." That only validated my denial that I had a problem with drugs or suffered from the disease of addiction. I was just medicating my feelings of sadness and despair.

Darren began to change as I changed. He saw me trying to crawl out of that hole and recognized that our relationship was contaminating us. He decided to move home to Virginia and started thinking about his own future. Together we were too self-destructive. We packed up the broken-down, boxlike apartment he'd lived in and cried. We knew it was for the best. We had become as addicted to each other as to the drugs we took together. We said our good-byes, and he left. Now I would have to go through college alone. No more Cloud or Darren to hide behind.

I was not the only Putignano going through rough times. My brother, sisters, aunts, uncles, and parents had been working hard to keep the restaurant open during the recession. Bad business choices combined with a decline in customers brought devastating results to the family—Giovanni's Avon Towne House closed during my sophomore year. The loss of the restaurant left everyone unsure of their lives. We had been born into that industry, and it was assumed that it would always be there. My father had deep shame about losing the business, and I think my mother was even more heartbroken because she would no longer see him at the bar. Even though they hadn't been together for years, I think it comforted her to see him as she passed through the smoke and gin. It wasn't just a place of business; the restaurant was our family's body, where we bled and bonded, for better or worse, and now our family crest had been shattered. Our livelihood was turned into a Chinese restaurant, mocking us as others succeeded.

I had a few days off from rehab for Christmas and went home in an attempt to make my way back into the family. I stayed with my sister Trish, since my mother and I still had issues. Returning home was painful, like slipping into an ice bath, freezing and numbing. The quaint town I'd grown up in was still the same, but also changed, as my ghosts and demons reemerged and threw themselves on me. The beautiful birch trees that once welcomed me now rejected my being, and I felt a bottomless pit of despair. When my sister went to sleep, I curled up on her couch by the Christmas tree. The twinkling colored lights and tinsel became the backdrop of my tears. I cried so hard I almost vomited. I couldn't believe what I had become, and I was unable to slow it down. I prayed to God, to anyone, to anything.

I felt like a helpless child. I hoped and wished and prayed that there was a miracle waiting for me inside one of those perfectly wrapped Christmas presents.

I returned to rehab to finish the program and cobbled together over two months of abstinence. I was allowed to return to Staunton College, but everything was different without Darren and Cloud. All alone, I continued on my path of recovery. The whole school knew I went to rehab. Kids would walk by and shout "drug addict," which I didn't really care about. It was better than being called a fag.

The campus felt different, like it belonged to the good students. I knew I stood alone. I knew I was still seen as the freak. My few friends from the gymnastics team didn't share even my nondrug interests, and hanging out with them felt more like they were babysitting me, keeping me out of trouble. I continued going to an aftercare program from the rehab and passed all the drug tests.

I was better physically, but mentally I was falling apart. I started jogging at night in the athletic center, a massive circular hall that made me feel like I was inside a UFO. Listening to techno music, I ran until I felt high, but my past would creep up behind me and ask, "What went wrong?" I kept jogging, running to reach redemption.

Depression continued to torment me, and I felt no different with the medication my psychiatrist prescribed. I became her lab rat. My anxiety kept me up at all hours of the night, and I was on 80 mg of Prozac for my suicidal thoughts. One of the men in my aftercare group with the same psychiatrist told me she prescribed Klonopin for him, which was a favorite of mine. He came into group therapy slurring words, stumbling, and pilled out, and when the counselor called him out on it, he'd say, "It'sss jisssst my medication." He never failed his drug test, even though it showed benzodiazepines in his system because he was prescribed those pills by our rehab psychiatrist. A small crack of light opened up when I heard this. I knew I could manipulate my psychiatrist to get me those same pills. When I called a friend and told her of my plan, she laughed and said, "Joe, there is no way she is going to prescribe those for you." The challenge had been set.

Aside from a short relapse with Xanax and mushrooms, I thought I was doing great in my recovery (no denial here), but my anxiety was seeping through my flesh. My psychiatrist saw the pain I was in and had grown tired of watching me battle with myself. Her desire to help me find peace within was met with my ulterior motives as I walked into her office to see how far she could be pushed.

She worked in a square, sad cube of an office, and deep in her eyes I saw my depression mirroring hers—years of studying, and she had ended up there. As she sat in her uncomfortable chair, she peered down at me like a specimen under a microscope.

"How are you today, Joseph?"

"Not good."

"What's going on?"

"I still can't sleep." I slid down in my chair.

"Did you try the trazodone?"

"Yup."

"The Serzone?"

"Kept me awake for a day."

"Really?"

"Really."

"How about the Buspar?"

"It was awful, made me feel even more anxious."

"Well, that can happen sometimes with that medication. What about the Elavil?"

"Gave me the worst headache ever."

She looked pensive, angry at the pharmaceuticals. I knew I looked restless, and was putting on the greatest act of my life. Then she asked casually, "Have you ever heard of a drug called Klonopin?"

B I N G O!

I couldn't believe she had asked me that. I almost exploded like a smashed piñata. There it was, the golden opportunity my friend said was impossible. Afraid to talk for fear of screwing up the situation, I pretended I'd never heard of it. I said it back to her in a long, confused manner as if the syllables were difficult to pronounce. "Kaa-lonnny-pin? Nope, never heard of it, but please, only if you think it'll work. I can't take this anymore." I restrained any signs of happiness and steadied my nerves by staring at the floor like a lifeless doll. And then, she did it. She wrote a prescription for twenty Klonopin.

The prescription was written for one pill a day. I ate two in the car on the way back to campus. I was to call her after a few days, and if it was working she'd prescribe more. I held the orange-brownish bottle tight in my hand like a trophy. I would use as much as I wanted, but had to control my insanity; otherwise she would know I was abusing them and would stop prescribing them.

By the time I made it back to campus, the pills had already hit. I was calm and lubricated. On my way to a friend's room, fate presented itself. During all this wintery madness I'd had my eye on an acquaintance. His name was Nick and he was tall, masculine, strong, and popular—everything society told me I wasn't. Having him would make me what I always wanted to be. I remembered one night we had done coke together. It had been his first time, and after a few lines his leg had started twitching like an impatient man with too much energy. I had found this cute in my drug delusion, and was sold. He was still experimenting with drugs, so my abstinence became the threat that kept me from him. Now that threat was gone, and there he stood in front of me.

He said hello, and I immediately held out the bottle and offered him one. He smelled stoned, so I knew he wouldn't turn it down. His eyes lit up and he asked what it was. I gave him a quick rundown of the wonderful side effects and gave him one, then gave him "one more for good luck" as I tried to pull his essence into mine. He then invited me into the world I had never been a part of—the other side of his bedroom door, where his friends hung out and smoked pot, drank, and partied. I had never been invited in before, and now was my opportunity.

I went in to find three other guys who looked slightly drunk and stoned. The pills were working, removing my anxiety, allowing me to relax and be myself, or at least who I thought I was. Nick poured me a beer from their mini-keg. I drank it as fast as I could, filled my plastic cup again, and made myself at home. As we listened to Phish, one of the guys asked me about some of the drugs I'd taken, since I had the reputation of being a drug addict. They were interested in getting to know me, not make fun of me, and for the rest of the night I felt accepted. I gave each guy a pill, but only one, since I needed the rest—though I secretly handed Nick another one. We drank more beer, listened to more music, and smoked pot. I ate a few more pills and told the guys my sordid drug stories like we were kids sitting around a campfire.

A day and a half had gone by and I woke up in the same chair, dressed in the same clothes—ripped rave jeans and a black hoodie. I looked elusive and mysterious, like a boy who played with matches. I reached down into my pocket, making sure the pill bottle was still there. It was. I shook it, hoping for the dull rattle of remaining pills. I couldn't believe I hadn't eaten them all or given them away in my calm euphoria. I looked up at the bunk bed and Nick wasn't there.

Alone in the room, I heard the door open, and it was him, returning from class. I said drunkenly, "Dude, how'd you go to class?" He said with his raspy, deep voice, "I dunno. I sat in the seat and fell asleep the whole time. I never miss class, no matter how fucked up I am or tired. I'm always gonna be there."

"Shit, man. I don't know how you did it; I can't even move my legs!"

We both laughed and I stood up, embarrassed and confused, because I didn't know how long I had been asleep, what day it was, or how much time had passed. I was afraid to ask him if it was Wednesday, but I knew I needed to take a pill fast. Reality was starting to crack through my comfort, and the anxiety was leaking through the medicated state of my brain.

I reached down into the jeans I had been wearing for months and handed Nick another pill as I left for my room. "Here's one for later." As I walked through campus, I thought about Nick's smile. I liked him, and acknowledging that fact brought a small trace of sunlight back into my gloom.

I walked into my room, and the depression hit me like a thunderclap. My room was dark, disturbing, and lonely. No one ever came in; it reeked of sickness, like a cancer ward. I didn't even bother to decorate the institutional white walls. My turntables were thickly layered in dust, and my clothes covered the floor. My chessboard always made me laugh. My mother had bought it for me. I loved playing when I was younger, but over the years I had lost the pieces. I replaced those lost pieces with prescription bottles full of antidepressants, useless antianxiety pills, and painkillers. Instead of warriors fighting to save their queen, it became an addict's playground—last pill bottle standing wins to take all of the remaining pills, surrendering his life to overdoses. There were no rules.

I called the psychiatrist a few days earlier than she had expected. I told her that the pills were working, though they seemed a little weak. I was fishing for a stronger strength. She paused for a moment and said, "I know what to do. What is your pharmacy number?" I quickly searched the bottle for the number that had nearly been rubbed off by my tight, sweaty grip on the bottle. She called in for the next dosage. The pills I still had were yellow 0.5 milligrams, little SweeTarts, but now I graduated to the green ones that were double strength. On top of that, I had a brand-new prescription waiting for me at the pharmacy. I picked them up, ate a few, and made sure to save a few for Nick.

My phone rang, which was usually my counselor since no one else called my room. I had slammed it down in anger so many times that it barely worked, but on the other end of the line was Nick. I smiled. He asked what I was up to, and I didn't know if I should tell him the truth or not. I was getting fucked up all by myself. He had just taken the pill I left him, was feeling the effects, and would bring some beers over. We talked into the night. He came from a caring family.

I felt like the black sheep in the conversation. I wasn't even twenty-one and had been to one rehab and was already into my second. He seemed to like all the bad things I'd done; all my destruction made him laugh. And then it happened.

We kissed, and it felt like my first kiss ever. The kiss I'd never had, the one I heard my sisters talk about when I was younger, the one I heard Tara and her friends mention a million times—that special kiss that made them teenagers. The weird thing was that I knew Nick wasn't gay. He was just fucked up, just another straight guy experimenting. Drugs make people more intimate and allow them to cross boundaries they normally wouldn't cross. I loved drugs even more, because they made that moment possible. I was so alone for so many months, and for the few moments that kiss lasted I felt cared for, attractive, and desired. All the things I had been washed away. Even though I had secretly wanted that moment and carefully prepared for it, the kiss shattered me. I smiled from deep within my being and it shone through my eyes and penetrated through the drugs. For a brief second, my soul and essence broke through the darkness I had covered myself with for years. For the first time in a very long time, I felt human.

20

CALVARIA

THE CALVARIA OR SKULLCAP IS THE UPPER PORTION
OF THE SKULL. WHEN SOMEONE SUSTAINS A BLOW
TO THE HEAD OR HITS THE HEAD AGAINST A STATIONARY
OBJECT, A CONCUSSION CAN OCCUR. A CONCUSSION
IS AN IMMEDIATE BUT OFTEN REVERSIBLE TRAUMATIC
PARALYSIS OF THE NERVOUS FUNCTION IN THE BRAIN.

I became a new fixture in Nick's room. We had sex on more than one occasion, but only when we were extremely intoxicated. We would whisper the words "no regret" to each other, verifying that although we never spoke of it afterward, we understood that it happened. Most of the jocks partied in his room, and I had painted them all wrong. I had judged them because I was never part of their conversations; however, they found me interesting and dark, with a sardonic sense of humor that made them laugh. I realized that there was more in common than not between us. We all felt the same pressures to be the best.

I had stopped attending group meetings at rehab, started to miss my appointments with my college counselor, and had no intention of showing up for classes. Every day started the same—I would shower, throw on my Ralph Lauren polo shirt and big baggy jeans, eat some pills, take a short walk over to Nick's room, and then start to drink. I'd take a nap while Nick went to his classes. We took every drug together, from ecstasy to acid and mushrooms to mescaline.

After Darren left, I contacted one of his dealers and started getting coke for the other guys who hung out with Nick. I loved it. My phone rang all the time, and for the first time I had tons of new friends, but I was a horrible coke dealer. I would get their stuff, steal a few lines out of it, and then cut their bags with baking powder to make it look like a large amount. Everyone knew I was a shady guy and buying coke from me was risky, but it's just the way it went. I wasn't going to justify anything to anyone. I had to feed my own addiction first.

I stopped talking to Darren and realized that we never had much in common; we had basically driven each other crazy in a bizarre struggle for power and acceptance. I spoke with Piper now and then, and even gave Cloud a call from Nick's phone. After I told him so many Cloud stories, he finally let me use his calling code to give her a call.

Still in design school, she answered the phone and her voice was disturbing. At first she sounded happy to hear from me, but then there was no one there, as if she had fallen asleep in midconversation. Then she woke up, completely forgetting that I was on the phone. Whenever I took about thirty pills I sounded the same way, but this was different; she sounded more anesthetized. What I could hear sounded like heroin. That same scratchy, soft, opiate voice that came out of junkies in the street begging for change now came out of Cloud's mouth. My counselor's voice echoed in my head—"Someday you will return here as a heroin addict"—and now I hated heroin even more. It seemed to have taken Cloud, and my voice couldn't wake her from her deep sleep. There she lay, somewhere in Portland, phone in hand, asleep in the void between life and death, an unkissed Sleeping Beauty.

One night a friend of Nick's came into the room and told us he was driving up to Maine, and invited us to come along. In my pilled-out state I grabbed this invitation and, like a harpy, convinced Nick that we should go. He was powerless under my spell. We grabbed a case of beer and my beautiful pill bottle, and headed for Maine.

They were going snowboarding, but not us. I wasn't going to waste precious drug money to play in the snow. I just wanted something to do, and, maybe in my own insanity, I thought this would be a romantic trip. Even in hell they decorate, right? Even in my dirty, grungy life and demented thoughts I wanted romance and love. We were two demons moving closer to the candle flame. After all, for me this was romance: beer, pills, cold Maine air, and the man I was deeply in love with but who would never admit his true feelings for me. It didn't matter to me if he didn't love me back, just as long as he was there by my side. He could wear any disguise he wanted, but I knew at night, in the darkness as the rest of the world slept, he was snuggled in close to me.

We partied, drank, and talked all night, and Nick woke me up in the morning to drive back. In our mutual delusion I convinced him that we had taken too many pills, and without coke we would fall asleep at the wheel and die on our way back to campus. We had to find *real* Maine snow. We woke up a guy who was from there and asked him if he knew anyone. "I don't know . . . maybe someone at the high school knows somebody." He rolled over and went back to sleep. My fucked-up mind translated that as "Someone at the high school has coke on them and we just have to go there and find them." When I tried to stand up, I almost fell over. Nick could barely walk either, but I knew a few more pills would straighten us out and get us thinking clearly. It didn't. On a spectacular Monday morning in a small Maine town, Nick and I were completely fucked up. It was pure romance.

We got into his old pickup truck and started swerving through the little curved lanes. We had no idea where we were going, and somewhere inside me I knew we were playing with fire. The walls between my sanity and my true self were getting thinner. I started to have a complete psychotic breakdown on those pills. I started to believe my own lies. We drove until we found a school, which wasn't difficult in a small town, then pulled into the parking lot and watched teenagers file inside. I knew this was crazy, but I couldn't stop it. If there was a glimmer of hope to score, then it would be worth it.

As the teenagers marched in with their book bags, we got out of the truck and walked in with them. Nick and I still looked young, so nobody would think anything of it as long as we just kept walking in alongside the other students. I decided to just ask a random student if he knew where I could find some cocaine. We both started asking a few teenagers, and they seemed completely scared of us. I found that confusing, since we weren't monsters or doing anything wrong—we were just inquiring about a certain something. I continued creeping up to groups of kids and interrupting them, asking, "Hey guys, do you know anybody selling coke around here?" I couldn't understand their awkwardness and fear. We continued deeper and deeper into the school, until ten minutes into the search two teachers ran down the hallway toward us. We started running and pushed through a few students in our way, and then ran through the doors and into Nick's truck.

We peeled out of the parking lot and gunned it down the street toward the highway, afraid the cops would soon be chasing us with that obnoxious siren. As we drove faster along the curved streets, arguing about what a stupid idea that was, we took a tight turn on a dangerous curve and saw a car coming straight at us. Nick's reaction time was in slow motion, and nothing could be done. A huge bang slammed my head hard into the dashboard, which blocked me from shooting through the windshield. Nick's side of the car was smashed in, but he was similarly saved by the steering wheel. The woman driving the other car was okay and came to my side to see if we were injured.

The impact of the crash furthered the loss of my senses; I opened my door and started swearing at her. "What the fuck were you doing driving into us!" She looked confused, since we clearly had hit her. Even though we totaled her car, she seemed all right and more concerned about us. But I was not all right. I continued cursing her at the top of my lungs at eight in the morning in the cold streets of a city in Maine. The police and fire department arrived with the expected sirens. When the firefighters asked my name, I replied, "Reese's Pieces," convinced that was truly my name. They asked me what town I was in, and I said, "Holyoke." My usual conniving brain had really been knocked around, and everything was confusing. Normally I'd be lying about my medical situation to get some painkillers out of these guys.

We watched them tow away the wreck that was Nick's old truck. Still majorly fucked up on pills, I got into the back of the ambulance. All I remember after that is a room with bright lights and being diagnosed with a concussion. A guy from the party picked us up at the hospital and we went back to the apartment we had partied at the previous night. We had no way to get back to Holyoke. Nick's truck was never leaving Maine again unless it got recycled into beer cans. The doctors told Nick not to let me sleep because of the concussion, but I was so tired from all the pills, there was no way I could stay awake. So we decided to take the rest of the day easy, and took the remainder of my pills and drank.

Nick's uncle came all the way from Brooklyn to pick us up and drove us back to Holyoke. I can't imagine how awkward and awful it must have been for him to see his nephew hanging out with his dirty, drunk, pilled-out, face-pierced friend, Joe. The drive back to Staunton College was the longest silent drive of my life, as Nick's uncle punished us with slow, deep, concentrated breathing.

Back at school I felt horrible about Nick's truck, but worse than that was coming down from taking so many pills over such a short span of time. I had taken an entire month's worth over the weekend. I was so scared. For some reason the transition from being high to being sober affected me more this time than it did the others, and I would do whatever it took to ease the comedown. The goal became to never come down at all, no matter what. I would beg, steal, or lie to stay on the cloud of calm, because the Klonopin withdrawal was unbearable.

That week was awful. I went to the pharmacy to refill my prescription, but the pharmacist wouldn't budge, so I devised a plan. I would call my psychiatrist and tell her someone had stolen my prescription. Since I felt a true state of anxiety coming off the pills, it would be easy for the phone call to sound like a real state of emergency, complete with tears. I told her some kids came into my room pretending to be my friends, and then stole my pills. As a drug of choice producing euphoria, this situation could certainly occur. When I had used every weapon I had in my manipulation arsenal, she finally believed me, sounded terribly concerned, and called the pharmacy immediately to refill my prescription. The next problem I had was that I didn't have the twenty-seven dollars to pay for the script, and no one would lend me money. They all knew I'd spend the money on drugs and would never repay them.

In my desperation I went into one of my teammates' rooms, started up a conversation, and surveyed the place for something valuable and easy to steal. A portable CD player caught my eye, easy to stick down my pants and walk out with. I sat down near it and talked to him about how well my recovery was going and how happy I was to have the team's support. I waited until he turned his head and stuffed the CD player in my huge, baggy jeans. I knew he didn't see me take it and quickly said, "Shit, man, I gotta go. I'm late for something," and ran to call Nick.

We borrowed a friend's car and I promised to give him a pill for the drive. I pawned the CD player for forty dollars and picked up my prescription. I didn't even wait to get back in the car; I tore open the stapled prescription bag right in front of the pharmacist, took two pills, and chewed them up waterless. I knew these pills would keep me safe in my own head for another twenty hours.

I had been missing gymnastics practice, and the coach would tell the counselor, and then I would have to go in and meet with her. I went back to practice, telling them I had been out for mental health issues, which they knew about and honored from my previous leave for rehab. I wasn't competing that season, which allowed me a semester to get my head and skills back together enough for the competition level.

I warmed up on the vault, going through the basics, back to that moment of flying through the air, untouchable, beautiful, and free. I was doing a layout Yurchenko, a round-off entry to the vault, back handspring onto the horse, and pushoff to another elongated flip. The old-style men's vault faced lengthwise, and I ran toward it as fast as I could and did my round-off back handspring onto the horse, but my hand slipped off the side. I must have taken off crooked from the board. I knew in midair that I didn't have the muscle strength to pull it around, and the force of gravity took me crashing down, digging my ankle into the mat. My landing sounded like I had just stepped on a brittle branch, and the bone screamed its very first word: "Snap!" Everyone heard it, and I immediately curled into a position of physical pain, wiggly and writhing. I knew it was broken. And I knew a broken bone meant Percocet—an opioid painkiller.

I knew I had broken my ankle as a direct result of all the pills I had taken. My mind and muscle synapses were all out of sync. Even though I wanted my body to pull the flip around, the message came too late, dulled by residual Klonopin.

Our physical therapist brought me to the campus medical center, and they transferred me to the emergency room. The X-ray came back showing the broken bone, and I was given a prescription, with a refill, for Endocet, Percocet's cousin. The doctor seemed sympathetic to me as a gymnast with an ankle injury, so I decided to see how far I could push my luck. I told him my back hurt from a car accident the weekend before, and he added carisoprodol (Soma), a mellow muscle relaxant. Doctors always seemed to treat athletes differently from civilians, aware of the great pains we put our bodies through. As a gymnast on the team I consistently received more time, care, and desired meds, and I took full advantage of that. It was raining pills, and I would be in oblivion for the next month.

Nick and I didn't leave my room for a week. We took so many downers that I decided we needed some cocaine. I thought the downers would be more enjoyable while we were awake, but we had no money and no car, just a lot of pills. I managed to find a good source of mushrooms that I planned to sell off, so I went around campus taking orders and collecting money from students. Now that I had money, I had to get to Southie, a long two-hour drive away. I also had to find a new cocaine dealer because I had burned my bridges with my old guy. On top of that, for my fundraising I went around campus selling fake ecstasy to kids who had no idea what it was, telling them they had to drink a lot with it to feel the effects. I took regular pills like Advil and ex-lax, rubbed the print off, and gave it a new name like cinnamon or sunshine for thirty dollars a pill. Ex-lax was the easiest, since all I had to do was scratch off the print except for the letter X, standing for ecstasy. That unquestionably clinched my place in hell.

The money was sorted out; now all we needed was a ride. We asked one of my friends from the team who sometimes lent us his car. He said emphatically, "No way. You guys are too fucked up right now!" I changed the approach by offering a joint and a pill, which he took immediately. He relaxed and passed out by his computer. While he was fast asleep, Nick and I grabbed the car keys and left for the parking lot. We had taken so many pills that we were falling asleep ourselves by the time we found the car. I felt like I was in quicksand with my feet made out of rubber, unable to stand. My vision blurred and my heavy eyelids were pulled toward the ground. None of that mattered; we had the keys and the car, and it was now time to go get the coke.

We started our run onto the highway, a swerving metal death box powered by zombies, a steel-encased, ticking bomb. Nick was driving and I was the watchdog, making sure we stayed between the straight yellow lines and on the lookout for state police. About twenty minutes into the drive I lost the fight to not shut my eyes, and finally they succumbed. A blaring horn from a car we almost hit jolted me back awake. Nick was dead asleep at the wheel, swerving into another car beside us. I screamed his name and cursed him out to stay awake. I had taken double the amount of pills as Nick, so if he was swerving I wouldn't stand a chance driving the car.

Within minutes I fell asleep again, but was shaken awake by the horrid sound of the tires hitting the side of the highway speed bumps, suddenly going right off the road toward the guardrail. Again, I shook Nick to wake him up, but he was slipping into unconsciousness. How we weren't wrapped around the guardrail already is still a mystery to me. We were only forty-five minutes into the drive, and we had already nearly crashed twice. I had to take control of the situation. We pulled over; both of us stumbled out of the car, and then I harnessed all the muscle memory I had within my body so that I could drive. Every gymnastics practice was channeled into that drive. I swerved in response to a few honking horns, but luckily none of them were cops.

Miraculously, we arrived in Southie. I looked forward to doing the biggest line of cocaine ever to wake myself up. I found a girl to buy from who had been witness to my progressively quick decline. She handed me the bag of coke and I instantly said, "No, I need to get a little more, there isn't enough in here." She looked pissed but concerned. "Joe, I think you better slow down." *What the fuck . . . a drug dealer telling me to slow down?* Insulted, I told her it was for the long drive back and I didn't want to crash, so she threw in a free line.

The drive back was easier. I was alert and fresh, ready to push the pedal to the floor in the fast lane. We got the mushrooms and coke, and after a few pit stops along the way to do more lines, we made it back to college.

∞∞∞∞∞∞∞∞∞

I don't remember the rest of that semester. I remember people looking at me like I was completely fucked up, and if they said anything I just flipped them off and shouted, "Fuck you!" I was out of control, and the time came to leave the team. I couldn't use drugs and continue to train. Gymnastics was taking up the precious time I needed to drink and do other drugs.

I was devoid of all human emotions, and it actually wasn't difficult to quit. I called the coach and started an argument. I don't recall the words, only his confusion and anger. I remember being very clear that I could no longer do gymnastics and felt no remorse over that decision; after all, my gymnastics was the only thing truly standing in the way of my happiness.

Every moment without drugs was agonizing. A long time ago I had given everything over to gymnastics, surrendering my heart and body to its torture and beauty. Gymnastics had been everything I wanted, and I had given it everything I had. But now I had a new love—a love I loved even more deeply than gymnastics. There was only room for one, so my beloved gymnastics had to go.

It felt good to walk away from a funeral I was happy to miss. Not a single teardrop fell as I left behind all those first-place trophies and grand Olympic dreams. I was relieved it was over. The relationship between my sport and my drugs was painfully close—both shared the common bond of destruction. Training hard was as painful as a bad hangover. Both destroyed my body, and since I had to choose one, I chose drugs.

With all my free time dedicated to my new love, it didn't take long to reach disastrous new highs and lows. I think only a week had passed since I had quit the team, but my boundaries dropped dramatically and I bordered more perilously between sanity and insanity after taking too many pills. Toward the end of that long drug run, Nick passed out from the pills, fell back, and hit his head against a wall so loudly that a student two doors down came in to see what had happened. His head was bleeding, and I made him go to the medical center. My love, attacked by my other love—drugs were trying to take him down, and I would do everything I could to not let that happen.

It was 11:00 p.m. when we went to the medical center. As I waited for him to come out, I started a conversation with a girl. She was quiet, skinny, and smart-looking, with red hair and glasses that were too big for her face. I was so relaxed and intoxicated that I became completely intrigued by talking to a stranger, and told her everything. I told her about all the drugs, the rehabs, Darren, Nick, and the buying and selling. It actually felt good to get it all out. She listened contently to my confession, like a high priestess. I felt a weight lifted, and I started to cry as I filled in every detail of my life. I was so fucked up I couldn't contain my emotions, and just wept and hugged her. I loved her patience. It felt like she gave me golden wings. I don't remember her name, but I left the medical center completely absolved of my sins. It felt so good to tell another human the truth about what was really going on.

The next day there was banging on my door. I could barely open my eyes and vaguely remembered the night before. Nick was in my bed, and I opened the door to my school counselor, who instantly barged in and yelled, "What the fuck is going on?" She collected herself and said, "You have to meet me in the dean's office in an hour. You need to shower and get dressed." *What the fuck had I done now?*

I didn't even wake Nick up. I walked in the office and sat down. The vibe was different from before. This was serious, and their expressions left no doubt that I was in trouble—big trouble. The dean began reading from a legal document. They were expelling me for not completing the rehab program and because they had heard I was selling drugs.

I instantly reacted. "Selling drugs! No, I'm not! Why do you think that?"

The dean didn't even look up, and started reading from another paper. It looked like a woman's handwriting. It was a letter from the resident assistant of a dorm and went into long detail about things I had never told anybody. I turned white.

The priestess I had made my confession to the previous night wasn't my savior after all; she was a resident assistant, and worked for the school. Her job was to make peace and bring order to the dormitories. Typically, they were geeks, and the girl I had befriended the previous night had turned me in. *What a fucking bitch.*

It was true; I was guilty. "Okay. How long do I have to get my stuff out of here?" He said, "One hour."

"One hour! You can't fucking kick me out in one hour. Where am I gonna go?"

"I don't care, but if you don't leave, the police will escort you off campus!"

"Where am I gonna go?"

"Call your parents."

My parents were certainly not going to pick me up, bail me out, or let me live with them after this.

I said, "Fuck off! Both of you! You are so fucking stupid!" and slammed the door behind me.

I went back to my room and packed a bag of my most important possessions. I didn't think they were serious, that they would actually kick me out, but as I packed, the campus police opened my door and watched me. They were going to escort me off campus. As the cops led me off, I saw a guy from the soccer team and yelled, "Tell Nick I'll be at the park!" My dorm room was still full of many of my things, but there was no way to bring them with me.

I went to the park half a mile down the road to figure out what to do next. A horrid, quiet pain crept inside me as loud city sirens mixed in with the cold winter breeze. I couldn't believe I had no place to go, no place to live, and no way to contact anyone. Two hours ago I had been safe and warm, asleep in my bed with Nick, and then all of a sudden I was shocked into a new reality. I sat on the dirty green grass and cried.

21

BLOOD

BLOOD AND THE STILL-BEATING HEART ARE CENTRAL ELEMENTS OF SACRIFICE, USUALLY A RELIGIOUS RITUAL THAT INVOLVES THE KILLING OF ANIMALS OR HUMAN BEINGS, SUPERVISED BY PRIESTS. IT HAS BEEN A FEATURE OF ALMOST ALL PREMODERN SOCIETIES AT SOME STAGE OF THEIR DEVELOPMENT. A SACRIFICE WAS TYPICALLY OFFERED TO FULFILL AN OBLIGATION TO THE GODS. THESE SACRIFICES WERE KNOWN AS *blóts,* AND THE BLOOD WAS CONSIDERED TO HAVE THE POWER OF ITS ORIGINATOR. AFTER THE CEREMONIAL SLAYING, THE BLOOD WAS SPRINKLED ON TEMPLE WALLS, ON STATUES OF GODS, AND ON THE PARTICIPANTS.

I waited all day in the park for Nick. I wasn't sure if he got my message or if his friends finally knocked some sense into him to be finished with me and my disasters. As the sun set and I began to give up hope, Nick appeared in the distance, bundled up, with that adorable smile on his face as if to say, "Joey, what the fuck have you done now, you crazy bastard?" I loved that smile and will never forget it. Nick was there, and everything would be okay.

He sat beside me on the frozen grass and we talked about a plan to sneak me back into his dorm room. By now everyone knew of my expulsion. My school ID picture was on the desk of every dormitory's door guard, but I managed to walk by concealed in the center of a "penguin's huddle" of Nick's friends.

In Nick's room I felt safe and relieved, and planned to get as drunk and pilled out as possible to forget that hellish day. In my drunkenness,

I plotted my revenge against Staunton College. I believed I was innocent and the school had infringed upon my civil rights. I drunk-dialed a lawyer, explaining that my entire case was hearsay. He told me that I didn't have a case and would have to accept what had happened. In my deepening delusion I came up with another idea to call the dean and plead with him to reinstate me as a student. I called from Nick's room, so drunk that I didn't consider that caller ID would come up with the last name and room number. The dean's assistant answered. "I know you are in Nick's room. The police are on their way to escort you back off campus." I begged her and told her I didn't have time to get my things out of my room, but she didn't seem particularly sympathetic.

I hung up the phone and ran back to the park. I had a week's worth of pills left and took them all. The higher I got, the easier it was for me to live in the gutter. All my nighttime fears became comforts in the illusion of Klonopin. I, the Klonopin King, reigned from the throne over the enchanted land of heaven in my delusory state of mind.

Again, I had nowhere to go and no one to call. When holding drugs I was everyone's best friend, but when the pills and powders were gone, they forgot my name. I was terrified. I didn't have a plan for the next day, and I would soon be drugless and homeless. *I have no place to go. I have no place to go,* repeated over and over in my head, a ruby-shoeless-demented-Dorothy, fighting off the truth as my tears cascaded down my cheeks. Truth was not allowed in my Oz; I just needed my ticket back to a drug-filled euphoria.

Night rolled into the park and so did two friends I used to party with, who pleaded with me to stop using. This just made me defensive and angry. One of them handed me the harshest letter I had ever received. She wrote that I was destroying the beautiful light within me, and that she could see my inner glow withering from my drug use. She said with sincere honesty, "Joey, go home. Try to reconnect with your parents. Just go home. The battle is over. Look at where you are!" I hated her for saying that. I was unaware of much of what she wrote, since my pills hit me while I read the damn letter. At that moment I believed I was in a beautiful, lush park surrounded by a city of opportunity instead of the broken-down neighborhood I was sitting in. I exploded in anger at them for their drug-friend hypocrisy. They left after seeing they couldn't dent my denial or comprehend my slurred words.

Nick came back, as I knew he would, with beer and weed. We devised yet another *brilliant* plan of action. His uncle was coming to take him home for a long weekend, and I could get a ride back with them. I made it back to campus for the long weekend and saw Nick waiting for me with his uncle outside his dorm. He had to run back in and grab his bag. I had only a vague recollection of meeting Nick's uncle in Maine due to the concussion, pills, and alcohol, and was now embarrassed standing there alone while making small talk. My embarrassment grew as two campus police approached us. A residential assistant must have seen me crossing the large parking lot near his building and then called the police.

"Mr. Pu-*tan*-yano," one said, deliberately mispronouncing my name.

"Yes."

"You're not supposed to be here on campus."

"I know. I'm leaving. I'm getting a ride to my friend's place."

Then Nick's uncle chimed in, saying, "Yeah, it's okay, guys. He's coming with me."

Nick had not told his uncle what had happened; however, Nick's uncle figured things out and proposed that perhaps he should drive me back home. We naturally challenged him on that idea, and then he asked why I couldn't go home.

I said, "My parents won't let me live with them anymore," omitting the detail of not being able to stay drug-free for more than a moment's time. Instead, I brought up old memories of my parents, turning them into monsters to convince Nick's uncle that I could not go home. It was true my parents had problems with alcohol, relationships, and each other, and I had valid points and deep pain to crucify them to this man I barely knew, but my parents were doing the best they could. I knew in my heart that I could not go home, and remembered the many times I had tried to. I was so far from the human I used to be that both my parents made it clear on more than one occasion that I was not welcome in their homes.

Nick's uncle called my dad. After the conversation he turned to us and said I could go home, and that my dad wanted me to come home. I was pissed. This was not the father I knew—the heavy-handed Italian-American who was embarrassed by my clothes, my body piercings, and my nihilistic "hate life" attitude. I knew he was bullshitting, trying to pull off the good parent act. I was everything my father hated. He must have been lying, faking his kindness, and I couldn't figure out why. As soon as I arrived home, I knew he would tell me to leave.

I hated both men for making the decision for me. I didn't want to leave Nick and go home, but I had no alternative. The thought of being without Nick was a punishment worse than sobriety and made me want to crawl deeper into a pillbox and numb out to the rhythm of nothing.

The family beach house had changed. Every happy memory of playing there in the summers was murdered by the existence of my father's new family. Even though I loved my father's girlfriend and her two daughters, it was still painful to see them living together. The house's familiar comfort had changed into someone else's home where the memories my mother, sisters, brother, and I had shared were but a salted mist that evaporated over the sandy beach. I carried my one packed bag up to my room and cried as I desperately tried to cling to the past.

I had always felt so natural near the beach. I felt that if I could recover anywhere it would be there, by the ocean. But this time something inside me wasn't right, and the place wasn't easing the pain. A presence of evil had taken residence inside me that I could not control or get out; I was under its every command. Finding a way to quiet that roaring beast became my life's work—to reach a moment of peace from the debilitating depression, anxiety, and active addiction. If only I could drown that demon in those icy waters, under that fucking moonlight that had witnessed my entire descent, as that bright, soulless god of a moon withheld its divine intervention.

That night I poured myself a giant cup of vodka, and washed down another handful of pills. I was scared, embarrassed, ashamed, and cornered. I knew I could not continue to live this way, and yet I did not have the strength to change. I thought about my father upstairs as he was probably wondering where he had lost his son—that young boy who conquered fear and performed incredible skills, who won countless competitions as he continued to the Olympic Training Camp, that smiling, happy son full of spirit and life who was now a shell of the child champion he once knew. I kept crying and drinking and taking more pills, and then suddenly knew what I had to do. I had to end this and allow the icy-cold ocean to swallow me whole into its depths. I wondered if my father could feel my crippling pain shoot up through the floorboards into his room.

In pure desperation I grabbed the kitchen knife I had been using to open the moving boxes and began cutting my wrists. I was afraid at first, and the initial gash hurt, but then the pain felt good. I tore through my flesh, trying to release the veins out to the open air so they could bleed out my life. I wanted my soul to rocket through my skin and stain the floor where I once lived and breathed, to forever mark my pain, regret, shame, and anger. I wanted to fill the entire room in my pool of blood, choking on my past and floating to the top as my soul left my damaged body behind.

I kept cutting, trying to get deeper into the veins, trying to dig out the pain and sin. Blood trickled down my wrists and turned my stomach—there was no turning back, and I held my breath, tears streaming; I was hell-bent on severing the radial artery. I could taste in my tears the sadness this would bring my family. I didn't want them to have to clean up the mess, but I also could not bear to be in my skin any longer. My flesh quivered and my face froze. "Please, someone stop me. I don't want to die. I just don't want to feel the pain. Please, God, please help me. I'm dying." Hating everything about me and hating that I could not change, I knew the only solution lay in bloodletting.

While I was performing the surgery of suicide, my father came into my room. To this day I don't know why he was awake or what made him come into my room. He saw my wrists and screamed, "What are you doing?" I looked up at him, eye to eye, as the little boy I was—lost, alone, scared, teary-eyed—and said, "I don't know." His girlfriend came in, picked me up, put a jacket on me, and said, "We have to get you to the doctor." I didn't resist. I let go of the fight and let them help me. I don't believe I really wanted to die; I had just run out of solutions.

My father started his truck and waited for us to come downstairs, but I remembered all those pills upstairs. I told Lynn, "I'll be right back, I forgot something." I ran to my bed, cut a hole in the mattress under the sheets and pushed the pill bottles into the fluff where nobody would find them, and pulled the sheets up.

At the hospital, they waited for my blood alcohol to lower and then gave me Ativan, which brought calm and separation from my body. My father waited with me until the doctors returned. I was so relaxed, I told him everything. I'm sure it must have been the worst thing for any father to hear. I held back nothing. I exposed every private detail to him. I wondered if he thought, *Did I do this to him? Is this my fault? Is this because I left him when he was younger?* He sat there, a pained statue, waiting beside me for the heavenly nothingness to rock me to sleep.

22

CELL

Discovered by Robert Hooke, the cell is the smallest functional unit of life that classifies an organism as living. The cell is the building block of life. Hooke coined the word *cell* in 1665 when he compared the cork cells found through his microscope to the tiny rooms of monks. Cell is derived from the Latin word *cella*, which means "a small room."

I woke up in a strange bed. They had transferred me to a mental institution, and I could not recall anything. Did they wake me up and put me in a car? Did they drug me more and strap me to a gurney? I didn't know, but I was afraid. My father was not around, and I heard people outside the door. It sounded like a hospital, but I wasn't sure. I got up out of the bed to check out the situation, started recalling images of the night before, and considered maybe this was the right place for me to be.

When I opened the door, I saw a large nurses' station crowded with odd characters waiting in a crooked line for something. A large chalkboard had a list of names on it, including mine. I laughed as I thought, *Well, at least* someone *is paying attention to me*. I caught the eye of a girl who seemed to be my age, and before I could listen to my gut, which told me to stay away, she abandoned the line and started walking toward me. Stuck in place, I couldn't move, and gave her a slanted smile. She was clearly seeking some sort of affection as she started flirting with me, asking questions like "What did you do? How did you get here? Where are you from?"—you know, the usual pick-up lines heard in a mental institution. Luckily, a nurse saw me as I stood in my doorway, demoralized by my surroundings and being harassed by a patient. She said kindly, "Joseph, you can get in line with the others." She had a warm, Betty Crocker cookies-equal-love smile.

The bothersome girl kept talking to me and I noticed she was talking through her teeth, seemingly unable to move her jaw.

I asked, "Why are you talking like that?"

She said, "My mouth is wired shut," swishing her tongue around behind her teeth with a sticky, gross sound. She smiled proudly to show a row of metal wires locking her teeth together that formed into a big metallic block. I immediately knew I didn't belong here and I had to get out.

I then asked a very stupid question. "What happened to you?"

She said strongly, and somehow didn't slur through her grate, "DON'T EVER DO HEROIN!" This was the third time someone had told me that. I was thinking about that coincidence as she began publicly and shamelessly recounting her story while standing in line, for everyone to hear.

"I'm a junkie and I turned my roommate on to it. She ran out of heroin and knew I had some hidden in my room. She asked me for it and I wouldn't give it to her. She was dope sick and insane, so she came back into my room with a baseball bat and started swinging it at my face. She hit my face like a hundred times, bashing my teeth in, breaking my nose and my jaw."

The line had moved up to the smiling nurse behind the desk, and the girl talking about her tragedy grabbed a cup of red liquid from the nurse and threw it back like a shot of Hawaiian Punch. "Methadone," she said proudly, presenting her religion to me.

She continued on with her story. "When I woke up from being knocked out, I was in so much pain that I shot up and went to the hospital. They put me out and did surgery, putting my jaw and mouth back together. Then, two weeks later I ended up here." She smiled coyly. I was screaming inside to be released.

While I was still in shock from her heroin story, the nurse called my name and handed me a little white paper cup of two bright, shining Klonopin and a Prozac. I threw them back without water and, with a sudden change of attitude, I thought, *I love this place! I want to stay here forever!* It was slightly lower than my normal dosage, but I wasn't about to argue with free drugs. I took my pills and hoped they would calm me down. As they kicked in, I had to join a group meeting, where we were forced to look at one another and talk about our feelings. I fell asleep. Everyone fell asleep. It was amazing they even bothered trying to communicate with us. My attempt to listen was no match for the pull of sleep as my eyelids dropped. I finally woke up, covered in drool.

Later that night, I woke up in terror as the pills started to wear off. I tried going back to sleep but couldn't, and coming out of my fucked-up, comatose state I noticed something horrifying. I ran to the mirror and was furious with my reflection. It was true. How had I not noticed it earlier? *Shit,* I thought, *all of my holes are going to fucking close up.* Body piercing isn't like ear piercing—body piercings close up and heal themselves if left open for too long. Face, nipples, stomach, all the hardware was gone, and I didn't know what to do about the holes. Did they remove them while I was asleep? I had to find something to put in place of the steel rods and rings. Any object would do to fill in my nose, septum, lip, tongue, nipples, and stomach holes. They removed my armor and now I was bare, my only defense being the skin I was born in, weak, soft, and vulnerable. I searched my tiny, cell-like room for something to stick in the holes. I had a fortune invested in my piercings and would burn this place down if they closed up. I took a second and realized I had to calm down; one should not flip out in a mental ward, or it becomes a permanent residence. Though things were bad, I needed to try to keep them from getting worse.

Our cutlery was plastic to limit self-inflicted injuries, and I decided this might work perfectly. I broke the prongs off the fork, making little spears, and methodically inserted them through my various pierced parts. The plastic hurt like crazy because it was thicker than the flesh openings and it stretched the holes. Since my piercings outnumbered my four plastic fork plugs, I rotated them throughout the day and night, ensuring all holes stayed open. The hardest was my tongue; when I spoke the piece would fall out, and I swallowed it while sleeping. I collected forks at breakfast and stashed extras in my room as backups. I can't imagine what I looked like in group therapy: a sleeping, medicated, dirty boy with pieces of plastic forks running through his face. I began to think that maybe the wired-jaw girl was my soul mate after all.

Throughout the day I would call Nick collect, and then break down and cry. He would say positive things like "Everything's gonna be fine" and "You'll be out soon," which I hoped was true; those people were crazy, and I was just visiting. Jaw Girl continued her romance mission, asking me tight-lipped, "Why won't you be my boyfriend?" That question shut down my entire system. I quietly laughed at her—a broken-spirited girl desperate for a man's approval. And the man's denial fueled her desire even more. She became the failure she set her sights upon, and I now became her daily unachievable goal. But I wondered, *Wasn't I in the same shitty situation and blind to it? Had my eyes been wired shut?*

The next day when I received my little paper pill cup, I poured the meds under my tongue, quickly walked away, spit them into my hand, went to my room, and then hid them under my mattress. I took them before bedtime and started sleeping through the night. I continued to receive Klonopin for my deep anxiety and Prozac for depression; however, the staff couldn't figure out what made me so melancholy. In group meetings I began identifying with some of the other patients and heard my story in theirs. I saw a reflection of my own madness through them. I felt like I wasn't alone. The only way out of this place was to show some sign of progress. I started to pretend I was happy.

My case was reevaluated after two weeks, and I finally got discharged. I had never been so happy, and would never have to see that girl again or be haunted by her face. My brother picked me up, which was strange for us both. What is it like to see your younger brother saying good-bye to the other mental patients in the psych ward?

Michael battled his own demons, and I never could figure out how he kept it all together. He didn't do drugs, not even pot, but we drank the same way, and somehow he was able to handle life. I hated him for that. How come when I drank it put me out of commission, but he managed to get up the next day, function, and go to work?

He drove me to my mother's house, which was closer to the mental institution. I would stay with her for a few days. My parents were deeply concerned and wanted to spread me around the family to lift my sadness and help me as best they could. My mother tried to have patience with me, but her own inability to stay sober tore open the roof of my addiction—being next to her made my need to use urgent. We returned to our vicious relationship cycle of numbing, fighting, hating, and disappearing, and carried that toxic formula into our language. In my pain, I could not find any kindness to speak to her, and no matter how she approached me I subconsciously felt her hatred. I treated her as I treated myself and cut her down to a wounded woman, left defenseless and bare.

I found deep pleasure and satisfaction in my desire to hurt her. She deserved it; she was responsible for my despair; she was the woman who clipped my wings. Her boyfriend received the same treatment. I never missed an attack as he walked by, cursing him like I was a vengeful gypsy as I sent all forms of psychic torture his way. I was upset with Michael for bringing me to that house of darkness. Then I realized that despite our nonworking relationship, my mother was not pushing me out, but reaching out to help me in her own way. And I returned the touch of her kind hands with poison. If I stayed there I'd end up back at the nuthouse, so I begged my father for another try. I went back to his house, where he set some rules for me. It was like caging a hurricane, since rules were never part of my upbringing, but I agreed to them in an attempt at normalcy.

The house rules were no alcohol or other drugs. My father would keep my medication and administer the two pills like the nurses did in the crazy ward. I liked this plan, because we were trying to heal my wounds. He spoke with the pharmacist and told her he wanted to wean me off of my medication. She told him it might take a very long time and to be patient while we made little changes at first. I was defenseless against the overpowering urge to take more pills after swallowing even the tiniest dose of medication, and I didn't know why.

I told myself I didn't need any weaning and could do it like I did things in gymnastics and stop completely, and so I called upon the strength of my childhood warrior. I would find that pinpoint dedication to just quit and not use alcohol or other drugs, no matter how bad the detox got and no matter how bad I felt. As a gymnast I was stronger than most people, and would refrain from using those fucking pills that were killing me. The quickest way for me to start getting back on track was exercise—finding myself again through sweat and endorphins.

On a beautiful morning by the sea I started jogging toward my new destination, with anxiety trailing close behind. Inhaling the saltwater air, I watched the beach pass by as each stride drove a deep footprint into the soft sand. A small runner's high started to hit and I smiled, but panic was still there behind me. Then panic came through me, matching my pace and growing from the ground below me. It became so physical that I couldn't breathe. I began to shake and sweat, not knowing what had happened. I tried to catch my breath as my heart pounded in my chest. I would outrun this feeling. I knew I could beat it, knew I could get over this hump, so I ran as fast I could through the sand, pushing out the anxiety that was streaming through my veins.

As I ran along the curve of the waves crashing into the beach, the world suddenly went crooked and upside down like I was inside a snow globe. I tried to keep running and fight the dizziness, but the pressure inside my head was extraordinary, and my skull bounced onto the sand. I refused to stay down; a gymnast could handle balance in any situation, so I stood up, but was aggressively pushed back down. My body repeatedly smacked against the wet sand, hurling itself over and over, in complete powerlessness.

I don't remember standing up or going home, but as I walked through the front door my stepsister looked over at me from watching TV in the living room and said, "My god, Joey! What happened to you?"

I didn't know what she was talking about. "You're covered in sand and it looks like you threw up all over yourself." I looked down and noticed foamy puke all over the front kangaroo-pouch pocket of my favorite raver hoodie. I called the pharmacist my father had talked to earlier and she said I had had a seizure, and this was the result of stopping my medication. She insisted I slowly wean myself off the pills and that it could take months. I was scared because I knew I couldn't decrease the dosages. If I took even the smallest amount, I would lose all of my senses and go crazy.

After hanging up with her, I took two pills. My psychiatrist had increased the dosage after my suicide attempt; they were the strongest dosage made. As the pills hit, so did the desire to eradicate all emotions. I remembered my stash of pills in the mattress. I ate about ten pills and downed them with water because my father had locked up all the alcohol in the downstairs refrigerator. I had heard of people locking up their alcohol, but had never seen it before. But there it was, an actual metal lock on the side of our basement refrigerator with all the alcohol inside. I went down to confront the big white beast and tried to break the lock, but couldn't get it open.

I went back upstairs, surveyed the living room, and saw a bottle shaped like a woman. It looked like a decoration, but there was some sort of liquor inside; they must have overlooked that one when conducting the liquor lockup. I took the plastic wrap off with a knife and downed it, guzzling its warmth into my stomach. It felt so good and hit me hard like a lightning bolt. Filled with a rush of euphoria and freedom, I took more pills and finished the bottle. I filled it up with water and tried taping the cover back on, but just ended up repeatedly spilling and soaking the dining room table in my drunkenness.

I woke up the next day sometime in the afternoon with no recollection of the night before. I walked into the kitchen and could feel the ions had changed in the room. My father was sitting at the table, looking angry and distant. He asked, "What happened last night?" I honestly didn't know what he was talking about, and then he said, "Someone drenched the table and opened Lynn's bottle of liquor and tried to retape it." I knew I was guilty because I had done things like that without recollection so many times.

"I'm sorry, but I laid down the house rules and no drinking was one of them and you've already broken it. I'm sorry, Joe, but you can't stay here any longer."

I flipped out and expressed my fury in the most violent way I could muster. I screamed that if he hadn't abandoned me as a child I would not have grown up like this. I released my hatred in the most diabolical phrases to punish him forever. But even as I hurled those dreadful words, I knew deep down he wasn't responsible for my drug use. I had made the choice to take those drugs and I couldn't stop, but it felt good to blame someone else. I knocked him down with my words and cut him as deeply as I had cut my own arms. He just sat there and took it. In that moment of rage, I hated him and never wanted to see him again.

His anger began to rise, and I was surprised he didn't punch me in the face. Instead he said, "Get your things and find a new place to live. I'll drive you to the bus station."

I didn't know where to go, but I grabbed my things and decided to go back to Holyoke and wait until spring break to go home with Nick. My father dropped me off at the bus station and I called a friend from Southie, who brought me some pills. I got on the bus and headed back to Staunton—back to another place I had been kicked out of.

23

DIGITUS IMPUDICUS

IT WAS IDENTIFIED AS THE *digitus impudicus* (IMPUDENT FINGER) IN ANCIENT ROME, AND REFERENCES ARE MADE TO USING THE FINGER IN ANCIENT GREEK COMEDY TO INSULT ANOTHER PERSON. THE WIDESPREAD USAGE OF THE FINGER IN THIS CONTEXT IN MANY CULTURES IS LIKELY DUE TO THE GEOGRAPHIC INFLUENCES OF THE ROMAN EMPIRE AND GRECO-ROMAN CIVILIZATION. ANOTHER POSSIBLE ORIGIN OF THIS GESTURE CAN BE FOUND IN THE FIRST-CENTURY MEDITERRANEAN WORLD, WHERE EXTENDING THE *digitus impudicus* WAS ONE OF MANY METHODS USED TO DIVERT THE EVER-PRESENT THREAT OF THE EVIL EYE. DURING THE HUNDRED YEARS' WAR, THE FRENCH CUT OFF THE MIDDLE FINGERS OF CAPTURED ENGLISH ARCHERS SO THEY WOULD BE UNABLE TO USE THEIR BOWS, AND AFTER THE BATTLE OF AGINCOURT, THE VICTORIOUS ENGLISH SHOWED THE FRENCH THAT THEIR MIDDLE FINGERS WERE STILL INTACT.

The five days before spring break I stayed at a coke dealer's house, doing so much coke that my nose was raw. We weren't going to Nick's house for spring break as planned; instead we were going to Old Greenwich, Connecticut, to the house of a friend of his from the football team named Greg. We were going to stay with him because his father needed some help with landscaping and he was going to pay us for helping. Any opportunity I had to make drug money, and I would be there. Nick and I thought it would be fun because we could smoke weed in the woods and then help out all day.

We started our first day of work. Greg's father, a man of few words and much action, rented one of those giant wood chippers. He was clearing out a big section of his backyard. A supervisor accompanied the machine, making sure it ran properly, and once Greg's father saw we knew how to use it, he left for work. Our job was to feed tree branches into the chipper, and every now and then I would overfeed it, to which the man would give a stern "No, that one is too big." After returning him a dirty look, I'd search for smaller ones. The warden left after an hour, leaving his mechanical kraken unguarded.

Greg went inside to get some beer, and Nick and I thought the quicker we finished working, the sooner we could get high. Greg told us he had a good source for coke, and we would get some later that night. That motivated us to work harder and faster, so we decided to push everything into the wood chipper all at once. The machine made a huge coughing sound, and we burst out laughing. That inspired us to gather more things unsuitable for chipping, like rocks, bricks, and tree stumps. Laughing hysterically, on the count of three we threw our pile of unbreakable objects into the spinning blades. The machine let out a sharp zipping sound, and the rocks ricocheted back at us as the stump and bricks got stuck in its mechanical grasp. Next, a horrible sound like screeching train wheels blasted out from the machine, followed by a huge plume of black smoke. We fell to the ground in laughter. The machine was dead.

We ran into the kitchen to tell Greg the machine wasn't working, and on the kitchen counter was a prescription bottle written out to his mother for Percocet. This was too good to be true. I picked up the bottle, found Greg, and asked, "Dude, can we take these?" He said, "Sure." We each took three with a beer. I said calmly, "There is something wrong with that machine. It's not working right." We walked back to the site and could smell the last wisps of smoke emanating from the engine. Greg tried restarting it, but it wouldn't budge; there was no resuscitation. Nick and I began picking out the rocks from the front of the chipper to remove any evidence, and then Greg asked, "Wait . . . where did that guy go?"

"I dunno, he just took off."

"Well, it's his fault; he should have been here with his machine."

The man seemed drunk when he came back, and started yelling at us for breaking his equipment. We met his drunkenness and anger with the same and told him he should never have left us alone with that expensive thing.

With our work finished, we showered and got ready to find our coke connection. It was a friend's friend named Katherine, a pouty, hippie-wannabe girl who resembled Cloud, but only in her clothing. She was kind and quiet, and I was taken in by her gentle smile. She brought us to her friend Angela's apartment in a seedy part of town.

The place looked like animals lived in the walls, with dirty floors and huge clouds of cigarette smoke hanging in the air. A vapor of a woman came crashing over to us with long, red, fake nails and a raspy voice that sounded like she had been screaming since the day she was born. Her eyes were pretty, but all her beauty had been tainted by something I couldn't yet figure out. It really didn't matter, though; she had the coke and was the most radiant person in the room—in fact, she was stunning.

We paid for our cocaine and she invited us to hang out and drink for a while, which I was into because Katherine seemed nice. The coke was weak, but still something to sniff. We stayed at Angela's all night and she got in close with Greg, which was sweet since he never seemed to connect with the college girls.

For the next few days we made money doing yard work (sans the chipper), and blew it all at Angela's house every night. She became more and more irritating as she writhed around the room like a pathetic, disturbed doll seeking attention. Socially awkward, she savored her delusional world as she shouted out her sexual desires. She would dance into the living room in frilly negligees, do a line of powder off her fake, fire engine–red nails, and then saunter away. Her addiction wasn't to drugs, it was to attention. And it pissed me off how she disrespectfully toyed with the cocaine, doing it off her plastic nails. *Was she crazy? What if she dropped it?* Her nails weren't even big enough to do the right amount. She bounced around the room, desperate for a man to look at her.

Her brother started joining in with his own array of shady people. Those people cast a skin-prickling energy throughout the apartment. But I was there for the drugs, not the company. Angela and her brother seemed more like lovers than brother and sister; he overbearingly protected her while she carelessly flung herself around him. Greg and Angela, meanwhile, were growing closer, disappearing into the night and returning like two teenagers in the dawn, but something about her was off.

One evening a downpour got us off work early, so we had a head start on partying at Angela's. Her smeared makeup and dark "Hellooooooo" invited us in, but she quickly ran to the other room as the phone rang. Twenty minutes later there was a knock on the door. A man in red-and-black plaid came in, and without introduction he and Angela went into the bedroom for fifteen minutes; then he opened the door and left. At first I thought nothing of it, but when it happened again an hour later, I understood. Greg was too stoned to realize his new girlfriend was a prostitute. All her attention-whoring and sexual innuendos made sense, but I felt bad for Greg, who had finally connected with someone. The sad twilight that cracked through her dirty apartment cast a light on her painted face for all to see who she really was—a version of me. Her essence was completely dismantled in the light, while she covered it up with painful amounts of makeup and perfume. Her pain fired up her skin, creating a glasslike quality of porcelain, too strong for any emotion to pass through.

Spring break was ending, and so was my living situation. With homelessness as my alternative, I called my mother. Working for Greg's dad and sounding sober during the phone call helped me build my case, and I convinced her that I was trying to change. I asked if I could come home for a few weeks until summer, and then I'd go to Brooklyn with Nick. She agreed. I think somewhere inside her, guilt gnawed at her to give me another chance. We drove back to Holyoke and I got on a train home.

I missed Nick every day, but was happy to see old friends who had either flunked out of college from partying too much or had just given up. In the year since I'd last seen them, I had been on a concentrated diet of beer, cocaine, and benzodiazepines and had attained my desired pilled-out, lost look—a dehydrated waif with deep, black moats around my eyes. I was ecstatic when my psychiatrist transferred my prescriptions to a pharmacy in my mother's town. Now I had refills all over the state of Massachusetts.

After we hung out for a few days, I noticed my old friends were not enjoying my company. Standing at his front door, I heard a longtime friend say, "Dude, don't let him in here. He's a complete mess. I don't know what happened to him, but I don't want him in my apartment."

I didn't care. I'm sure I did stupid things; I just didn't remember. I did find Piper and the old Southie addict crew. Everyone was taking something new called Rohypnol. I had heard horror stories of girls being slipped "roofies" and getting date-raped, but didn't think people took them recreationally. We had gained such high tolerances for pills that roofies didn't knock us out like they did civilians. My first roofie high was amazing, and I bought as many of them as I could afford and went back to my mother's house.

The next month I spent completely anesthetized, with little recollection of what happened or what I did, just glimpses of people, laughter, and fighting, like beautifully illusory, never-ending dreams. But it finally ended with the sound of my mother's screams. Who knows how long I was asleep? I was untouchable, safe, alone, and happy—until her voice penetrated my broken bedroom door, calling me to war. I tried fitting pieces back together, but I had nothing to work with. I didn't remember returning to the house I swore I'd never return to, wanting only to escape from her demons. I looked around my clothes-strewn room, the high school posters and fist holes punched into the walls, knowing it was about to get ugly.

I could feel her energy approaching. *What did I do this time?* I didn't know, but I put my clothes on, downed a handful of pills, waited for them to hit, and made my way out to the living room. Like a samurai sharpening his sword, I was now ready for battle, confident her disease could not penetrate the prescription shield of unconsciousness, for I was the Chemical Master. Without a chance to explain whatever evil I had summoned, she told me through clenched teeth, "Get the fuck out of my house." I didn't argue. When she left the room I grabbed a bottle of liquor and chugged it in my room as I packed and called Nick. The semester was almost over and he was picking me up in a week, but I made it clear he had to come now. Since we had totaled his truck on our romantic Maine trip, he needed to convince a friend to make the trip. "Just ask him what drugs he wants. We'll stop by Southie and I can get anything. Piper has sugar cubes, they're insane."

He convinced some friends to make the trip, and they would be at my mom's house in a few hours. I returned to the living room to resume the fight. I felt nothing from her aggression; my roofie armament made me invincible. I was a zombie; words were my bullets and I used them gallantly against this other human being—against love, hope, and goodness. I felt no love for or from my mom. It was disease versus disease, and my disease was winning.

I kept drinking and packing my things as a fire inside me melted my flesh. After a few phone calls, several addicts in Southie knew to meet us at a friend's apartment in Mission Hill. Nick and his friends arrived at my mother's, and we packed the car like I was moving out forever. Once again, I never wanted to return to my childhood home where the God of Movement's arrow first shot me. I was a drunken, pilled-out monster who looked like a pathetic, homeless raver carrying boxes of junk.

Somewhere in my delusions I believed I was moving in with the man I loved. Nick was not open to his friends about our developing relationship, and I always respected his decision, but on that day it weighed on me and stuck like a splinter in my brain. I was so trashed I made the proclamation that Nick and I desperately loved each other. His friends fell silent and looked shocked, and so did Nick. He had walked straight into the tornado of Joe, having no idea of my capabilities for destruction—and sadly, neither did I. All I knew was that I needed some coke or crystal to clear my head; I was starting to fade away. Nick looked furious and was amazed at how messed up I was. He whispered, "Dude, shut the fuck up," and I stayed quiet for a moment.

We drove to Southie where every drug desired was waiting for us, but even my addict friends were shocked at my condition. I had surpassed them and was now partying with something evil. A girl I used to date said, "Joe, man, you have to slow down, seriously . . . take it easy." I looked at her like she was crazy and asked, "Who has the roofies and who has the coke?" Nick's friends bought a lot and I got my roofies and coke, which turned out to be some other powder with no stimulating effect, but I sniffed it anyway, burning out my nose for a desperate high.

As we got into the car and headed toward Brooklyn, I took two roofies and everything slowed down. As I did with everyone now, I started a fight with Nick in front of his friends, challenging him and unearthing our secrets for public viewing. I don't remember much after that except a long, five-hour drive telling everyone in the car to go fuck themselves. Through the grace of God I finally passed out in midargument and woke up in Brooklyn—my new home of opportunity.

Once again I woke up not knowing where I was or how I got there, but recognized Nick's clothes and felt safe. He wasn't there, so I assumed he was with his friends and would be back. Still embraced in the arms of the pills, I saw Nick's aunt and introduced myself with comfortable, slurred words. Nick had mentioned that his aunt took Xanax for anxiety attacks, and I felt so connected to her through pills that I said, "I'm having an anxiety attack. Do you have some extra Xanax?" She silently left the room, I thought nothing of it, and then Nick showed up.

He said angrily, "Do you remember anything about what happened?" I didn't, but now within seconds I would find out. I had entered his house, had fallen asleep while walking upstairs in front of his aunt and uncle, and then had continued making a complete asshole out of him in front of friends and other family members. Way too fucked up, I told him the argument with my mother had upset me so much that it had made me cross a line, and I promised I would slow down. Nick was only a few handfuls of pills behind me on the path to disaster.

I convinced him that I just needed some strong uppers to straighten out my head. We made a call and secured some crystal meth. Afraid I'd embarrass him again, Nick left me at home. Sadness and shame swelled up inside me as I sat in his basement and cried, coming down off a mountain of pills.

Nick got the crystal meth, but his friends confronted him about the devil he had brought home with him. They hated me and wouldn't come over if I was there. I was partying above the level of fun and was literally trying to kill my body and soul. The fun had stopped for me a long time ago, and I was trapped in a riddle: how many pills does it take to kill the human spirit? I would find out. If I wasn't gone in a few days, his friends threatened to escort me back to Massachusetts. I laughed at that; my years of training plus pills made me feel fearless and invincible, though the truth was I couldn't even see straight and would have fallen on my face in a fight.

Nick and I snorted all the meth in one line each. We weren't meth-heads but we used it occasionally, and this was way beyond our recommended dosage. Instead of calming my anxiety, it created an urgency of raw fear in the form of physical energy, resulting in the need for more downers. Nick, on the other hand, was overdosing, seeing spirits trying to take us away, going in and out of a seizure. Somehow I was the more sober one, and made the decision that we needed to go to an emergency room.

After we left for the hospital, Nick's friends contacted his parents to arrange an intervention for Nick and to restrain me, but they couldn't find us. The ER nurse called Nick's parents after our intake, so the cavalry would soon be on their way to rescue and destroy. The nurses searched us for drugs, but we were clean since we had already eaten every pill, and then they made us take a drug test. Nick dunked his urine cup in the toilet water to dilute it and told me to do the same. Before any results came back they took Nick away as I waited outside the emergency room. I paced the floor, filled with terror that he would overdose and die. The horrible question stung my heart: *Did I kill him? Is this my fault?*

His mother arrived, yelling, "All of Nick's friends are after you, so you better just leave." I didn't care. I felt macho and tough. My body's chemical rage would keep me standing like a scrappy street thug. I was ready for a fight and would die proving my toughness.

I argued my way back to Nick and saw him throw up the activated charcoal they had made him drink to absorb the drugs. The nurse told him, "You're either going to have to drink more or we'll pump out your stomach." A stomach pump should be on every human's "Things to Avoid in Life" list, like being choked to death and forced to vomit simultaneously. He looked horrible, sheet-white, sunken eyes and sickly, his entire body writhing in pain.

What if he died? I loved him so much. I had never loved anyone like that. My body filled with guilt, remorse, self-hatred, and sadness. I looked Nick in the eye and saw his God. It spoke louder than my own and echoed to my core, "Joe, let him go. Leave him to save him." I would never tell Nick what I heard, but I knew his relationship with me was killing both of us. I loved him and I left him. It was the hardest thing I had ever done in my life. I left him in that emergency room, covered in black vomit and with tears in his eyes, to drink his liquid charcoal alone. I walked out of the hospital and down a double-laned street, not knowing where I was going or what I would do.

Down the road I passed a police station and walked in. Still intoxicated, I pulled myself together as the situation approached a new tragically horrible reality and said, "I don't have any money or food. Is there a homeless shelter around here?" They gave me a bus ticket and a coupon to a grocery store nearby. I bought a bagel and water, and got on the bus.

The bus driver told me where to get off. In the middle of the danger zone behind a broken-down building full of street people was the homeless shelter. I walked straight toward it, ready to receive the next orders of my life. It was time to stop.

I walked through the door and saw a beautiful woman with blonde hair. I began talking to her and fell apart. I'd never shattered into so many pieces. Every aching cell in my body shrieked with an urgent need for help. I cried my heart out. The woman looked shocked at my breakdown and kept telling me it would be okay. I don't think she had ever seen anyone fall apart so completely. I couldn't stop crying, and as I told her my story she sat beside me, holding my hand and listening. God met me there at that shelter, holding me and caressing me, a broken-winged angel at the bottom of the Earth, suffocating and dying.

24

INNOMINATE

THE INNOMINATE OR HIP BONE IS A LARGE, FLATTENED,
IRREGULARLY SHAPED BONE, CONSTRICTED IN THE CENTER AND
EXPANDED ABOVE AND BELOW. IT HAS ONE OF THE FEW BALL-
AND-SOCKET SYNOVIAL JOINTS IN THE BODY—THE HIP JOINT.
IT COMES FROM THE LATIN *innominatus*, MEANING "NAMELESS."

The woman tried to calm me as we walked to another room, where she sat down and asked questions about my past. Her voice soothed me, and I didn't want her to leave. The shelter was surprisingly clean, starkly different from the rest of the neighborhood. We walked upstairs to a room filled with bunk beds where I would sleep. When I saw the other guys, I immediately stopped crying because I realized I wouldn't get by on tears in that place.

The cafeteria was next on the tour, and I got in line for food. The gymnastics team had volunteered once at a soup kitchen in downtown Holyoke, and now I had graduated to the other side. Surprisingly, it wasn't soup but a giant container of chop suey behind a small glass panel, a dish that made my stomach turn; but I was starving and ready to eat my own fingers.

She came by again and asked if I was on any medication. I wiped away the slop of sauce on my face and quietly told her Klonopin and Prozac. She told me they would keep me on my pills to avoid seizures and hold and monitor my meds, but I was relieved to know my prescribed dosage still gave me a good buzz.

I found out from the guys in the room that I could only stay there at night. One guy said, "For the first two weeks this is how it works: You have to stay outside during the day and come back by eight o'clock at night for curfew, then you get a bed. After that, if you're following the rules, you get more privileges." *Outside?* I thought to myself. *That doesn't make sense. Isn't this a homeless shelter? Can't I just stay in here all day?* Then I turned toward a man who drew me in; my preternatural radar went on high alert. His dark eyes glimmered, and I knew he had something I needed: drugs. We talked quietly. He fronted me some Xanax when I told him I was getting my prescription later that night and would pay him back.

I took the pills and went outside into the dirty madness of the city. I found a building to lean against, frightened among all those people on the streets. I slid down the concrete wall into a ball and watched the city's busy flow, always changing, never the same. People filled the street corners, sometimes in arguments, sometimes in laughter, and it reminded me of PBS's deep-sea documentaries about dazzling fish in coral reefs. The big fish always ate the smaller fish and so on, and the different fish were born with different mechanisms of defense. I was the smallest, weakest fish hiding between two buildings on a pavement full of broken glass, the soundtrack of chaos pulling me toward sleep.

When you have no place to live, nature mocks you. A dandelion tried to rip through a crack in the sidewalk, its bent stem repeatedly trampled on, but still trying to thrive. I tried to embrace its beauty there among the filth, crime, and noise, but its simple charm began to wrestle with my humanity and it was no longer a flower, but rather all I had lost—desensitized and destroyed. The pills hit me hard and the destructive soundscape turned enchanting, freeing, and comforting. All I hated and feared became strength and desire. I was now a fish with power. I lay on the city street, confused and alone, thrown in with the graffiti and the sirens. I fell in and out of sleep to those soothing sounds. I missed my curfew and a bed, clutching my things in my hand, and slept like a dog whose eyes pop open at the slightest sound.

The next day I thought hard about my life and knew I needed to change, but still didn't know how. I had failed so many times, and always returned to the drugs. I didn't know what happened to Nick, if he was alive or dead. Did the charcoal work? Did it save him? I couldn't remember the hospital we were at, so I had no way of getting any information. My heart was broken and all the soft poetry we had made crumpled—smoldering against the fire of our lives. I prayed he was okay.

I saw a pay phone spray-painted black and white across the street. Hoping it still worked, I approached it and picked up the broken handle. There was a dial tone, and, remembering a commercial from when I was younger about teenage runaways, I pressed zero. I was finally the star of my own show. The operator answered and I told her I was a teenage runaway who wanted to let my parents know that I was okay. The operator was kind and concerned; I could have talked to her for hours. She connected me to my mother, who hung up as soon as she heard my voice. I slammed the phone and disconnected inside, fighting back tears so as not to draw attention to my weakness. Crying at that pay phone would have been like holding a neon sign: "I'm weak! Come beat me up and steal my clothes. Please." I didn't think I could hate her any more, but I did.

I looked around the street corner next to the homeless shelter, behind a dilapidated church, in a neighborhood full of ghosts, horrified at the contrast between my past and the present, with no concept of a future. How had I fallen from standing on the first-place podium in gymnastics to sitting in the gutter of that trash-piled street? The dirty pavement was my podium now. I was the newest piece of shit, and the sewer welcomed me with open arms. At least I was loved and cared for somewhere.

One day, after I got used to the place—even hell gets comfortable and normalized—I walked into my bunker and there was Nick, looking sober and handsome. My heart stopped, and all breath escaped my body. There he was, an angel out of heaven, with that old spark back in his smile.

My eyes watered in disbelief and he said, "Hey man, my mom's outside, she's going to drive you to the bus station so you can go home to your mom."

I started crying and said, "Nick, I thought you were dead, I didn't know what happened to you."

Nick, now abstinent and unable to communicate his real love in the world without the illusions that had held him up, said, "It's okay; don't cry. I'm all right. Just get your stuff and let's go."

I knew he wanted me to stop crying in front of the other homeless guys in the room. We couldn't show our true feelings for each other. I couldn't believe he was alive. I just wanted to jump into his arms and hug him and give him the heart-warming welcome of my fantasy. I said, "I can't go home, my mother hung up on me. How did you find me?"

"You know my mom, she's resourceful. She found you and talked to your mother who said you could go home."

I didn't want to go home, but I didn't want to stay at the shelter either. And, if it meant a chance to see Nick again while we continued our relationship, secretly or in whatever bizarre way he wanted, then I would do it.

He said, "Come on, my mom's gonna take us for lunch before you leave," which seemed very strange. *Was this my chance to make amends? Could I somehow rectify the situation and at least explain my inability to stay sober to this woman who saw me as pure evil?*

I went to the front desk and told them I was going home. The woman behind the window handed me a brown paper bag. I asked, "What's this?"

She said, "Your medication. You're going to need it."

"You're damn right I will," I said, grinning from ear to ear. Jackpot! I hadn't even considered that. I figured they would keep it there, but they would be responsible if I had a seizure without my pills. After all, I wasn't there for addiction, I was there for homelessness.

Nick and I went into the bathroom and we both took a handful of pills. I grabbed my book bag and made it downstairs to the car. By the time we sat down for lunch I was a mess. I had been restricted to two pills a day while in the shelter, and now I was back to my natural super self. We went to a small Chinese restaurant, and in my comfortable, bordering-on-comatose state, I slurred my colorful past over moo goo gai pan and spring rolls. I secured myself in his mom's eyes as the most dangerous, destructive, and ill human being she would ever meet, as her face contorted with shock and disgust. Eager to rid herself of my presence, she made it clear that Nick and I would never see or speak to each other again. But I had something over her—I knew Nick's true feelings for me. Whether he was gay, straight, or bisexual, I owned his heart, and I wasn't going to let it out of my filthy claws.

On the way to the bus station, Nick and I sat in the backseat trying to figure out how we would see each other again while keeping our teary emotions under his mom's radar. They walked me down to the bus, making sure I got on, and I grabbed Nick's mother and hugged her, crying and thanking her. I didn't know if I was crying for her or for Nick, but every now and then a shred of humanity burst through my darkness, and I said to myself, "I'm still here, Joe." I hadn't yet turned into stone. I hugged Nick one more time as I tried mentally to stop what was happening once again.

I got on the bus and my mind wandered to the pills in my bag. Someone in my family was picking me up at Boston's South Station, but once home I had no place to hide them from my mom. I did the only thing an addict can do: I opened the huge bottle of Klonopin and gazed at all those pills. I would never take them all at once; there were too many. But my mother would trash them if she discovered them, not understanding I would die without them—but I could die taking all of them. I looked at the bottle and started eating them. I ate them all, no water, just chewed and swallowed them all down, wondering if I'd be found overdosed upon arrival. As they took effect, I no longer cared if the pills killed me. I was back on my throne, once again reigning over my Klonopin Kingdom.

I don't remember getting home or seeing my mother. I remember smoking a cigarette in front of her, which I would normally never give her the pleasure of seeing. I considered cigarettes the ultimate weakness, and blamed her smoking for my asthma, but here we were, joined in vice.

I remember the scream. "Where are the pills, Joe?! They said they gave you your medication when you left. Where is it?"

I smiled and fell back into my kingdom. I woke up two days later in my old room. The holes in the walls were patched and the carpet was still a matted mess, still stained in the corner from the night I had tried tattooing my foot. Holes and stains personified me. Once again the pills served their function, erasing my memory of the past weeks: the homeless shelter, Nick's overdose, and even the trip to Greg's. My brain was rattled and blurry.

I walked out of my room feeling shaky and sick. My mom was on the couch smoking a cigarette, and pretended not to notice me standing there. I was already starting to have withdrawals—heart racing like a grandfather clock ticking out of control in my chest, louder and louder. It was coming on fast, and I needed to intervene. I needed to take something, anything, but the only thing that could stop this was a new prescription.

I told my mom I needed to see a doctor, and with a confidence I'd never seen before, she said flatly, "You aren't going to any doctor or anything. In fact, you aren't leaving this house."

The oxygen in the house disappeared, the air in my lungs evaporated, and I freaked out. I would die without those pills. The detox would be too much for my body; seizures were on their way. I pleaded with her. I cried my heart out, begged her to get me to a doctor, yet she sat there motionless, reading the news as a blue smoke trail floated by her face. Just a normal day at home with a son detoxing and tearing at his skin. Oh, how I loved Sundays with the family. She was dead-set in her decision. Dammit, she must have read a pamphlet on tough love while I was away setting the country on fire.

I went to my room, in fear, and cried myself to sleep, bracing for the storm. I could feel the strong tide of emotions rolling in, raw and exposed to the world. I lived a horrible detox for the next few days: shaking in my skin, flesh crawling under the shock of recovery as evil wafted through my room, poking and picking at me. Sweating in bed as my drug body slowly died, I faded in and out of hallucinations: chanting, scratching, clawing, and being dragged into a torturous underworld. Small demons encircled me, tying my body to a pole as a hot, sweaty fire grew beneath me and danced to the rumbling of a drum.

The next day I cried and pleaded with my mother, but she remained adamant. She was going to detox me in my room. My monster had grown in strength, and I swore, cursed, and hated her with all my might. This was my mother's test of unconditional love, as she saw the eyes of the beast peering through mine, knowing I couldn't defeat it myself. The withdrawals worsened at night as the demons paid me a visit and brought with them a new entity—tall and cloaked in shadow, its face concealed as it crouched at the foot of my bed and guarded the door. Death said, "I warned you I would be back."

Those moments lasted for days, alternating between calm and turbulence, starting in again when it seemed like it was done, beyond all previously experienced physical and mental anguish. A month went by, and I was only a fraction of the human I used to be. I felt a hundred years old, dizzy and feeble. Speaking with Nick on the phone once a week helped me continue on, determined to start over in a sober life. He cut out the hard drugs, but kept smoking pot and drinking—I had no idea how he could pick and choose his drug use.

A few more weeks of abstinence passed, and my mother told me it was time to get a job, time to slowly piece things back together. I applied for a job with Johnson & Johnson, and to everyone's amazement (especially mine), they accepted my application. I was offered a high salary and insurance with 401k benefits—not bad for a college dropout. All I had to do was pass the drug test. I couldn't wait to tell Nick, proud to have an opportunity to be the man I always thought I could be. That gave me an even greater desire to stay abstinent, and all I had to do was pass my drug test on Monday morning.

Nick arrived on Thursday. I was so happy to see him. We both swore to remain abstinent while together. As we watched TV in my room and talked about how much better our bodies felt without taking those damn pills, Nick asked if I wanted a drink. I thought, *Well, one drink couldn't hurt.* My mother's house had booze all over, and stockpiled in the basement from when the restaurant closed. We went down, grabbed a bottle of Grand Marnier, and started drinking. Nobody would know if I had a little drink, and it would help with my anxiety and depression. While I was mostly a beer drinker and rarely drank hard liquor, I made an exception.

I chugged the orange liqueur and instantly remembered a refill left for Klonopin at the pharmacy near my father's house, an hour away. I called the pharmacy to ask if they could transfer it to one near my mom's, and they agreed to do it. Now we just needed money and a car. Just like old times. I asked my mom to borrow her car, and since I appeared to be sober and trustworthy, combined with her already being tanked, she said okay. We didn't have enough money, but the pharmacist gave me four white pills to tide me over until I had cash to fill the rest. I think she realized I could have a seizure without them, so she was really doing this out of pure kindness. And man, was I appreciative. Two pills wouldn't be enough to screw up my drug test on Monday, and I had a prescription making it legal—I had that relapse all figured out. I had been so convinced I would never use those damn pills again after that detox hell. I couldn't believe it was happening again.

The pills, combined with alcohol, were amazing, and I was instantly a god, wanting everyone around me to feel good. Nick was fucked up too, and we went home and drank everything in sight. Apparently we went to my brother Michael's house, slurred words, fell down, and woke up back in my room with a hangover tearing apart my brain.

After we struggled to open our eyes around two in the afternoon, I heard the familiar alarm of my mom and sister screaming that the downstairs smelled like pot; smoking would have been nice, but we actually had no pot. The weed accusations escalated, and so did my temper. Still buzzed from the night before, I jumped in the ring ready for a fight. I launched a verbal assault on my sister that quickly progressed to physical violence, which resulted in me once again getting kicked out of my mom's house as she threatened to call the police. Nick and I grabbed a bag of stuff and left.

I decided we should beg for money, and then walk to the pharmacy when we had enough for the whole prescription. There were pills waiting for us that would help me cope with sleeping on the street— homelessness is easier in a lubricated state.

We headed toward the pharmacy, which was far away, but oblivion is a great incentive. We passed a health clinic and made a quick manipulation stop for more pills. Lingering gymnastics injuries that looked bad on X-rays, mixed with my extensive medical vocabulary and puppy-dog eyes, always resulted in painkillers and muscle relaxants. I told Nick to use some old sports injuries, and between the two of us we should be able to leave well stocked.

I got Ultram and Soma, the same muscle relaxants I got after the car accident. I was hoping for Percocet, but we could still get completely messed up on those.

It was a warm summer day and I was happy; as soon as we got money and made it to the pharmacy, all our problems would dissolve. After a nice pill lunch, the beasts within would direct our next course of action. On a whim, Nick checked his bank account and there was a surprise hundred dollars in there—we think Nick's mother deposited it in case he needed a quick escape bus ticket from me. Now we didn't have to beg for change outside the local supermarket. That summer day turned to Christmas for the damned.

We filled up and feasted on our new windfall, relaxing into the calm sunset. With no place to go, we settled on a parking lot dumpster, cuddling together side by side under a flannel shirt blanket. We were deeply in love, at the ends of our Earth.

Something wet and cold startled me awake, landing on my face; I wiped it away, and then another drop followed. I opened my eyes to a New England thunderstorm, and I knew within moments we'd be drenched. We sought shelter back in the pharmacy, reading Hallmark cards to each other as hunger started to peek through the pills' haze, but most of the money was gone. My medical training taught me how to relieve the symptoms: get more pills, get more messed up, get less hungry. Little white stapled bags full of treats lined the counter behind the pharmacist, and, unlike at other pharmacies, the bags were close to the register, within an arm's reach. With my great dexterity, when the pharmacist turned his back I would reach over, take a few, stuff them in my pants, and casually leave our friendly neighborhood pharmacy. Nick's assignment was to steal Hershey bars for dinner, breakfast, or whenever we decided to eat something less chemically based.

I stalked the movements of the pharmacist like a cheetah preparing for a hunt. I learned his patterns. He turned around and went toward the back, and I lunged over the counter, reaching beyond my body with my Go Go Gadget arms, grabbed a bag, and stuffed it down my pants.

"Gotcha!" stopped me dead in my tracks. I was still calm but trapped and cornered, with no place to run.

He calmly said, "I've been watching you for twenty minutes. Let's see what you almost got." I could have gotten anything else, antibiotics, diuretics, or anything, but playing the addict's pharmaceutical lottery was hoping for a higher payout like Valium or better. He ripped off the top of the bag and laughed, "Well, this is what you would have gotten. An old lady's neck brace."

I sunk inside myself with embarrassment, shocked that I actually felt an emotion. Stealing prescriptions is a federal offense; I couldn't believe I did something so stupid, risking years in jail for a fucking neck brace. I waited for him to call the police, but a moment of grace intervened, a miracle that to this day I still have trouble believing actually happened.

The pharmacist looked me in the eyes and said, "You have to leave." I don't remember thanking him. I darted out of there and back into the pouring rain in absolute gratitude. Nick pulled out our breakfast, lunch, and dinner of stolen chocolate bars. I told him the tale in the cold rain, a dim streetlight glowing across his face, the two of us shivering and laughing, eating chocolate, and me thinking to myself, *We are pure poetry.*

We slept in the nearby woods, and the sun rose with our idea of selling some pills to get cocaine. We called a cab service to go to the mall, where I had worked during high school at the music store. The driver seemed cool and, thinking we could barter, I reached my hand through the small, protective window and offered him some pills. He turned cold and instantly afraid, so we ate our pill offering.

I called Piper in Southie and offered her a great deal on pills for coke. She would meet us that night, so with time to kill we went into the mall. But first we mixed together huge handfuls of pills for breakfast—addicts' granola first thing in the morning hits fast and hard. As we walked around the shops Nick kept falling asleep, passing out while standing up, right in front of moms and kids. I shouted at him and tried to keep him awake.

"Nick, you're gonna fucking get us arrested, dude. Wake the fuck up!"

He tried but he couldn't. I moved him against a wall and he slid down as his eyes rolled back in his head. I was pissed. He would get us caught. I dragged him outside onto a bench to sleep off some of the effects, and had to somehow hide all the prescription bottles we were walking around with. I left him to buy a can of Pringles.

I woke Nick up from his bench sleep—slumped over between his two legs, inches away from falling flat on his face. I dumped the chips out, poured all our pills in, and covered them up with chips. If the police stopped us they would never find the pills—I was the smartest pill popper ever.

We waited in the parking lot for nightfall, as Piper pulled up in a white van filled with Southie kids, alcohol, pills, and coke. We partied until the sun came up, clinging to that youthful mad paradise, praying it would last forever.

The next afternoon we woke up still in the mall parking lot. Piper must have left us there. A cop car approached us and asked, "Are you

Joseph Putignano?" Any fear in our bodies was medicated away; we were untouchable.

"Yeah, man, that's me."

"We've been looking for you."

"Well, here I am."

He got out of the car and said, "You have to come with me, you have a summons for your court appearance."

"When?"

"Now!"

"Are you serious?"

"Yes. Very."

Surprised, and slightly amused, I grabbed the Pringles can and Nick, and we got in the back. He seemed cool for a cop, and I asked how he found me. "We got a call reporting you missing and possibly in danger of hurting yourself. Then a cab driver called, telling us about two guys stumbling around in the streets. He was concerned because he said you two were really messed up, but seemed like good guys."

"Good guys, huh?" I had no idea what he was talking about. We arrived at the courthouse and they walked us to the back. First my feet were shackled, and then my hands. I was enraged, yet curious to see what asshole had disrupted my day of tranquility. I was escorted into the courthouse and saw my sister Trish and her husband. Nick was there too, sitting on the pew-like bench, and then it went from strange to surreal. The judge spoke in his judicial lingo, but all I heard through any of this was that my sister wanted me detained and committed to Norton State—a mental institution. That place had been a local ongoing joke growing up: "Someday you'll end up at Norton State!" I didn't need another regional disgrace; junior college was enough. Pride and ego sobered me up as I planned my tale.

My sister stood up and told the judge her side of the story. As she spoke I looked deep into her eyes, my dark circles of vengeance cursing her with hate. After all she saw me go through, all my turmoil with our mom and dad, now she was the one trying to commit me. Drugs had torn apart our once-close relationship. She was seven months pregnant and had gone in and out of labor from the stress of watching my downward spiral. She stood rows away from Nick, right in front of me, and sobbed, "My brother is sick; please help him. I can't bear to lose him. Please. He doesn't know what he's doing; he's a good kid. Please help him!" The pills' residual effects put a haze over the experience for me, but she did highlight a few horrid details from the past two years.

Then the judge turned to me and said he would like to hear my side of the story. The shackles hurt; they were painful inside and out. I stood up and stared at my sister, centering all my anger in her direction.

"Trish, I cannot believe you are doing this to me." My eyes filled with tears and I began to create the most convincing fable of victimization. I was the black sheep of my family, a successful gymnast whose parents' alcoholism had pushed me out the door. I recounted to the judge the many times I had gotten kicked out of my mother's and then my father's homes, as I continued to look to my sister, begging her with my glares to release me.

The judgment was made: I would not go to Norton State. I was victorious. I was retained for twenty-four hours, most of which I slept through. At my release, the police officer at the front desk returned my belongings from a plastic container, handing me my sweatshirt and the Pringles can. I shook it and heard the beautiful holiday chimes of pills ringing inside. I couldn't believe the court system returned my fully loaded handgun. I laughed to myself and thought, *What a bunch of idiots.* I was so proud of my clever, diabolical skills. I met up with Nick and popped open a celebratory breakfast of bitter pills and greasy chips.

∞∞∞∞∞∞∞

The next week was spent in a pilled-out fog, and somehow we met up with an old gymnastics friend from the Staunton team. His father owned a popular gymnastics club attached to the back of their house.

191

I had known his entire family since childhood, and we went to his place.

I had competed and trained often at their gym when I was younger. Thomas, my old teammate, brought us in, and his older brothers were drinking beer. With our pills, I figured we'd be welcome in their home. We drank through the night and took more.

I had the great idea of going into their gym and flipping around. It was empty, silent, and challenging me. The stale chalk covering the equipment shimmered in the dim light, and I heard a low growl escape from the sprung floor: "You are no longer welcome here." I stood my ground. I knew every apparatus better than my own body. This kind of precompetition silence could kill me a thousand times, and in my drunken, pilled-out bliss, I was home.

A voice from above called out my name. It was Thomas's dad, Mr. Harris, and I was too high to feel remorse or embarrassment as I stood below the man I admired, in his gym, the boy champion he had watched grow. He knew Coach Dan well, and in that moment I was challenged, like God was towering over me in judgment. Somehow his appearance cracked through the chemicals. There I was, a dirty, pierced, staggering, pill-popping drunk in his gym, in his church, confronting my now-jealous addiction—two lovers battling over one heart. God above and I, the Devil, below, capable only of saying "Hello." He just walked away. His sons, laughing like the little demons from my detox ritual, went to shoot pool as I walked over and lay down under the high bar, falling asleep as my memories of gymnastics bliss warmed my cold heart.

I woke the next day to the usual routine of not knowing where I was or how I got there, afraid of what I had done or said the night before. I still wasn't used to that sensation. The sunlight beamed through the window like a laser, stinging my hung-over head. Hearing an argument from the next room, I got up off the couch, grabbed my jeans, and did a quick pat-down for drugs. I already needed something to calm my nerves; reality was setting in and I needed protection. As I chewed a Klonopin, Thomas rushed over to me, and before I could ask how he got in my room, he said, "My father wants you out right now."

I was completely confused as to how I was in Thomas's house. I looked around the room, full of people I didn't know, put my clothes on, ate two more pills, grabbed Nick, and started walking toward a road. The sun was killing me, and I really needed some coke to cope with the exhaustion.

We realized parking lots were in our immediate sleep future, so it seemed logical to get as comfortable as possible—we had a lot of pills left. Nick and I split the pills, leaving a few of them, and then headed for the road. I needed to undo the memories that had surfaced between gymnastics and Mr. Harris, and I knew all those pills would eradicate any human qualities I had left.

What I remember after that are only fragments. I recall seeing old friends from high school, the backseat of a car, and moments at my mother's house. I was on a medical table in a police station surrounded by scared cops, my body being pulled up a flight of stairs, with the back of my head hitting each step as it went up to the top. I remember my mother yelling, "Wake up! Wake up! He's foaming at the mouth."

And then, a wonderful feeling—looking down at my legs and thinking to myself, *I have never felt so good in my whole life.* I was so warm. There was no panic, no pain, just tender protection. I was complete, satisfied, and finished. Yes, I felt finished—as if God came down and told me to rake up all the leaves on the planet and I had just captured the very last one, adding it on to the biggest pile that ever existed. I was loved, held, and cradled, and as I sat in that warmth, bathed by the foundation of my soul, the timeless moment seemed to go on forever, but lasted only seconds as I drifted into a well of nothingness.

I realized that all along I was a spirit pretending to be human, and I heard the most pleasurable silence enveloped by a golden heat surrounded by what appeared to be stardust. It was perfection. And then an unwelcome sound came rushing in, an unwelcome sound that blew my pile of leaves across the planet by the mightiest wind. As my eyes opened, terror gripped me. I heard beeping sounds, saw lights; then heard machines and talking, and then nothing.

I was back between awful white hospital walls, not knowing what day it was, how I got there, or why I had been ripped from heaven. I got out of the bed. I was still wearing my favorite Ralph Lauren striped shirt, which was bloodstained. My piercings were gone, *all of them*, no nipple rings or labret. They were all gone. What the fuck? Medical suction cups covered my chest—were they monitoring my heart? My heart! Did it even beat anymore?

I walked out of the room, heard a nurse talking, and got the familiar sick feeling that I'd been here before, that once again I'd be treated like some asshole, some drug-addicted asshole. They would look at me like I was meaningless, awful trash.

I heard a voice devoid of any kindness or humanity. "Mr. Puttanyanoh," she said, completely mispronouncing my name. Her fat fingers attached to fatter hands extended from her nurse's uniform, hair overdone like a blonde biker helmet, and avoiding my eyes, she said, "You have an appointment with the doctor later today."

I didn't bother to ask any questions. I walked over to a chair by the nurse's desk and tried to put together the pieces of what day, month, and year it was, the city and state, and who I had alienated. This one was big. I did something truly awful. My gut knew something life-altering had taken place, but I had no recollection of what it was—just faint memories of a white van, leaves, a doctor's office, a mall, and an incomprehensible warmth, a happiness far away, at the other side of a tunnel. I hoped the doctor's clipboard would give me some insight as I struggled to grasp what I had done. My bones felt different, altered, and I felt misplaced—like my soul just rode a roller coaster and now I had to pay for the ride.

25

PUBIC BONE

According to Hindu text, there are seven chakras, or energy vortexes, in the body. The second chakra, called *Svadhisthana*, means "dwelling place of the self," and is located in the lower abdomen, below the navel and over the pubic bone. It controls the emotional and sensual aspects of our lives. Excessiveness in this chakra energy may lead to frequent emotional drama, poor boundaries, and sexual addiction.

I walked into the doctor's office expecting to find someone I could easily manipulate. A wall full of achievement plaques framed the large, black desk he sat behind, surrounded by paper-stuffed manila envelopes. He was old and stubborn-looking, and I could tell immediately he was beyond my controlling abilities. I was feeling too many emotions and needed something to calm my nerves. For some reason, being abstinent felt harder this time.

Right away I told the doctor I wasn't feeling well, but he looked at me with disdain and said, "Shut your mouth and listen to me. Do you know why you're here?"

"Not really," I said, playing it cool and using my charm. I wanted to sweet-talk my way into his compassion. He was uninterested in me; his interest was in why I was there and how he could treat me. All my glorious gymnastics stories would have fallen dead in that office. He said sternly, "I'll tell you what happened."

He looked me in the eye and said, "You were clinically dead, twice." I didn't shudder. I wasn't shocked. I felt a massive sense of accomplishment, like a hero dropping into the underworld, finding death, and then walking away, making me truly indestructible. That lifeless form had mocked me since I was a boy. Once again it had tried to steal my breath, and once again, it had lost.

I looked back at the doctor, doubting his information, and said, "I don't believe you; you're just trying to scare me into staying sober."

But he repeated with perfect conviction, "YOU . . . WERE . . . DEAD! All the drugs you took stopped your heart. Not once, but twice, and you are lucky to be sitting here in front of me."

Somehow that sentence hit me harder, and the comedy of the situation blew up in my face, as if someone had thrown a grenade at a clown instead of a whipped-cream pie. Maybe I did need to calm down and take this recovery thing seriously.

The doctor used barbiturates to detox me off the benzodiazepines. Good god, barbiturates—it would be like trying to heal cancer with chamomile tea. I'd have no euphoria. His message still didn't quite penetrate my disease until he said, in a way only old people with years of life experiences behind their words can, "I am not going to change your medication, so don't even ask."

The next few days were a nightmare for me—a nice corner in hell would have been better than this place. I detoxed next to my filthy roommate and tried to call my mother collect, but she refused to accept the charges. I discovered I was in a mental ward in Rhode Island. I had destroyed every relationship in my life, with friends or family, and was crippled by loneliness.

I made an honest attempt to listen and learn while I was there. If a solution existed to stop me from ending up in places like this, I intended to find it. Adding to the humiliation of being in the crazy house, I had arrived with no shoes and had only hospital paper slippers to shuffle around in. My parents continued to reject my calls, making the mystery of the chain of events seem even more ominous. *What had I done?*

Somewhere between heaven and here, my piercings had disappeared, so I returned to my finely honed skill of using the prongs of a plastic fork to reopen the holes in my skin. I wasn't embarrassed about plastic prongs sticking out of my face since the place was swarming with falling-down drug addicts, alcoholics, and people with serious mental disorders—some spoke to shadows, some drooled endlessly onto their laps, some ate chess pieces, and some insisted on spinning in circles while shitting. I made friends with a few people, and during medication lineup we would swallow, show the nurse our tongues, remove the pill from under our tongues, spit it out, and switch pills later in desperate, unfulfilled hopes for a high. Once I got methadone from a girl who was on her fourth visit to that resort. Was being admitted to a psychiatric unit what my future held for me? As we made the pill switch, she warned me, "Don't ever do heroin!" . . . *Why does everyone keep saying that?*

I couldn't wait to get out of there. They helped me create an outpatient plan to continue my recovery in the outside world, but recovery was not in my plans for the immediate future. That desire had burned out. Nick and Katherine came to pick me up and I ran out to meet them in my torn-toe, paper slippers. I was so happy; I couldn't believe people I knew had actually shown up for me.

We planned to stop at my mother's house to pick up some of my things before heading on to Katherine's house. I thought my mother would be relieved and happy to see me, but a woman in a screaming rage welcomed me at the door. No longer mother and son, we were now the worst of enemies, and she told me if I didn't leave fast she would call the cops. I ran to my room, got my things, and tried to remember where I had hidden that damned can of chips. She stood by the door and fired into my heart, "Oh, by the way, that huge amount of pills came in the mail. I called that bitch psychiatrist and told her to stop sending them here 'cause they're fucking killing you."

I froze. I had completely forgotten about those hundreds of free pills still being sent by the state. Fuck! How did I screw up that mother lode and not redirect the mail? I shot back, "Where are they? That's my medication! You can't do that! I fucking hate you!"

She threatened again to call the cops. Didn't we do that exact dance just weeks earlier? We were in a perpetual cycle of hatred, debasement, and destruction. I grabbed my stuff and left, with the Pringles canister remaining lost in the shipwreck.

The plan was for us to live with Katherine's parents. They were extremely kind and took us in, as if we were part of the family. Whatever details Katherine had created as our backstory, it worked. They gave us food and a place to live, and even drove me to my doctor's appointments.

After two weeks, my addiction returned in the form of a panic attack. My first trip to the Delmar emergency room got me Xanax. Katherine's parents began to see that something wasn't quite right with the new family portrait. Their new pets had dark secrets— bloodthirsty, ravenous beasts would soon be at the doorstep, primed to destroy their family values. It began, as usual, with me stumbling around their house, scientifically exploring the balance between gravity and chemicals. I would overcompensate every movement, exaggerating the form of the human body—a man walking through a dry ocean, working against the force of invisible waves. As the alcohol on their shelves began to disappear, so did their trust in us, and the time came for us to leave. They kindly asked us to go, and, without confrontation, we understood.

When Angela let us stay in her attic, we entered the prostitute's lair. My addiction was moving up in the world, becoming my medal of honor. Released of all worldly obligations, no bank account, no clean clothes, addiction was all mine, and it deepened every day. Even though my bones were tough as granite and my heart grew colder with each breath, my relationship with Nick flourished. We were falling desperately in love with each other—or with each other's addictions. Our disease united us as our corruptions intertwined, staining and blurring our realities. To be without Nick was to be without breath; we were happy together, upstairs among the clutter and the cobwebs.

Life in Angela's house was exactly what one would expect in the home of a prostitute and an addict. No real happiness lived there, just a perpetual state of existing. We stopped asking ourselves how we got there or what had happened to our childhood dreams—the children in us were dead. We accepted our fates, nurtured our darkness, and displayed our black petals as we made the best of that horror. We were all trying to die. Well, at least I was.

I became angry at and jealous of Angela because of the power she held over us. Jobless and broke, we were at her mercy for drugs, and I hated her for that. I needed my own money to reclaim control of my cocaine. I realized that her prostitution gig paid well, and having lost my self-respect, I began to think her job wasn't so bad: have sex with people, get money, get coke. Maybe I could do that.

When human hands touch a flower, it will often wilt. Would strangers touching my flesh absorb the last drops of my vitality, my humanity? Was I willing to wager that for drugs and peace? Would I hate myself even more and finally sell my soul? Those thoughts paled next to the luminous mountain of coke I envisioned on the other side of my plan—I could do it; it would be easy. Nick was completely against it until he entertained my vision of Mount Cocaine. I told Angela I was interested in selling my body and saw her face light up for the first time. She knew someone I could talk to the next day. I had already fallen so far from that first-place podium; I wondered, how much farther was there to actually fall?

A big street carnival was in the center of town and we were going to attend as a family outing, in celebration of nothing. I was happy; tomorrow might bring a new job and I would no longer be under Angela's control. Some drug days hit quicker than others, and the pills today were hitting me hard.

Angela bought our first round of warm draft beers, and the carnival fun began. I spotted a group of raver-looking kids and started in with my usual bullshit. I asked if they had any K, which was out of character for me—I never liked ketamine. I blacked out for a few seconds, and, once conscious again, I was convinced I had already handed over the money, even though I had no money to hand over. Nick and I started yelling and screaming at this group of guys I'd just intruded on, and after I started pushing them around, the cops arrived. I was sure that I had been wronged and that it was my right to fight for my drugs and money.

In the mix of breaking us up, I heard a cop call one of us a faggot, so I took a swing. After connecting somewhere on the cop's body, I immediately flew into the air. Pain crashed through my chest and stomach when I landed on the street. My eyes filled with dust and tears of laughter as cops kicked me and dragged me, facedown, bleeding, and finally under control. They cuffed me and threw me into the back of the squad car, and still I couldn't stop laughing. The golden thread with reality had been severed.

Nick and I were placed in cells next to each other. They stripped me down to my underwear and took my sneakers away because I threatened to hang myself with the laces. I told a cop I was having a seizure and needed to see a doctor fast; he came closer and, like a violent, untamed animal, I spat on him. I saw that once on TV, and, somewhere inside my fucked-up head, I believed all this was make-believe.

In the calm of the night, Nick and I reached through the bars and grabbed each other's hands—beautiful lovers, clasping hands through the iron bars, our hearts kept apart by the guard outside. We savored our dream of a nightmare. Addiction is the only jail cell where the key is on the inside, impossible to find in the darkness. In my oblivion, I sobbed, knowing the world still did not approve of us and that we were the last two people on earth harboring a dream.

In the morning Nick had vanished. I didn't know why I was in my underwear or where I was, except that I could tell I was in jail. It was cold and my head hurt. I called for help, and it hurt to breathe; it felt like my ribs were broken. I had dried blood and dirt caked around my lips and fingers.

A cop came in and said, "Oh, loudmouth, you're awake! Seems like you've sobered up."

They threw me my clothes; I got dressed and was released. I had to promise to return the next day for a court hearing. As I walked out the precinct door, I realized that I was badly injured and knew those cops were responsible. I spotted a pay phone near the door and called 911, not realizing that the call was actually being directed to the very building I was standing in. I told the operator I wanted to press charges against the cops who beat me up, and when they saw I was making the call from the pay phone in their station, two cops rushed over, grabbed my arms, opened the door, and catapulted me out. It felt like I was back on TV, lying facedown on the pavement with the warm sun hitting my back. I saw a hospital across the street and walked into the emergency room.

After I waited for hours to be seen, the doctor said I was too intoxicated to be given pain medication. But when she left the room I stole vials of injectable lidocaine, which had no euphoric side effects, but just taking anything relieved my anger. I was exhausted and pissed at Nick because I didn't know where he'd gone.

Somehow I found Angela's apartment and crawled up to the attic and onto our dirty mattress, curling up next to Nick. He had been asleep, but rolled over to ask me where I'd been, which started a fight. I screamed at him, wanting to know why he abandoned me by not waiting for me at the jail, and I told him I never wanted to see him again.

I closed my eyes and drifted off to safety until horrible shrieks woke me up. Paramedics huddled over me, shaking me, yelling, "Wake up! Joe! Wake up!" Katherine stood next to Angela, holding an empty prescription bottle I'd filled a few days before.

The paramedics asked if I'd taken all the pills at once. "Yeah, but I always take that many. I'm fine. I'm not overdosing. I just want to sleep," I told them.

I looked over at Katherine. "What the fuck is wrong with you? Did you call them?" Scared I was going to overdose, she'd called the paramedics, but I'd finished those pills twenty-four hours before, so if I had taken a lethal dose, I'd have been dead. They knew I was right, but said I had to go to the ER. Using my TV medical education, I told the paramedics that I was invoking my right to refuse medical attention, but they disagreed and took me back to the same hospital I had just left hours earlier. I was placed under strict observation. The nurse treated me like I was a serial killer, and made it her life's work to make me feel like shit about myself.

A few hours later I walked back to Angela's apartment. All I wanted to do was sleep. When I arrived, Angela's brother and his crew of dangerous elves were sitting there, waiting for me. Their energy was in protection mode, and it felt like I was walking into a lion's den. I went up to the attic to lie down, but everything was gone except my teddy bear, Oatmeal. He was the only one left that had not abandoned me. We'd begun to resemble each other—generally filthy, with torn noses and matted hair. A few pieces of my clothing were thrown around the attic, but when I went to pick them up I found huge tears across them, slashes from top to bottom. Someone had had playtime with box cutters at my expense.

Angela's brother came up to the attic with his mob and told me I had to leave. I said, "Not without my journal. Where is it?" He found it and handed it over. There I was, with everything I owned: Oatmeal, my journal, and the clothes on my back. The rest of my things were gone and it was clear I wasn't getting them back. I was bone-sober at that point, with nothing to protect me from the pain.

I heard rain strike the attic's roof and realized if I didn't leave immediately I'd be drenched. I asked Angela where Nick had gone. In her nastiest voice, primed from years in the sex trade, she responded, "You don't remember, you crackhead? You broke up with him. He called his uncle to come pick him up."

All I remembered was a fight, not a breakup; I loved him. I left before my conversation with Angela and her brother and the elves could escalate to a fistfight, and walked out to the streets, back to my now "usual" hospital to ask my favorite nurse if there was a shelter in the neighborhood. She wrote the directions on the napkin that had been underneath her Styrofoam coffee cup. I wasn't even worth wasting a piece of paper on.

Exhausted and broken, I went to the shelter and got a bed in a huge room full of other homeless men. Two large fans were on full blast at the end of the room; it was the most soothing sound I'd heard in a long time. It reminded me of my father when he lived with us; he couldn't sleep without the soft sound of a fan. He was there with me, the white noise cradling his broken child. What was he doing right now? I wanted to see him. I couldn't believe I was in another homeless shelter, alone, scared, gripping every ounce of teddy-bear life out of Oatmeal. Listening to the hum of the fans, I fell into one of the darkest sleeps I had ever known. I hit a new bottom that would be my watermark in the well of my life. I felt I could only go up.

I awoke and faced the sunshine in perfect fear. The other men were kind to me; everyone had a version of being broken by the system, drugs, families, and life. There were twelve-step meetings, and I went to one; on Sundays we had to attend church, where a crazy guy tried to baptize me and force me to accept Jesus Christ as my savior. I wouldn't do either of those things, and it pissed him off, but he said God still loved me. I was thankful to hear somebody still loved me.

I had nobody left to call. Feeling completely alone, I remembered talking to Darren a few weeks ago during one of my meltdowns. We had moved far away from each other, and neither wanted to see the other again, but I called him and begged him to pick me up. After I cried and pleaded, he finally agreed and said he would come in a few days.

I was so happy to see Darren, but he was shocked at the sight of me. He knew I was in trouble. He convinced his mother to let me move in with him. I was terrified of using again. I would do everything possible to get into recovery and change my life. I was a desperate, dying boy, and though I wanted to cry, I didn't. I climbed into the backseat of Darren's new car and fell asleep as he drove home to Virginia.

26

CEREBRUM

THE CEREBRUM (LATIN FOR "BRAIN") IS THE LARGEST
AND MOST HIGHLY DEVELOPED PART OF THE HUMAN
BRAIN, WHILE ALSO BEING THE MOST RECENT IN EVOLUTIONARY
TERMS. IT IS ASSOCIATED WITH ALL THE HIGHER COGNITIVE
FUNCTIONS, INCLUDING THOUGHT, MEMORY, IMAGINATION,
PERCEPTION, INTELLIGENCE, LANGUAGE COMPREHENSION,
AND PERSONALITY. THE BRAIN TAKES THE LONGEST OF
ANY ORGAN TO DEVELOP AND UNDERGOES THE MOST
CHANGES. ON AVERAGE, IT LOSES FROM 5 TO 10 PERCENT
OF ITS WEIGHT BETWEEN THE AGES OF TWENTY AND NINETY.

Sitting in the backseat of Darren's car, I was surrounded by my truth.
I was beaten up, and had crashed and burned into bits of debris
and despair. In the past, I would have pulled myself together to
mentally and physically connect with Darren, but at that point in
my life all human interactions had been reduced to an animal level.
After all those years I had bought into and cultivated a dangerous
look, investing in body piercing, clothes, and tattoos to speak for
me, I now saw my darkness reflected in the fear in Darren's eyes. I
no longer needed to hammer into people's hearts, "Fear me." I had
become fear.

Darren lived with his mom, and I would be allowed to stay in
their basement. It took a few weeks to get back to a state of mind
where I could think normally. Even simple thoughts were difficult
to articulate.

I called Nick to make amends, begged for his forgiveness, and asked him to believe in me and believe that I was finished with using drugs. He was skeptical, but I was determined to prove that I could leave my former life of destruction. We made a loose plan that if I stayed in recovery, worked hard, and saved money, we would find an apartment together. I even contacted another college that had expressed interest in my gymnastics before Staunton, but got no reply.

Darren still partied, but kept it under control. While I was reemerging as a functioning human being, I wanted no more drugs in my life. I found a counselor who guided me in writing letters of amends to my family, begging for their understanding and acceptance of my apologies. I didn't dare call them because I knew they were through with me. I would only be able to repair the damage by showing them—over time—that I had changed.

I was looking for a job when my brain started clearing up, and I found one as a waiter at a sports bar. Never a morning person, I started my first shift at 7:00 a.m., pouring coffee for a group that rented a function room every weekend. I couldn't imagine what kind of people would regularly meet so early and have coffee in a crappy room, but I needed every cent and my manager said they all tipped a dollar.

That first weekend shift was an absolute shock. Late to arrive and get the coffee brewing, I rushed into the room and heard someone speaking. Trying not to interrupt them, I looked over and saw some books on a table. I had seen that book before, but couldn't remember the context. I knew the setting too, but paused in confusion in an effort to jog my brain for memories. It was a twelve-step meeting, a meeting for the disease people believed I had. I poured the coffee and stood outside the room, listening to their stories through the closed doors, desperate for help, too terrified to talk. Could I tell them I might have a problem? Would they tell my boss? I was grateful to be entrusted with the job and couldn't afford to lose it.

I was in the room cleaning up cups when the chairperson asked, "Is there anybody new here who would like to introduce themselves?" I wanted to speak, to scream, for all the flesh to melt off my bones, exposing myself to them, but I didn't. I just stood there in silence—the silence that kills a person, the silence only the destroyed and damned understand. My body heaved in defeat as I filled a woman's mug. I wondered what it would have felt like, divulging my truth to those strangers. I left the room and pressed my ear against the door, eavesdropping for hope.

Then a woman spoke. When she came to the meeting, she said she thought the doors of heaven were opening, but realized it was just the Gates of Hell closing behind her. She had left the underworld and was ready to live a life of honesty and recovery. Tears streamed down my face as I clung to the door separating me from them, my Gates of Hell—which side was I on?

Instead of embracing the help of those recovering addicts, I opted to switch shifts with another waiter. I could no longer hear their truths on one side of the door and live my lies on the other side. Hearing the honest emotions spoken at the meeting was too painful, and I didn't see success for me in their program. I felt my disease was unique. *My* addiction was more malicious than theirs. I knew if they heard how truly evil I was, they would never let me stay in the group. I still wanted recovery, but it felt like a theoretical heaven, a place people talk about but never reach.

I did the same thing every day of every week—work, come home, and put my money under my pillow. The more time I spent drug-free, the more I wrote, mostly poetry, endlessly scribbling words in my journal about Nick and the pains of separated love. Nick had peered too closely through the keyhole of my soul. My bender frightened him and illuminated my potential danger to us both. He never thought I would succeed and see our plan through to the end, but I vowed to prove him wrong. We would live together, in secret from his friends and family; I would reside as the phantom ghost, the invisible love of his life. Forever.

The Virginia summer slowly passed, and I began to feel my welcome at Darren's waning, though his mother tolerated me sulking around her home. As I put some time together in recovery, I forgot how bad I was, especially my last horrible fiasco, and slowly started partying again. I placed strict guidelines on my using: no pills from a pharmacy, but illegally obtained substances were fine.

By summer's end I'd saved enough money to move in with Nick, but Nick had decided to move on. He would continue living with his parents and return to college. I was beyond outraged. How could he do that to me after I had worked so hard? I hated him, but still loved him, and kept to my plan of moving. I would find an apartment close to his new college. He was hesitant, but okay with my idea. He said he would help me move and visit me all the time. I forgave him for changing his mind. I couldn't believe I had finally accomplished something. Darren drove me to Brooklyn to apartment-hunt and then to find a job. Most apartments I liked turned me down. I wasn't that surprised, because I suspected my credit was bad. There was one place left to check that was close to my old homeless shelter.

The apartment was a total dump, its floors covered with dead leaves that blew in through screenless windows that wouldn't shut. The carpet beneath the foliage was moldy and the door frames were slanted and warped. A small, dust-covered chandelier vied for attention in the center of the room, reminding me of my parents' restaurant. The landlord didn't run a credit check; it was reasonably close to Nick's college and within my price range. I said, "I'll take it."

There was a second bedroom, and I said to Darren, "You know, we're forty-five minutes from Manhattan. Do you wanna move in with me and split the rent?" I knew he wanted out of Virginia and was just waiting for me to ask. He wanted in, but wouldn't be able to move until he sold his car and gave a few weeks' notice at his job. Driving back to Virginia, we were both proud of our first apartment and amazed to spend money on something other than cocaine and pills.

I moved in November, and as I opened the door to my apartment found it dirtier and ice-cold. The lights and heat didn't work, and there was a grimy outline where the refrigerator once stood. Nick was supposed to help me unpack, get settled, and find a job, but he didn't show up.

I was alone in my first apartment with no food, heat, electricity, or the man I loved. I called the utilities company from a pay phone across the street to figure out what had happened to the heat and electricity, only to learn that my new landlord hadn't paid his bills. It would take two weeks and a large deposit to get service.

Trying to turn this around, I went to a store, bought a case of beer and some candles, and got drunk. A group of cockroaches in the bathroom found a five-course meal on my toothbrush, nibbling between the bristles. Fearlessly, they continued eating as I stood in the candle's flame, seeing my drunken face in the cracked mirror; my life was reflected in those roaches, hard to kill and surviving on filth. Even with a heavenly glow, the apartment was a nightmare, a perfect replica of where and who I was: broken, empty, dirty, and depressing, but with a slight glimmer of hope, as represented by the dusty chandelier.

With no success in finding a waiter job in Brooklyn, I tried Manhattan. There is the world and then there is that other planet called New York City. I already hated it, and nothing would change my mind, but my love for Nick kept pushing me to try. After many failed attempts, I found an Indian restaurant that stood out with white Christmas lights around the glass storefront, making it seem cozy and warm. I walked in and a very nice woman quickly greeted and interviewed me. After I told her of my lengthy restaurant experience, she said I would be right at home here, since it was also a family business. I got the job and would start immediately, right there and then. For the next eight hours I ran beautiful Indian dishes back to tables, learned the menu, and met the other employees.

After the shift I took the subway back to Brooklyn. I went home exhausted and proud, slept, and got ready to do it all over again, in New York City.

27

PITUITARY GLAND: PART I

ENDORPHINS ARE PRODUCED BY THE PITUITARY GLAND
AND THE HYPOTHALAMUS IN VERTEBRATES DURING EXERCISE,
EXCITEMENT, PAIN, CONSUMPTION OF SPICY FOODS, LOVE, AND
ORGASM. THEY RESEMBLE OPIATES IN THEIR ABILITIES
TO PRODUCE ANALGESIA—THE RELIEF OF PAIN—AND WORK AS
NATURAL PAIN RELIEVERS. THE TERM *endorphin* CONSISTS OF
TWO PARTS: *endo* AND *orphin*, WHICH ARE SHORT FORMS OF
THE WORDS *endo*GENOUS AND M*orphin*E, COMBINED TO MEAN
"A MORPHINE-LIKE SUBSTANCE ORIGINATING FROM WITHIN THE
BODY." "ENDORPHIN RUSH" REFERS TO FEELINGS
OF EXHILARATION BROUGHT ON BY PAIN, DANGER, OR OTHER
FORMS OF STRESS. WHEN A NERVE IMPULSE REACHES THE
SPINAL CORD, ENDORPHINS ARE RELEASED TO PREVENT NERVE
CELLS FROM RELEASING MORE PAIN SIGNALS. AFTER INJURY,
ENDORPHINS ALLOW ANIMALS TO FEEL A SENSE OF POWER
AND CONTROL OVER THEMSELVES, ALLOWING THEM TO
CONTINUE STRENUOUS OR AGGRESSIVE ACTIVITIES.

I was twenty-one years old and celebrating New Year's Eve in my own apartment with Nick and Darren, smoking pot but not taking pills or drinking alcohol, staying within my definition of "recovery." Darren had moved in after Christmas, and Nick, attending a new college, was visiting more often. Darren landed a great job waiting tables at a restaurant downtown.

I was happy and excited to be working at the restaurant because it was a whole different clientele than what I was accustomed to. Cross-sections of new people piqued my brain to consider different human experiences. People's dreams created and ran the city and started fueling some of my own dreams, which had been suppressed through years of refining only my addiction. Everyone was aspiring to be an actor, model, musician, or writer, or to simply rise above where they were in their lives. That atmosphere with everyone working hard started to push me out of my long-term grave.

It was the most professional restaurant I had ever worked in, and they ran a tight ship. Mistakes with food orders were deducted from our pay, and everything had to be accounted for on the table to prevent thefts, including water. At the end of the night we pooled our tips, which made us all work hard to make the most money we could as a team. That way we cared and thought about all the customers, not just our own tables. The owner definitely knew how to run a business, and strangely enough, I loved having strict rules in my life.

I joined a gym and started working out again. My self-esteem got a little jolt, but I never spoke of my athletic past and didn't want to have any connection to gymnastics. I had buried that love and passion and would not exhume it for anyone. I looked into attending community college, but since I owed almost twenty thousand dollars to Staunton and an inordinate amount in student loans, I wasn't welcome to register.

My mother forwarded two years' worth of mail to my new apartment—it was mostly a huge pile of bills from mental institutions, ambulance services, hospitals, and rehabs. The pile remained untouched for weeks, but I had to make a dent in it in order to move forward. Ripping each envelope open was like tearing scabs off old memories, a paper trail of the demoralizing things I had done to myself and others, a concrete map of where I had gone and the insanity of my actions.

A new concept crept into my now-abstinent world—credit. I had never considered the notion, especially after taking a handful of pills.

But now I needed credit. Naturally I could not get any because of my past "investments" of money. I didn't really know what credit was, but I knew mine was bad. All those bills added up to a massive amount of money. There was no way I would ever have that much, regardless of how many tables I waited on. Doomed from the start, why should I even try fixing any of this? After reaching the bottom of the pile, I calculated I owed over forty thousand dollars. A lawyer I contacted through a number I found in the Yellow Pages suggested I file for Chapter 7 bankruptcy to cover the hospital bills—the student loans were all mine to keep.

My family sent me Christmas cards and asked me to come home and visit. After I had been kicked out of my mother's house, we had talked occasionally, and the recovery my family heard in my voice, along with no new arrests or creations of destruction during the last few months, spoke volumes to them.

Finally, I was behaving and functioning moderately well within society. I bought things I had never wanted before, buying into the illusion that having things made me somebody. I was part of *their* world, having conversational input about VCRs, TVs, Nintendos, and other objects, rather than substances, which gave people pleasure. I wasn't sure if my new consumerism gave me pleasure, but buying things seemed to be an acceptable way of filling the void. And the more things I acquired, the happier, healthier, and more functional I appeared to others.

A new guy from New Mexico, Stoop, started at the restaurant and we became friends. Since he couldn't stop talking at the restaurant he was soon fired, but he quickly got a new job delivering weed. Stoop's company only delivered pot, but it was the best pot I'd ever experienced—pure and dark with a deep, pungent odor. That weed was a rarity, the perfect, seedless kind of bud. Darren, Nick, Stoop, and I hung out and smoked all the time.

I didn't love New York, but I did start to find some comfort with it, taking advantage of the many free things the city had to offer, like museums, parks, shows, and art. My life was slowly repairing itself.

The warm spring air energized New York's inhabitants; flowers bloomed, and so did my asthma. After working all day, I began to frequent the city's emergency rooms, back on the whole regimen of asthma medication I had taken as a teenager. But now, without insurance, and trying to avoid another pile of bills, I had to pay for them in real time. All my proud savings were again going to pharmaceuticals—but this time to prednisone and antibiotics, which made me break out in hives.

I would chug liquid Benadryl that would stop the hives and allow me to go to work without itchy splotches all over my body, but all the medications made me somnolent. My lungs felt like knives were lodged between them, and each breath cut in a little deeper. I was finally diagnosed with pneumonia, which demanded a long recovery time, but I couldn't miss work. Struggling for air to soak into my lungs, I fought for each breath as I worked my shifts, pushing through the pain to keep homelessness at bay.

Another new guy was hired on at work, a tall Egyptian named Asten. Everyone disliked him—he was always late, got orders wrong, and fell asleep during meetings, and the owner constantly told him he smelled bad. I didn't smell anything bad and knew what it felt like to be the underdog, so I tried to befriend him. I would keep an eye on his tables and back him up to keep him out of trouble. He seemed withdrawn, always looking at the ground, and I wanted to help him.

One night, while waiting for the subway, I saw him standing in line and said, "Hey, Asten, you live in Brooklyn?"

"Yeah, I've lived there for four years." His achy, scratching voice was familiar, and I recognized it, but couldn't recall why.

He seemed embarrassed when he asked me, "Joe, do you think I could borrow eighty dollars? I'll pay you back at the end of next shift. I need to get my phone turned on and can't do that without a deposit."

Since I had gone through the same thing, I said, "Of course you can, man," and handed him the cash.

He never paid me back, and I assumed he needed it more than I did; he was always kind of a mess. There was something off about him, something almost gruesome that I could never figure out. He reminded me of a zombie—a heartbreaking, soulless man who came out of his crypt to wait on tables.

One night, Asten was in a surprisingly great mood. Looking at him, I noticed his eyes were different, dark brown with pinpoint pupils—the Devil's eyes—so dark I almost fell into them. I guessed that he was on some sort of painkiller, perhaps Percocet or something, so I asked him to get me some pills to help me breathe. He told me he wasn't taking pills; he was using smack.

After a month of constant, extreme pain in my lungs, I didn't think twice about handing him forty dollars to get me some. I liked the sound of smack; it made heroin sound so somber. I gave him a ten-dollar service fee, and after the shift he came back with two bags of heroin, shoved into an empty Marlboro Reds pack. There was a smudged skull stamped on the wax paper and the word *crossbones* printed below. After all that time of wanting to be the gymnastics champion with heroic qualities, the gods bestowed upon me a powdered invitation wrapped in wax paper, bringing my "hero-in"—my crowned heroine.

Finally I held heroin in my hands, and I couldn't wait to bring it home to Nick and Darren. Trying a new drug with friends was always exciting, the unraveling of a beautiful mystery together and discovering a new feeling. Apparently the heroin makers intensified the potency so we wouldn't have to shoot it; we could just sniff it for the high, making it less dangerous. I wanted to stay abstinent, but I wanted to try heroin more.

When I came home to the apartment, Darren looked shocked, almost angry, but intrigued at the little bags clenched in my hand. We carefully unfolded the wax paper, pouring the dirty brown powder onto a plastic CD cover, our usual stomping ground for coke. We cut two small lines from the mound; a bit of the powder still clung to the paper. We didn't know how much to do or what it would feel like, even though we'd done opiates before. But this was the source; this sniff would take us all directly back to the enchanted poppy flower.

How many warnings had I received not to drink from the sacred well of the world's most divine water? I could hear the serpent calling my name from the Tree of Knowledge. How could we know that a single drink would leave us forever thirsty, make us sick and insatiable? How could we know that it would take away our lives, money, and future? That one drop of nectar would never allow us to stop?

Before I sniffed the small line, I saw a future before me: birthdays, Christmas cards, clothing sales, long shifts at work that made me look forward to a weekend, growing old, running with a dog on the beach, a quiet evening with a cup of steeping tea. And from my slow progression upward, out of darkness, I willingly gave it all back. In that moment, leaning toward the table, holding the straw to my nose, I sniffed my new life straight up to my brain. I sniffed hard and heard an angel sigh.

The powder stung my nose and I could feel it ball up in my nasal cavity, like a rotting cobweb lodged in there, and the bitter taste dripped down to the back of my tongue. Its bitterness was the taste of an unsatisfied life and the reward for a new beginning. The three of us silently waited for the high to alter our existence, and it did.

When it hit, it felt warmer than the sunshine and deeper than any hug. An intense, itching sensation filled my body, especially across the skin of my nose, and scratching it felt magnificent. Closing my eyes blocked out the slight nausea that camped in my stomach. Darren reached over, put his hand on my shoulder, and asked, "What have we done?" Even though his skin was on my flesh, I was untouchable. I was falling in love, and the rapture exploded in my blood.

I lit a cigarette, grounding myself in the plumes of smoke, and found my lungs perfect, uninhabited by the air-stealing beast. I had just sniffed the secret and the answer to life. Growing up as a gymnast I had accepted agonizing tests of endurance, but at that moment I finally found my weapon to annihilate those years of mental and physical pain. And I vowed I would never live my life without it.

Inside that warm elation, I sensed a distant presence, not the usual demons I knew so well, but something stronger, more eternal, reeking of forever, and calling me closer. I knew that would not be our "first and last drink" from the well. I would forever be peering down that stone circle, wishing my arms could reach the heavenly water to freely cup it to my mouth.

As I sank quietly into the safety of our dirty carpet, every violin and piano chord reverberated and chimed through my skin and senses. As an experienced addict, I had to plan carefully and meticulously to never get physically addicted. I had to discover a scientific way to use occasionally to avoid the depletion of opiates in my body. I would never surrender to the horrible withdrawals and malicious sickness that seem to torment every heroin addict. Both God and the Devil had a place in my life, and I willingly invited the Devil in, heeding none of the many dire warnings. I believed I could use heroin in moderation and refrain from ever shooting it into my veins. I deemed I was strong enough to obey that order and keep smack in my life forever, but under my control.

Disappointed in me for bringing another drug into our lives, Nick, I felt, needed to be properly introduced to my new love. Despite his initial protests, he sniffed without question, but didn't find the same romance as I did. During one night of using, I set our sheet-covered, cardboard-box dinner table with the CD case; three perfectly cut small lines for each diner. Nick accidentally moved the sheet with his leg and the plastic serving platter flew into the air. Losing my cherished smack turned me into a crazy, screaming monster. I grabbed my straw and started sniffing anything that resembled powder off our disgusting, moldy carpet. Nick and Darren watched silently, glimpsing my future.

Sniffing heroin didn't send me out of control like the pills had; in fact, I almost appeared to be sober and extremely happy. The only telltale sign was my eyes. Pupils normally widen or narrow, like the aperture of a camera, in response to light, but opiate users' pupils stay like pinpoints. Still, I could walk a straight line, go to the store, and do my laundry, all without making a complete fool of myself. A favorite activity became doing a line before going to the gym and running on the treadmill.

My new love kept me warm as winter approached, but I had to keep a close eye on our relationship. The voices of that distant underworldly presence were getting louder, and I began to detect an aroma of cinnamon and ash. I continued my research to beat the side effects by grilling my addict friends with questions like "How did you know you were dope sick? If you had to do it again, how would you avoid it?" They must have known I had picked it up. I avoided writing in my journal—putting it down on paper would mean I really *was* using smack.

I found a new job waiting at Gabriel's on the Upper East Side. Despite warnings not to work where the rich and cruel clientele would treat me like a slave, I left the Indian restaurant that had welcomed me to the city for less hours and more money: the perfect recipe for an addict.

The restaurant was famous among locals and tourists for its brunch. Tables were dressed in white linens, and two enormous flower arrangements separated the dining areas. The countertop in the bakery area was pristine and gave an atmosphere of dignity, respect, and warmth. On my first day I saw Woody Allen cross the street, and decided to tone down my heroin use, afraid it could interfere with my new job and clientele.

A tall, beautiful girl named Diana with huge, sparkling eyes and an amazing singing voice became my new work friend. Her unstoppable charisma made everyone around her happy, and I knew someday I'd be saying, "I knew her when." As summer approached, Diana said she needed to find new roommates to help pay her ridiculous Manhattan rent on the Upper East Side. She invited Darren and me to move in. But the rent would still be too expensive with just the three of us, so I called my first rave and piercing partner, Randi, who lived in Boston, to see if she wanted a life change. She did. It would be difficult not living as close to Nick, but he could visit on days off, and we both saw the move as an opportunity to expand and further my life.

In June of 2000, Darren and I moved to the Upper East Side, which turned out to make everything incredibly convenient for the work commute and living in general. Darren and Nick were both a little nervous about another convenience: living closer to Hell's Kitchen, where I got my heroin.

Eventually, Asten got fired from the Indian restaurant for stealing from the tip jar and leaving syringes in the employee bathroom, exposing his heroin persona—but he remained my faithful heroin connection. He was sickly, skinny, and dirty, with an odd sense of fashion. His plodding gait was not from injury, but from the deep spell cast over his system from shooting up. He always wore ridiculously oversized hats and smelled like mothballs. And I looked like a little boy at his side.

Notoriously late, always borrowing money and never paying it back, Asten was hard to track down, but could usually be found nodding out in McDonald's or Starbucks toilets—the modern junkie's shooting gallery. Despite all his shortcomings, I found him to be kind and like a big brother. He joined the legions of others who had warned me to never inject heroin. The process of getting my heroin was like crawling through a septic tank, but that was the gateway to my heaven, and he, my Papa Legba, opened the doorway to the other side, to my newfound loa spirit world.

28

ACHILLES

WHEN HE WAS AN INFANT, ACHILLES' MOTHER TRIED TO
MAKE HER SON IMMORTAL BY DIPPING HIM IN THE RIVER STYX,
GRIPPING HIM BY ONE ANKLE. AS AN ADULT, ACHILLES PROVED
HIMSELF AN INVINCIBLE WARRIOR AGAINST THE TROJANS UNTIL
ONE ARROW FOUND ITS MARK IN THE ONLY VULNERABLE
SPOT ON HIS BODY—THE HEEL. TODAY, THE GREEK MYTH
LIVES ON IN A MOST FITTING NAME FOR ONE OF THE TENDONS
MOST SUSCEPTIBLE TO INJURY IN OUR BODIES.

Summertime in the city. We had moved into a small, two-bedroom Manhattan apartment on a sun-drenched street lined with tight-fitting trash cans kept from trespassing onto the sidewalk by small iron fences. Each night, dog-sized rats would break through the bars and scavenge through the garbage, practically taking over the neighborhood.

Our place was across the street from a playground, and mornings brought the sound of children laughing. The surrounding tall buildings allowed no natural light inside the apartment, but I didn't need that warmth—sniffing heroin created my own source of heat. Sniffing the brown powder off a CD cover immediately renovated the dark space into an enchanted aquarium as Nick and I sat, feeling invincible, in my ocean-blue room, high up on my loft bed.

I was opiate-filled to the brim, and every scent from the city intensified my lust for Manhattan. It had grown on me, and I found that I loved everything about it. The trash, the homeless man on my corner, the aroma of street-cart fresh-brewed coffee—all those things made New York feel like a giant college campus full of interesting people, with something new always around every corner. It was the college experience of my dreams.

Nick and I had our routine. He would meet me at my apartment and we would then find our way to the Port Authority and Asten, sniff a line in a McDonald's bathroom, and walk back to the Upper East Side through Central Park. The intensity and newness of everything sparkled and seduced me into a land I never wanted to leave. As we walked through the park, we talked about growing old together and sharing a small country house with rocking chairs on a big front porch. Heroin strengthened our relationship—or so I thought. We were perfect, and our lives would forever be the beauty of that special summer. I didn't think I could be any happier. Denial had snaked its way back into my life.

I turned twenty-two and called my party planner, Asten. I told him for my birthday I would need a lot more heroin than usual. Asten always answered the phone as if the phone line had shocked his corpse awake from a hundred-year sleep. He kept falling asleep on the phone, even as I kept asking him if he was okay. Finally he woke up, promising he would get my stuff, but he needed me to pick him up in a cab.

I buzzed his apartment and he came down, walking out the door slowly—something about him was different. A prehistoric, oversized suit made him look like a skeleton wrapped in purple fancy rags, and huge, dark, movie-star glasses made his head seem shrunken. Olive-colored undertones rose up through his ashy skin and his lips were cracked dry, the sides of his mouth caked with a dull, white crust. Walking toward my waiting cab, he stopped and seemed to dry heave into the air, but kept walking, making the unnatural natural. It was a beautiful and dreadful image: the dead crawling toward me.

I opened the door for him and asked if he was all right, but he didn't answer. He made a low, gurgling noise and dropped his head back. His bones poked out from underneath his skin. I asked him again what was wrong. He leaned forward, and in a twisted motion vomited yellow bile into his hands, then flipped them over, letting it ooze onto the floor of the cab. He stuck his head out the window and started puking uncontrollably, his body shifting as the vomit streamed out his mouth, running down the side of the glass in a smeared, drippy mess.

My god, I wondered, *does he have the plague?*

Moaning, he tried wiping away the stomach fluid from around his mouth, but just smeared it across his face and continued barfing into his hands, shivering in the warm summer air.

The driver had no idea what was happening until another cab pulled up at a red light and told him his fare had thrown up all over his backseat. He started yelling at us as Asten continued emptying his guts of whatever he had managed to recently digest. Do the dead even eat? Tears filled his jaundiced eyes as he whispered through the gurgling, lapping sound in his throat, "Joe, I'm dope sick. Don't ever get this bad, don't ever start shooting this shit, don't ever." He curled over in a convulsing position and emptied the remains of his stomach juices on the floor.

Yes, that scared me. He was not a well man, and the words *dope sick* sank in, along with the smell of vomit all over everything. That was my first experience with the words dope sick. He seemed to be dying from a horrible disease right there beside me. How could the absence of drugs do that to a person? The driver jumped out of the car when we got to Forty-ninth and Eighth and started screaming at me through the window, apparently thinking I was the more stable and responsible one—forty dollars quieted him. Asten almost fell out of his door and into the street, but I propped him up, gave him $300 in cash, and told him to get as much heroin as he could.

I walked to the closest Starbucks, ordered a black tea, and sat down, waiting for Asten to return. The worst part was always the waiting. It usually took Asten fifteen minutes to score some dope—fifteen horrible minutes, each second tied down with anxiety, despair, and fear. I feared that he might never return with my stuff, and the excitement I generated from scoring could only be taken down by using. I feared that he would get arrested and not come back, which happened once, and it left me waiting by the phone for two days. I feared that I would get arrested when he returned and wouldn't be able to get high before going to jail.

After half an hour, I saw a crazy man resembling Asten crossing the street, but it couldn't have been the same corpse that had shared a cab with me. Singing opera at the top of his lungs, he sauntered through traffic, with cars honking and swerving around him. Blood re-pulsed through the veins of his mummified body, and other than falling asleep mid-aria, and apparently overmedicated, he looked like a well, happy, healthy man. I wanted what he had: to be fluid, happy, calm, and healed. I grabbed the cigarette pack from him containing the power to resurrect the dead, and hurried into the Starbucks toilet. I cut the top off a straw with my key, stuck it in the powder, and sniffed my salvation. The powder stung, but I didn't care—the heroin's bitterness paired well with the aftertaste of my tea, creating a blend that would keep the green mermaid in business forever—heroin-blended tea, my perfect summer-signature drink, the foundation of my dreams.

Twenty-two was the best birthday ever. Everyone I invited came to my party, and most ended up doing heroin, which made me happy— nobody wants to sit in hell alone. The more demons I had around me, the more accepted and justified I felt in my drug use. I brought my friends over to my side of the mirror so I wouldn't be forced to stare at the ugly reflection of reality all night.

Vicky, my newest friend, was an aspiring painter with a warm smile that made me want to hug her and never let go. Vic was pretty, smart, and skinny, with strawberry-red hair, and we shared the same love of alternative music.

I was excited, but hesitant about exposing my heroin use to my new friend. Asten always told me, "Don't turn anybody on to this; there is a God above us and he won't be happy with you if you share this secret." But didn't he turn me on to heroin every time he got me more? In my own boundary-less euphoria, I invited her in for a visit to the dark world. Vic took right to it, her face and skin effusing love. That night I was wrong in facilitating the permanent staining of her nose and brain, and it is a moment I will regret for the rest of my life. The heroin always runs out and the party always ends.

I used more and more, outside the watchful eyes of Darren and Nick. Unable to come off heroin without more heroin, I always set an extra bag aside for the day after our "social using." While they seemed content smoking pot the next day, I needed to taper off to make a more gradual descent—Heroin Light, for a smoother landing.

∞∞∞∞∞∞∞∞∞

While walking home from work one day, I saw a torn, mud-covered poster stuck at the bottom of a storefront window with the word "Gymnast" on it. I stopped dead in my tracks. It was an audition for Disneyland in Florida; they were looking for dancers and gymnasts. I had never seen a connection between gymnastics and a job before. Competitive gymnastics seemed separate from the acrobatic performance world, and I felt it would be like selling out. Simply staring at the audition poster made me nervous. I was just a gymnast with no dance or performing experience, and probably too old for the job. What if I auditioned and didn't make it? What if everyone there was a better gymnast than me? I didn't need any more humiliation in my life, and I tried to ignore the invitation. But that poster loomed as a huge reminder of my failure, and seemed to follow me everywhere I went. I wanted to tear them all down. After a week of dodging those posters, I decided to go for it.

The audition was in three days, so I still had time for self-dissuasion. That night Nick came over and we went downtown, met Asten, and then faded into our romantic, black-hearted love triangle: Nick, me, and heroin. We used all of Friday and even Saturday morning, the day of the audition.

I went to the Manhattan Gym, and, despite being well medicated, was still a shaking mess, terrified of reentering the temple I had desecrated. I had pledged never to return, but my legs carried me toward some desperate hope for change.

Huge windows lined the gym overlooking the Hudson River, and seeing the equipment through the glass made me want to turn back. Instead, I walked through the double doors and headed toward the "Audition Here" sign, though I interpreted it as a warning sign that said, "Joe, you're an ultimate failure. Go home." I stood in the back of the room and watched a few guys stretching before signing my name to the audition list; I had to study the situation before committing to the audition. Looking over the silent, warm bodies on the floor, in a state of meditation with their muscles, I envied and loathed them. The woman behind the desk asked for my resume and headshot. High on heroin, with a thick cloak of cigarette smoke around me and my Boston accent, I responded with "What the fuck is a headshot?" She was not amused.

I proceeded to the warm-up room, but when I recognized two guys from my gymnastics past, my feared humiliation began. Did they know what had happened to me? Did they know of my drug-fueled madness and destruction at Staunton? And now, years later, with two large holes pierced through my ears, on heroin, there I was, trying to audition for wholesome-as-American-pie Disneyland. I felt busted even though no one had seen me, let alone recognized me. Even worse, one guy from my past was helping to run the audition. Would he be judging me on all levels? The headshot woman said, "Okay, Mr. Put-Ig-Nano, you can get in line with those guys." I looked at her coldly, not because I didn't like her or for mispronouncing my name, but because I was having a mental breakdown.

I laughed, shook my head, grabbed my coat, and stormed out the door, hailing a taxi to go back to Nick, who was on my couch, nodding out from the heroin that was holding his bones together. I did a huge line and curled up next to him, pushing the shame and self-hatred away, placing that memory where all my other bad memories went.

Nick felt my body next to his and asked in a cool, raspy voice, "How did it go?" I told him I hurt my Achilles tendon while warming up, knowing that from his years of football he'd understand no one could tumble with an injured Achilles. A tear fell from my eye. Nick couldn't understand why I was so emotional over a hurt tendon. And I couldn't tell him how gymnastics equipment was the stone foundation of my church, how the high bar and the pommel horse had shaped and molded me, and how I loved them. The way a painter falls in love with his paint and a dancer loves movement, I loved gymnastics but had repeatedly condemned my church before my God. I had set one foot back in my holy place, only to feel rejected by its spirit. My heroin, however, would never reject me or cause me such humiliation. Heroin would hold me in its warm embrace, and in return I entrusted it to fill me with the light of God and protect me. Nick and I shared that love, and our love was perfect. I would never know a relationship as deep or as powerful. My dreams weren't crushed, because I didn't have nor did I want any.

Since I wasn't going to Disneyland, I decided to go back to school. That summer Nick and I went downtown and applied to the community college for the fall semester. I was happy and couldn't wait to start, figuring that school would help me stop using heroin. I didn't feel like I had a problem since I was only sniffing it, and I knew I would never use needles. I loved body piercing, but sticking a needle in one's arm to get high seemed like a sad, dead-end road.

Vic and I hung out more often and our friendship quickly grew stronger, as most friendships do with drugs. She would stay the night and we would use heroin together. I got to know her on a deeper level, and she disclosed her horrible eating disorders. That information sealed the deal for our friendship. We were the same—both with our personal demons that wanted to use us, kill us, and never allow us to know peace. She would never question my disease and I would never question hers, both of us accepting each other's destruction. She was never addicted to heroin like me; she only did it to make herself throw up. She had been repeatedly hospitalized, intubated, and force-fed. We were fallen angels expelled from heaven; only God knew why we had to keep living like that.

As I started using more, I started feeling sick coming off my highs. Asten told me to buy a bottle of methadone and sip it for a few days, and it would get me through between sniffs. I got a few backup bottles from him, and didn't mention it to Darren or Nick. The deep-red, strong elixir did the trick. With a methadone chaser, I would never have to face the sickness again.

School was annoying. It interfered with my drug use, and I could never wake up for my early-morning classes. I needed to get help. An ad in the back of the *Village Voice* said "HELP: HEROIN," so I called the number and got the Substance Treatment and Research Service of Columbia University. I went to the STARS clinic and was told the detox used Klonopin, and after that I would be put on naltrexone, an opiate antagonist, to block the effects of heroin. But I had to be abstinent for fourteen days before starting the naltrexone pills. If I took them while opiates were still in my body, I'd go into immediate withdrawal and get an illness worse than being dope sick. That scared me. I didn't like the idea of detoxing off heroin with Klonopin—one pill would send me off on a horrible bender with unknowable repercussions. I found another place in Greenwich Village that offered group therapy and one-on-one counseling. I decided to give it a shot.

Asten was also going through a rough time. He got kicked out of his Upper West Side apartment and moved back to Forty-ninth Street. I hated calling him there, because some woman would answer the phone and call me "Chico" in her raspy voice. I didn't even care if she knew Asten was my heroin dealer.

At the end of that fall I got terrible news: Asten, my faithful drug dealer, was leaving New York to enter recovery in Arizona. I was happy for him, but unhappy for me. I took that as a sign and believed without Asten around to supply the drugs, I too would be able to stop using. How else would I get heroin?

The door between heaven and Earth was closing. The whole gang bid farewell to our heroin use and closed the opening of the well. I continued with school and was happy to do something besides waiting tables. The air around us changed; it was getting colder. I wasn't seeing Nick as much, but continued to hang out with Vic and Darren. We were all secretly pissed that Asten was gone and thought he would come back someday—but he didn't.

29

FIBULA

FIBULA IS DERIVED FROM THE LATIN WORD *figo*, MEANING
"TO FASTEN," AND DENOTES A BUCKLE, BROOCH, OR CLASP.
THE RELATIONSHIP OF THE FIBULA TO THE TIBIA IS THAT OF
THE NEEDLE TO THE BROOCH — A SKELETAL FASTENER.

A few weeks of abstinence had gone by and I was free from the
restraints of heroin. I physically felt better; no more runny nose and
achy bones. Using made me feel as if I had a constant cold or flu.
Even though I had not used heroin in a while, I was not completely
opiate-free. I endured a botched root canal and was experiencing
extreme pain, which gave me a new hobby: dentists. I would find
different dentists, show them my tooth, lie about the pain, and then
receive medication. Afterward, I would make an appointment to
fix the problem and never show up, traveling to another dentist to
repeat the cycle. I was getting Vicodin, Percocet, Roxicet, Endocet,
and Tylenol with codeine, which was my least favorite. I would take
about fifteen to twenty pills and go to work, trying to catch the same
feeling I got from heroin.

Vic was my only remaining drug ally; she would smoke pot with
me and talk about how we could find a new heroin connection now
that Asten had moved away. We thought maybe it was possible to
randomly ask people on the subway who were obviously nodding
out. Or we could go to a club and ask around, but fear kept us from
going through with any of those scenarios. I told her about Asten's
old roommate, the odd woman who answered the phone whenever

I called him to buy drugs. She was the secretary for the damned. Maybe it was possible to call her to see if she knew someone.

Vic and I figured we would at least try to find someone else, but we still didn't have a solid plan. Should we just call this woman we didn't know and ask if she knew someone who could get us heroin? Did people do those sorts of things? Vic begged me to call the woman, but I couldn't because I was terrified. What was I going to say? "Um, hello . . . I don't know if you remember me, but I am Asten's friend. Um, he used to get me heroin; can you get me some?" But that is exactly what I did, though when I said the word "heroin" she quickly said "coffee," letting me know her code word to use on the phone. Yes, it was coffee I wanted and coffee I was after. She sounded inebriated, with a hoarse voice, as if she had begun smoking in utero. She said I would have to buy her a bag for getting me one. I didn't have a problem with that, and we made plans to meet in Hell's Kitchen.

The joy of finding a new dealer after weeks of forced abstinence felt like Christmas. Vicky and I stumbled over each other to catch a cab and told the driver to go to the Coffee Pot at Forty-ninth and Ninth. Upon our arrival I scanned the tables, going over each person, wondering which one held the golden key to my nirvana. I spotted a woman staring down at the floor as if she were going to start a fight with the tile. She was chubby and disheveled, and had a bandana wrapped around her head. She was dressed in oversized men's clothing, with large eyes, greenish skin, and beads of sweat dripping from her forehead. Her hand was tightly wrapped around a black cane that had taken its own beating. Our eyes met and I prayed to God it wasn't her, but of course it was, and she waved to me and said loudly, disturbing the quiet environment, "Hey you, Chico, over here!"

Oh no, oh God, it is her, I thought as I smiled and happily waved back. I anxiously walked over to the table and sat down, acting like we were longtime friends. The heroin had soullessly united us. It was critical to establish a friendship with this woman because she would be replacing Asten's role in my life, and I couldn't afford to lose that connection.

Vicky joined us at the table and we talked about random things. It was around two o'clock in the afternoon and the woman, named Kimi, was blind, stinking drunk. The vodka burned off her breath like a chemical fire, making my eyes water. She circled the table while the sweat continued to trail down her face, despite her sopping it up with a dirty, tattered, plaid handkerchief. She was making me nauseous, and I wanted to hose her down. The awkward moment came when I had to exchange the money for drugs, but it was a smooth transaction because we were both professionals and well educated in the field. I told Kimi I'd be right back and left Vicky alone with the insane woman. I got high in the bathroom, and it tasted as good as I'd remembered.

When I came back to the table, the effects had begun to hit me, and all that I had thought was hideous about Kimi changed. In my high, her sweat didn't seem gross, and what I saw before me was a kindhearted woman with a cane. In my euphoria, her wide eyes sparkled and everything she said was funny. Maybe I had misunderstood her earlier. Vicky and I said our good-byes, took a cab back to the Upper East Side, and broke the news to Darren about our new contact, bringing back an extra bag to soften the blow. Though the bond between Darren and me had been sealed through drugs, over time those drugs would become the poison that destroyed our longtime friendship.

I was the only one allowed to go over to Kimi's apartment to pick up the heroin. Dealing with her was difficult because she was a complete disaster. Even though I would speak with her on the phone an hour before I was due to arrive, she would answer the door in an alcohol-induced blackout and not be able to remember why I was there. In her drunken paranoia, she would hide the heroin somewhere in her destroyed apartment, and we would have to dig through trash to find it. When you're dope sick, the urgency to use heroin is extreme. The fact that the heroin was lost in her apartment and she couldn't find it was like being in that cartoon of a cat surrounded by hundreds of cans of tuna without a can opener.

Kimi lived in a one-bedroom apartment hidden beneath the clothes of her girlfriend Eva, a petite, abused Greek woman who was experimenting with her sexuality at the ripe age of forty. She had had a terrible past with crack and switched to heroin when she moved in with Kimi. Their relationship was beyond dysfunctional and always seemed to be in some sort of a crazy, codependent crisis. It was obvious to me that Eva had been abused many times in the past, and the glue that held their relationship together was the sticky sap from the opium flower. They were always fighting, but Eva never argued with Kimi; instead she responded as if she were a baby, complete with childlike tone, weeping before her mother. Kimi had infantilized this woman into a little, abused girl and played the roles of both the abuser and the manly protector. Kimi was the threat and the hero. I don't know what kind of romance they had, but I believed Eva was not a lesbian. Rather, she was a diehard drug addict who would become whatever anyone needed—something I related to. This allowed her to get close to the source that kept her alive, but man, what a price to pay! Some say people who marry for money earn it, and I guess it's the same for people who marry for heroin, because to be in the same room with Kimi was like waltzing with a poltergeist.

Kimi had her own terrible past, and on the shelf of her dusty apartment was a copy of Sylvia Plath's *The Bell Jar*, next to a copy of *Alcoholics Anonymous* (also known as the Big Book). The familiarity of that book stuck out like the hand of God reaching through the darkness and chaos of the room; however, we all ignored it. Back in the 1980s, when Kimi worked, she got into a bad car accident, resulting in the now-infamous cane that she never walked without. She had seen many doctors since then and had perplexed them all; they could find no reason for her back pain.

If I had been dying from a rare disease and the cure was to hang out in that apartment, I wouldn't have been able to do it; but I endured that kind of madness for my heroin. The more I stayed, the less frightening Kimi and Eva's place seemed. Was I becoming more like the apartment, or was the apartment becoming more like me? I needed to get high in their bathroom just to be able to make small talk with the two of them.

One day I was in Kimi's room and a huge box of syringes fell out from behind the wooden doors of her closet, which were cracked open. It freaked me out because I assumed that she sniffed the drug like I did. I asked Kimi how often she used heroin and she said, "Only on occasion," because she was a lifer on methadone. The amount of methadone she needed was too high for the heroin's effects to break through, but if she skipped a day or two of methadone, she could feel it. Every day she hobbled from her cave with her cane, scuttling over from Eleventh to Tenth Avenue to the methadone clinic next to Duane Reade. If I couldn't find Kimi at her apartment, I would walk up Tenth Avenue and see her hanging out with her clan of methadone addicts, waiting in line. They all had canes of their own, and for a moment, when they were all gathered together, it looked like the dead had crawled out of their graves to form a line in front of the drugstore. Kimi would never get off methadone, and in a sad way her life enslaved her to the red liquid and confined her to the island of Manhattan. That was why I had to be careful whenever I detoxed myself. *Never take too much methadone over a long period of time,* I warned myself, or I would end up with my own cane in that same line. I wondered who used those needles up in her closet, and then the thought darted into my mind, *How much worse could it be? I've already died twice.*

I had been recently kicked out of my group meetings at the halfway house because I kept relapsing; they required at least thirty days of abstinence, and I couldn't even maintain a full week without using. I continued to see my counselor Derrick and enjoyed talking to him. He saw past my addiction and told me if I could manage to stay in recovery, my life would blossom. He believed that somewhere inside me lived a good guy who had the potential to do something positive with his life. I didn't believe him, but I wanted to. He said things that shot straight into my heart. "Joe, if you are serious about recovery and you truly don't want to use, you will have to leave your boyfriend because the relationship has become codependent." *Leave Nick? Was he crazy? After all we had been through together—homelessness, rehabs, mental institutions—how could I leave him? I loved him, and couldn't imagine a life without him.* Derrick continued, "Neither of you will get into recovery if you stay together. Your addiction ties you together, and you have been through so much that a bond has been created through the trauma of your lives." That made sense to me, but the thought of leaving Nick was unbearable.

Derrick was constantly bringing up the past and my gymnastics glory days when I trained at the camp at the Olympic Training Center. "Don't you know how much you accomplished at such a young age? You know that potential still lives within you." I didn't want to talk about gymnastics again, and the memories of those times made me want to bust open a vein right there in his small therapy cubicle. Even though I secretly thought about the sport, and longed for it, I would never admit it, because I'd failed. And every day, for the rest of my life, no matter what I did, I would be a failure. I continued to see Derrick because he spoke the truth, and I was so far from honesty that I needed to have a dose of it in my life or I would have forgotten what it was.

New Year's Eve was approaching, and I had invited many of my old friends from Southie to celebrate the week in Manhattan. My roommates were going home to visit their parents for Christmas break, and so I told Piper, my good friend from Boston, to bring as many people as she wanted. She had recently come into a truckload of pills, more than I had ever seen, and when she arrived I bought a hundred Xanax. I vowed not to take any Klonopin, but that went out the window after the first Xanax hit me.

I don't remember New Year's Eve or the entire week after, but somewhere in that madness I spent my rent money on cocaine, ecstasy, pot, pills, beer, and heroin. I have a few memories of that week, but only horrible ones: hailing a cab on the Upper West Side, trying to hit on a straight guy who had killed his girlfriend a week before in a drunk-driving accident, throwing up in my kitchen sink that was full of dishes, and endless stories that Piper comically recalled. When I finally woke up, all my friends had gone. My roommates had returned and accused me of puking in the sink on their dishes without cleaning it up. I denied knowing what they were talking about, even though I was guilty of doing exactly what they accused me of. My recollection of that week was vague, but I was so grateful I didn't end up in jail, even though it would have been much safer than my freedom to roam around in New York City.

∞∞∞∞∞∞∞

Darren began to rethink his life as he saw me spiral down a destructive path of debauchery and full-blown addiction. He decided to move back to Virginia to start over and to remove himself from the drugs and crazy lifestyle they brought. I felt terribly alone when he left.

Nick wasn't visiting that much because of his work schedule, and Vicky had started her classes at a school in New Jersey. I was sniffing a lot of heroin and trying not to use before school. I had an early-morning biology class and would go out into the city's freezing-cold winter, sniffling and dizzy, and get on a packed subway car downtown to Chambers Street. Once on the street, I paused before the Twin Towers for a moment, in awe of their ascension into the sky, before continuing to walk to school while cursing the morning and the happy people in the streets drinking their coffees. Those early morning risers' ability to pull themselves together amazed me, and I figured they must be using cocaine since their appearance was so well put together. After class I would go home, get high, paint on my wall, and wish that all those I had fought with would return. Sometimes I snuck into my roommate's room to steal a bunch of her Ambien to catch a buzz, but I had hit a plateau from all the medications I continued to ingest. The drugs were no longer doing what they used to do for me. It was getting harder and harder to erase the pain of my reality.

One day I left for school during one of the city's rare snowstorms when the snow actually stuck to the ground. It was difficult to walk on the slushy sidewalks, and my socks were drenched from the numbingly cold, melted ice. Every pay phone I passed screamed at me: "CALL KIMI . . . and end this dreadful day with warm, beautiful light!" I tried to avoid them, tried to get to my classes clean and unharmed, but there were too many pay phones. Before I reached my building I was dialing her number in desperation: the storm had won. Kimi answered the phone and told me I needed to rush back to her apartment because the guy who drops off the bags was going home early due to the storm. Apparently even drug dealers have snow days. I fled to her apartment as if my life depended on it.

Kimi opened the door, telling me to come in. The room was ice-cold and it didn't smell as bad as it had before; winter's air had frozen the stench of body odor and trash. Her closet door was still ajar, and I saw that box of syringes sticking out like a song whose tune I knew, but not its title. When she came back with my stuff, I said cautiously, "Sniffing isn't really working for me anymore . . . is there something I can do to make it better?"

I heard a sound in the distance, beyond us. I continued, "It's not making me as high as it used to and I still feel pain in my body." Kimi knew I was fishing for an intravenous fix, pushing her to introduce the title of that song I could not recall. I heard that sound again, as if something otherworldly were pushing its way through a vortex. I said, before she could say anything, "I want to shoot it." Again, that damn sound. *What was it? Why couldn't she hear it? Is the sound coming from me?*

She said, alarmingly, "Oh, Chico . . . really? No, you don't want to do that . . . do you?" She was warning me, but also tempting me. I could hear her despair pleading against her own voice, even though her words were the opposite of what she was thinking and wanted. She needed me to fall victim to that mess for her own selfish reasons. If I fell, then she would appear to be taller and it would justify her own madness and place in her chaotic life. It would be financially beneficial for Kimi to have me strung out, because she would make money off every order I placed.

I was in pain and ready to go deeper into the high, and confidently said, "I'm ready! Snorting hasn't been doing what it used to do for me, and I've always wanted to see what slamming dope was all about." She said, "Okay, but I'm going to skin pop it for you," trying to conceal a smile.

"What's skin popping?" I asked.

"It's when you inject it into a part of fat on your body, like the back of your arm, or even your ass. Oh . . . Chico, you have such nice arms; you don't want to mark them!"

But I did. I wanted to dig holes into them like a prisoner gone mad in his cell, trying to crawl his way out through the ground, to show the world my scars, evidence of my battles lost. I wanted to defile the flesh that once covered my thick, muscular arms from all those years of gymnastics.

She said, grinning, with a warning in her thick Spanglish accent, "Chico, promise me something, okay? . . . Never mainline this . . . never stick it directly into your veins."

"Okay, I promise," I said, happy that I was about to walk through another dimension.

She grabbed the box down from the closet and took out a few syringes. She continued with my lesson. "These are all new needles. I use this gauge; it's bigger, but you could probably use this size, that's what Eva uses." She held up the syringe with a bright orange cap and base. I couldn't tell what gauge she was using, but I would find all that out in time.

"So first we fill it with water, up to the 20 cc or 30 cc mark; it doesn't really matter. Then we carefully push out the water onto the spoon, and open the bag and drop the powder onto it. You can do it the other way around, but sometimes you spray the powder off from the force of the water. Then you gently shake it around in a circle while lighting the bottom."

In that moment I saw her for what she was. She was an ancient sorceress with the power to travel between worlds, and heroin was her potion. By the lit flame under the spoon, her eyes focused down on the brown liquid that gently smoked, and a scent arose from the fluid in the spoon. Her eyes never left the concoction, for she knew if she spilled even a drop, all hope would be lost.

"Then you drop the cotton into it to suck up all the impurities. If you don't have a cotton swab you can take the inside of a cigarette filter and tear a piece off . . . that works too." The small, white cotton hung from her sweaty fingers, and she carefully placed it into the murky brown substance. "Then tip this down into the center of the cotton." She purposely avoided the word *syringe,* as if saying the word out loud would disgrace the woman she believed she was.

"Now, Chico, slowly pull the liquid up the tube. It should be nice and brown like this. Then flick it to make sure the bubbles are out. You'll never get it perfect, but don't worry, those tiny bubbles won't kill you. Okay, Papi, straighten your arm."

Then she grabbed my arm underneath my triceps where there is a little fat deposit, and said, "Breathe out," and pushed the needle into my skin. It didn't hurt as she pushed the fluid into my body.

Like a professional nurse, she said, "It will take a few minutes to hit when you skin pop it, but if you mainline it, it takes six to eight seconds." As she was talking, I watched the snow fall from her fire escape. I wasn't sure what was going to happen, if she had even done it right, if I would feel anything, but I kept watching the snow and thought of my mother. My hands were still cold from outdoors and my socks were wet from the weather. Suddenly there was a loud sound—again, she didn't seem to hear it—like hooves on her kitchen floor, as if a giant animal had stepped into our space. I turned my head quickly, but saw nothing. I could smell the deep scent of cinnamon and ash.

Then I felt it, immediately spreading through my body like perfect heat entering my bloodstream. That feeling was a thousand times stronger than when I sniffed heroin. I was so hot, and there was a fire burning in my veins. The euphoria boiled up to a point in the middle of my head and escalated to dimensions I had never believed possible. It got stronger, and I became the fire, eternal and powerful, burning bright with absolute bliss. My eyelids became heavy with weights pulling them down into the underworld. I comfortably fell back onto Kimi's burnt futon, a surface I would have never lain on before. My eyes closed tightly, and then I felt it from within: the most magnificent hands touching my flesh, solid and powerful. Each touch sent shivers up my spine, wrapping me in a timeless moment, back to a fetal state, protected in the womb. Nothing would ever be this perfect, and I didn't dare open my eyes for fear that my sight would destroy the intensity.

Again, the hands covered my body, knowing each part of my physique. Yes, it was God, and the hands were lapping around my flesh and my soul. God was cradling me, touching the heart of my being and plucking my spirit from my body as we swayed back and forth together. Our energies intertwined through soft circuits of light. I was making love with God, and we blissfully walked through each other's beings. I saw everything, felt everything, and our small, ethereal mass flew up to the sky, spreading itself across the stars, absorbing the energy and power of the universe. The warm currents from the eyes of the Earth shot through me like rivers of orgasmic emotions quivering through my body. All my chakras opened and everything expanded. An intense itch covered my face, but I couldn't move my arms, because moving them would change this mosaic pattern. The hands continued to hold me, and I heard a voice that was more like a symphony. It said, "Look at me, Joe!"

"No, I can't. I'm afraid I will lose this feeling."

"Don't be afraid. I'll never let you go. I want you. I've always wanted you; you were one of my favorites. I remember when you were made flesh, and now we will always be together." Its voice was the quiver of a bow striking a violin, beautifully sweeping down and across the strings.

I said again, "Don't let go of me; I'm afraid of the pain. It never stops. It's always there. It's killing me."

"I love you, Joe, and I'll hold you forever. I've touched your soul. I've been waiting for you to call upon me, to open this door, and finally . . . I have you in my arms, and I will never let you go. I have your soul."

The pronunciation of the word "soul" came from an angry instrument and sent drumbeats of fear rippling through my body. That couldn't be God. I wanted to open my eyes and see who was holding me, and finally gained the courage to look. I wanted to see the face of God while it spoke in its mystical voice, and then I opened my eyes and saw the being that held me. It was the Devil.

"You're not God," I said in desperate confusion.

"No, I'm not," it agreed, holding me tighter in its grasp, wrapping its arms around my body as its hands changed into inescapable claws. I was powerless in its arms, and I heard a macabre laughter altering that beautiful, orchestrated voice. It was no longer angelic, but a terrible halting noise, mimicking the sound of a train wreck, or a horrible car accident that claimed the lives of humans. Its breath was like raw earth. It was beautiful, more beautiful than I imagined the Devil to be, almost perfect, except for its terrifying voice. I struggled and said, "Let me go; please!"

"Never! I've been waiting for you for many years. I thought I'd lost you a few years back, but you found the keys to my kingdom in that syringe. I will carry you away from all that pains you. I am the solution, the answer to all your prayers. Don't be afraid of me, I'm not evil. I just want you to stay with me forever."

"What do you want from me? Please let me go!"

"Nothing. I just don't ever want you to leave me. Stay with me forever, and I promise to make you feel good for the rest of your life. I love you, Joe. I'm the only one who truly loves you."

It leaned forward and kissed me tenderly on the forehead. I tried to yell and fight back, but my eyes opened and I saw myself staring at Kimi's ceiling. *It was just a dream,* I thought, and wiped a layer of sweat off my forehead. It almost seemed for a moment that I had stopped breathing. Kimi saw me stirring by the window adjacent to the fire escape with the fallen snow and said, "Chico! How do you feel?" Her eyes glimmered with a dark-red hue, as if she were perfectly pleased: another soul claimed for the Devil's embrace. Was she able to stay out of hell by escorting others across the threshold?

She asked again, "Do you feel good?"

I looked her dead in her eyes and said, "Yes. I don't ever want this feeling to end and I want to live in this memory forever."

30

PLATELETS

THE BLOOD CLOT IS ONLY A TEMPORARY SOLUTION
TO STOP BLEEDING; VESSEL REPAIR IS THEREFORE NEEDED.
THE AGGREGATED PLATELETS HELP THIS PROCESS BY
SECRETING CHEMICALS THAT PROMOTE THE INVASION
OF FIBROBLASTS FROM SURROUNDING CONNECTIVE
TISSUE INTO THE WOUNDED AREA TO FORM A SCAR.

I lay on my loft bed, high as a cloud, staring out my window that faced a brick wall. My room resembled an Egyptian tomb, and my love was the curse over Nick. He managed to get a couple of days off from work and came to visit me. I was so happy to see him after feeling so alone, his schedule keeping us apart. My love returned to me even after I had begun to put tiny needle marks on my body. He noticed small, circular bruises coloring the skin under my arm and asked me what happened. Obviously it was from my new adventures with Kimi, but he hadn't noticed it before. I told him I must have fallen into something, and this seemed to quiet his curiosity. I quickly changed the subject to something we both wanted to do: heroin.

We got our bags from Kimi, but instead of running to the bathroom with my straw, I went with my syringe, my sharpened sword, ready for battle. I was going to inject it in the fat in my butt because it was less noticeable than the arm. Nick asked me what took me so long in the bathroom; it took me longer to cook and shoot it than to sniff it. I told him I got sick and that my stomach was upset. He seemed suspicious, but after his own high had hit, he completely forgot about what he had asked me.

Nick was the sloppiest heroin user I had ever met. I'm not sure if it is because of all the training I had as a gymnast, or if it was the strong tolerance I had for the drug, but I managed to have more control over the effects than Nick did. We would take the subway back to my apartment on the Upper East Side, holding the metal poles while standing. Nick would be falling asleep on two feet, in midconversation, drooling on himself. I was constantly yelling at him, telling him that he couldn't do that in public, but every five minutes it would happen again. I'm sure I brought more attention to the situation than his calm, drowsy stance did, but he would do it everywhere; sometimes at dinner in a restaurant, while he was ordering his entrée, his eyes would roll back in his head and then his body would slump forward, as if he had narcolepsy. I would finish his order, and the puzzled waiter would shake his head. Nick and I were dreadful together. The two of us were a horrible pair.

But Nick would somehow pull it together where it seemed to matter, like at school and work. I was so envious and bitter that I could not do this. I could pull it together for the high alone, but failed in all other areas of my life. Nick was an exceptional worker and student. He never missed classes, got excellent grades, and would never call in sick for a shift. I was the complete opposite. I was doing poorly in school and, for the life of me, I couldn't figure out why.

I was trying to concentrate on the assignments in class, but I was rotting inside and could only concentrate on heroin. I would have to leave class to get high and then return completely out of my mind, trying to focus on the subject at hand. In my biology class I had a lab partner, and the poor girl could not figure out why she had to constantly explain what we had done the day before. She seemed confused as to why I couldn't remember where the microscope was kept, or the safety goggles, or everything else that she had explained to me over and over again. She didn't realize I was doing my own biology experiment, which was failing. I wanted to be a good student so badly. I thought if I did well, Nick would see that I could do other things and not just be a perfect drug addict. I wanted him to see the good qualities in me and to be proud of me.

In the end I got kicked out of college—once again—because of my drug use. In a way, I was happy I didn't have to go to class anymore; it was just getting in the way of the highs I wanted and needed. I didn't like my teachers, and I wasn't learning what I wanted to. The best part was that I no longer had to go down to Canal Street during that horrible, cold morning commute.

The time had come to move on to the next stage of my odyssey. I had climbed the great stairs of drug abuse and was ready to walk through the iron door—the door that had been scratched with warnings and prayers, had been stained with blood, fingernail markings, and the broken lives and dreams it had stolen. If you pressed your ear close enough to the iron handle, you could hear the screams of the souls it had already taken. I was bored with skin popping, and I wanted a higher high. I wanted more, and that deep smell of burnt cinnamon and ash pulled me to it. I wanted it in my veins. I wanted my body to become the map of stars over our heads, with my new needle holes and track marks forming the very constellations that astronomers search for—my future mapped out on my skin. I knew the place I wanted to mark first: the keyhole through the iron door. I had a deep vein below my biceps, a throbbing river over my muscle and bone. That vein was only there to be marked, to be opened for this very purpose. It was thick, intrusive, and all mine.

I cooked up the heroin as I had been shown, the thick, brown potion that boiled in my spoon. The spoon I used to eat with now fed my arms and thirsty veins. I drew the hot liquid into the needle, its tip so fine and sharp. I rubbed the spot on my arm with alcohol, a clean, medicinal smell somehow altering the macabre moment into a sterile environment that allowed my mind to justify what I was about to do. I was simply going to take my medicine as prescribed. I held the needle over the vein at an angle and plunged it into the river of blood. It was painless, sensational, and I pulled back the plunger as a dazzling display of blood danced into the heroin.

It ignited in the syringe like a liquid firecracker, thrashing through the brown, watery sky in its maroon magnificence. I was prepared to throw that firecracker into my bloodstream to re-explode in my brain, and I pushed the enigmatic fluid into my arm. I pushed and heard the deep hinges of the iron door opening, and wild wind swept through my hair. The vein bled as soon as I removed the needle. I wiped the blood away with the alcohol swab, and within seconds felt a tsunami of fire burning through my body. It was so hot, so good, wrapping me and holding me, clenching my spine, swirling to the tips of my tongue with such a pure, exquisite euphoria. This was the ultimate—the alpha and the omega.

There was no waiting, and the high was so much more intense than skin popping. This was it, the key to life, and I would never live without it again. In a crashing sound of cosmic bliss through the iron door, God returned. The room swirled around as God held me and cradled my body in his endless arms and gently covered my skin in tender kisses. Sweet and sublime, the sounds of each song in his voice told me everything was going to be all right. He rocked me like he had done in the womb and I was bathed in white light, never to return to the world without that tender armor.

I believed the feeling in that moment contained more peace than some people experience in an entire lifetime. I could smell and taste life all around me. God danced through me, making love to my cells, flesh, and bones, and our souls united again and again. In that moment I was the most powerful human being who ever existed. That odd smell returned to me, burnt cinnamon and ash, but I ceased to worry about its origin. My eyes shut and I went back to the place I had come from, back to the beginning of the music. If it hadn't been for my loyal heart pumping my blood, I would gladly have died in that moment. I would be okay with leaving Earth and my body because I was finally satisfied and felt finished. Like warm winds in a summer dusk, the feelings slowly escaped my bloodstream and mind.

I had found a new hobby, but I had to keep it a secret. I knew the spot on my body I would hit again like a dog marking its territory. That fat vein below my biceps, where my arm bent, was the target. The more heroin I used, the more I needed to work, because I was burning through money. I had to pick up an extra shift at Gabriel's to be able to afford my new hobby. I never had any reservations about using at work. I believed nobody really noticed if I was high because I had such amazing control over my physical functions. I imagine a few people at work knew something was not quite right with me, but it was New York City and everyone was eccentric and unique, with their own set of bizarre baggage. I felt a sick sort of pride taking orders from the overprivileged, rich Upper East Siders while ruined on heroin. My dirty secret contaminated their perfect, crystal-clear, wine-glassy lives, poking their enchanting dinner conversation with a needle.

One day we had a particularly full Saturday brunch. The weekend brunches were busy from 8:00 a.m. to 4:00 p.m. Table after table would fill up with a thunderous wave of demanding New Yorkers yapping about their hangovers and eggs. I had been so swamped with customers that I hadn't left my station in hours. I was wearing a dirty but pressed white Ralph Lauren button-up polo shirt and a solid green apron that tied tightly around my body. In our apron pockets we fit our mandatory sterling-silver wine keys, pens, and pads of paper to take orders. However, my apron had other things in it. I had a used spoon, stained from cooking, and a syringe.

A few times during a mad rush I had almost pulled out the syringe to write an order with, and it had almost spilled out on the table while I was searching for my wine key. I usually tried holding off on using until after my shift was over, but on that day my feet ached and I was consumed with terrible anxiety. Earlier I had messed up a table's order and forgot to enter a customer's item, and he had to wait forty-five minutes for an omelet. I couldn't handle it anymore and asked a coworker to cover my tables, telling her I had to go to the bathroom. The bathroom was pristine, with a huge mirror and wallpaper that had an exaggerated flower pattern on it. I used the sink counter as my table and prepared my own omelet.

I had to do this quickly, because being away from my section for a few minutes could alter the course of the day, and it would take hours to fix a mistake. I cooked the liquid in my spoon, smelling the sweet bouquet of heroin rise over the aroma of pumpkin waffles and coffee. I rolled up my white sleeves to reveal that beautiful vein, the median cephalic vein that swells up through the skin on our arms. My veins were like a dazzling gold mine ready for digging, I held the syringe and saw myself stick it into my arm in the huge wall mirror. I felt regret for a minute, with my whole body contained in the reflection, seeing myself first as a boy, hopelessly trying to be a champion in the number-one spot in gymnastics, then flashing to the present time: a sad man in a busy Upper East Side restaurant, with all the world outside the door, eating, laughing, and enjoying life.

I wasn't paying attention to my craftsmanship, and I pushed the needle too far into my arm and felt a large pain. I went too deep that time, and tried again. I slanted the needle, concentrating on my precision, gently entering the needle, painlessly, like a professional, and there we went—we had liftoff. I pulled the wild, colored blood back into the swampy brown heroin. This heroin was gonna be good because it was darker than normal, almost blackish. I pushed the liquid into my vein, sending a surge of energy throughout my limbs, and that memory of me as a boy vanished. I didn't need to be an Olympian or a college graduate, because now I was Hercules, strong and powerful, beautiful and eternal.

There was a huge bang on the door, and I remembered my tables. I had to get back out there, now. I didn't wipe the blood from my arm, but simply rolled down my sleeves, broke the tip of the needle so nobody could prick themselves, wrapped it in toilet paper, and threw it in the trash. I flushed the wax paper and heroin remains down the toilet: a sad good-bye as they swirled and spun to their death. I ran back out in an opiate haze.

Two new table groups sat down with smiles, happy that their hour-long wait for brunch was over. I couldn't believe people would wait that long for food. I pulled out my pen and started to take their order when I saw that, through my dirty, pressed, white tuxedo shirt, my blood was starting to seep through. The blood was brilliant, like a Rorschach test a psychologist would show to his patients. "What does this blot tell you, doctor?" It bled through the white shirtsleeve, perfectly over the top of my vein, forming a nice maroon pool.

I was distracted by the smiling girl's order for "seven-grain toast . . . and I would like jam, not that strawberry jam, I want something different, like peach, raspberry, or blueberry, or something nice." *Of course you do, sweetie*, I thought to myself. *Would you like a bloodstain on your toast as well, ma'am?* How I wanted to drip blood on the table to ruin their perfect breakfast. But I held it together and kept my arm bent to hold back the blood.

The girl's annoying order for non-strawberry jam gave me an idea. I would just smear some jam on my shirt, over the bloodstain. It wouldn't look perfect, but it could act as somewhat of an explanation. I took some dark blueberry jam and worked it into the crease where my arm bent, squishing it into the blood. It worked; no more bloodstain, and the blood had finally clotted on its own.

Things at my apartment had been rocky between my roommate and me due to the side effect of my new diet of mainlining heroin following a Xanax, which led me to unconsciousness. My roommate asked me to leave. I stayed with a friend who lived a few streets away, until she too asked me to leave, for the very same reasons. I had become a rare, toxic poison that was quickly absorbed through the pores of those around me. At first people didn't see it, but when they lived with me, I quickly contaminated their systems.

Once again I had no place to live; but, luckily, one of my coworkers, Kip, told me he had a room available on Forty-seventh Street between Ninth and Tenth Avenues. I couldn't believe how perfect that location was, because my drug dealer lived at Forty-ninth and Eleventh. I wouldn't have to take a cab anymore all the way down from the Upper East Side, and the money I saved on cab fare I could spend on dope. The rent was affordable, and I liked Kip a lot. He was a tall, slender man with a giant smile. Kip and his boyfriend, Keith, were aspiring Broadway actors and wanted to sing on the Big White Way some day. I knew nothing about musicals, and the very thought of them made me cringe.

I moved in with them. They had been together for a long time and had an enthusiastic, fun lifestyle that was nothing like my own. They gave me my own space, and I would sometimes hang out with them. They had no idea what I was up to, although I would shoot up in their bathroom with only a small, wooden door between us. I could hear them talking and laughing just a few feet away while I was sticking a needle in my arm, then would come out of the bathroom in euphoric oblivion.

Both Kip and Keith knew I had had a problem with drugs, but thought that I had straightened it out long ago. I felt bad about lying to them—they had been so kind, letting me into their living space. But I was too sick and scared to risk losing another place to sleep by telling them the truth. I also liked living in their apartment the most out of all the places I had lived in New York City thus far. It was in the Hell's Kitchen area and felt more like living in the city than the dreary Upper East Side. The neighborhood felt gritty and cool, mesmerizing to even the most jaded of junkies like myself. I could get high, smoke a cigarette, sit on my stoop, and watch the city unfold for hours.

The energy of Kip and Keith was infectious, and it helped me reevaluate my own life. They were happy together and had been with each other for such a long time. I knew my relationship with Nick would never come around to that stage. I would always be a secret in his life, and I couldn't live like that anymore. The more he was away, the more I ran to my other boyfriend: heroin. I didn't know what to do without Nick; he was the perfect guy for me. He put up with my unusual personality and let me entertain my own madness wherever I was. He laughed when I was in a store and squished and broke candy in its package. He knew that if I ever became a millionaire, I would buy a piano just to push it off a cliff to hear the sound it would make as it crashed. Who else would be entertained by such bizarre fantasies?

But my relationship with Nick was crumbling, and the last few times I had seen him he knew I was in bad shape. Those mysterious bruises had made their way onto my veins. The blue, green, and violet colors coordinated with the violence of my syringe. I knew Nick wanted out of the relationship. He wanted to do more with his life, and I was the heavy weight holding him back. After weeks of arguing and me watching him pull away, we broke up. Or rather, he left me.

I was devastated, and the loss sent me into an oblivion of Xanax, alcohol, methadone, and heroin. On the ensuing two-week bender, I left my safety net and ventured out into the city. The drugs helped me get over my fear of strangers, and I was able to visit the many gay bars in our neighborhood. Getting out of my own comfort zone made me realize there could actually be a life beyond Nick, to whose backbone, for years, I had nailed myself. Without him I was scared, but free.

I used until I ran out of money, and when I was finally broke, my body had been beaten to a lumpy pulp. My lungs felt like the insides of a coal furnace from the endless cigarettes I smoked. The place on my arms where I shot up ached, and without the opiates to protect me, I felt everything in my system. Running out of money was a beautiful grace that brought me so low that I decided to go see my counselor, who suggested I go back to twelve-step meetings. He also suggested I try the opiate blocker naltrexone. I thought that would be the cure for my disease. Imagine having something in my system that wouldn't allow me to get high even if I tried. I wanted it, and I was going to give it a shot.

31

THE CENTRAL NERVOUS SYSTEM

POLIOMYELITIS (ALSO CALLED POLIO) IS A CONTAGIOUS, HISTORICALLY DEVASTATING DISEASE OF THE NERVOUS SYSTEM THAT WAS VIRTUALLY ELIMINATED FROM THE WESTERN HEMISPHERE IN THE SECOND HALF OF THE TWENTIETH CENTURY. ALTHOUGH POLIO HAS PLAGUED HUMANS SINCE ANCIENT TIMES, ITS MOST EXTENSIVE OUTBREAK OCCURRED IN THE FIRST HALF OF THE 1900S BEFORE THE VACCINATIONS WERE CREATED BY JONAS SALK, ALBERT SABIN, AND HILARY KOPROWSKI. AT THE HEIGHT OF THE POLIO EPIDEMIC IN 1952, NEARLY 60,000 CASES AND MORE THAN 3,000 DEATHS WERE REPORTED IN THE UNITED STATES ALONE.

My bedroom was Kip and Keith's living room, which I shared with their little white dog, Keys. They lived a life that was completely unfamiliar to me, and I studied the relationship between them. They were caring, loving, enthusiastic, and drug-free. Every morning Keith would wake up to make coffee for everyone, and Kip would come out to sing a song from some musical he loved. I hated musicals and show tunes, but their excitement about those things made me realize that there were other things out there besides heroin. They were always practicing songs and going to auditions. They tried to inspire me to do some form of modeling, which made me laugh because I believed I was a monster—why would anyone want to capture that on camera? I took people's compliments as expressions of their pity for me.

It astonished me to see two gay men happier than any straight couple I'd ever known. Their days were full of accomplishment, while mine were full of failure. I was seeking something other than syringes and spoons, and Kip and Keith recommended I take a dance class, thinking I would pick up the dance steps quickly because of my gymnastics history. The city's energy somehow penetrated my self-made prison and pushed me to take my first class ever. New York has an amazing way of motivating even the dead.

I shot up some dope, put on my exercise clothes, and headed to Broadway Dance Center on Fifty-ninth Street. It was a basic jazz class, and I had no idea what that meant. Everyone was stretching outside the class, silently preparing. They seemed focused and ready for a fight, the way I used to be as a prepared athlete meditating before competitions. Why were they so focused? Wasn't this just a basic dance class? I began to feel threatened.

The other students already knew the spaces they wanted, and guarded their real estate. The teacher came in and everyone got quiet. As the class started, I awkwardly followed along, unable to understand their dance language, which was completely different from that of gymnastics. I turned the wrong way and accidentally bumped into the girl next to me, embarrassed for stepping into her sacred space. I tried to have fun and ignore my humiliation, but I hated myself for my ignorance.

The teacher made a small choreographed dance, and we learned it together. At first I didn't like it, but the more I moved, the more I lost the sense of myself. She made us do it again and again, and somewhere in the steps I disappeared, becoming energy, pumping blood, and life. It overpowered the heroin in my veins and shot straight into my heart. My body was hot, but not opiate hot. I felt alive, loved, happy, and eternal. In that moment I understood why dancers dance. It was like gymnastics, but different, a sharing of something very powerful and beautiful that I could not name. For a moment everything felt great and the world around me vanished. I was no longer an addict, but movement, pure and fluid.

Then, suddenly, I felt something strange move under my kneecap. My knee hurt every time I bent it, and I knew it must be bad because I was high on heroin and could still feel the pain. I became embarrassed based on an old belief from gymnastics that injuries are a sign of weakness. I stopped dancing, grabbed my things, and slithered out the door. I was limping and couldn't believe my bad luck.

I didn't have health insurance or a regular doctor, so I went to the emergency room at a hospital near my apartment. Every movement of my knee sent a pain through my nervous system. I waited in agony to see the doctor, and the nurse gave me two Percocet in a white paper cup. Pain meant getting painkillers, so, therefore, I liked being in pain. The doctor did a few physical tests, pulling my leg, turning it, and asked if those movements hurt. I said they did. He said I had likely torn my anterior cruciate ligament (ACL), but wouldn't know for sure until I had an MRI. There was no way I was going to get an MRI without insurance, so the doctor gave me a prescription for Vicodin, which was below my normal dose. I was a Percocet and OxyContin guy, and Vicodin didn't do much for my addiction.

I went to several different doctors, using my new ailment to obtain prescriptions for more painkillers. My injury felt healed, and I decided that I hadn't torn my ACL, but I was going to milk it as long as I could and avoid a truth-telling MRI. One doctor gave me a prescription for 100 Percocet, with a refill, and even I thought that was way too many pills to prescribe, but I wasn't going to tell him that. Taking my prescribed medication with heroin let me use as much as I wanted and avoid the usual dope sickness. I loved that aspect.

I was a mess on those pills, and one night I randomly decided to go to the Tenth Avenue Lounge, a bar in our neighborhood. I hobbled into the bar with my knee brace and crutches, chewing Percocet, and began drinking beers. The bar was dark and loud, just the way I liked it, so the noise of a song could muffle how medicated I was in case someone struck up a conversation with me.

A short guy with big arms in a beige Banana Republic shirt asked how I was doing. I have no recollection of our conversation, but I remember walking to my apartment with him, and instead of trying to kiss me, he reached out and shook my hand. There was something nonintrusive about that gesture, and it left a good impression. His name was Matt and he was only a few years older than me. I shook his hand and went upstairs to my apartment alone. When he walked away, I stopped using the crutches, because I knew I no longer needed them, but I kept using them in public to garner sympathy and pills.

The next day I received an email from Matt saying he wanted to see me again. He had a fun personality and seemed interested in getting to know me better. He was everything Nick wasn't, and I needed a fresh start. Matt worked for a prestigious law firm. He was intelligent and had his shit together. We made plans to hang out that night, but before I headed down to his apartment, I shot up and took some pills. We had a good time laughing and talking, and I told him that I'd had a brutal past with drugs, but didn't really do them anymore. I was a great liar when I was using—at least I thought I was.

I stayed the night at Matt's and woke up to the sound of his cell phone ringing in sync with his house phone. He immediately jumped out of bed and turned on the TV. I was still coming out of an opiate haze and heard the strange, nervous reactions of the news anchors who usually seemed to hold it together. What was happening? I didn't know, but I needed to shoot up, because the anxiety from the TV screen was already too much to bear. I needed to clear my head and pry open my eyes before letting that news in. Every channel was the same. A plane had just crashed into one of the World Trade Center towers.

Matt looked nervous and said, "I have to go to work!" I grabbed my things, said goodbye, told him to call me later, and left for my apartment. I still didn't understand what had happened, and everything around me moved in slow motion. The air was still, not calm, but frozen, as I walked home, unsure of the situation. Kip and Keith were watching the news, and by the time I got to the apartment another plane had crashed into the second tower. In confusion and fear, I went into the bathroom and got high. I lay my head against the wall of the bathroom, unconsciously eavesdropping on the sounds of human disaster coming from the living room. I shot up again, into my other arm, before leaving the bathroom. Kip and Keith sat still, staring at the TV with tears in their eyes. I wanted to have my own tears in my eyes, and knew if I were a human being with a heart I would, but I was empty. The devastation couldn't penetrate my disease, and I was numb to real human emotion. Then the towers fell and giant plumes of black, chemical clouds blotted out the sun. The apocalypse had begun.

"This isn't really happening, is it?" I asked myself. "We are Americans; this never happens in our country. We are always safe." The news anchor kept saying the word "terrorist" and I kept thinking, "No way. Nobody would do this to the US, and especially not in New York; we accept everyone here." *Why would someone want to do that to us here?*

I knew nothing about politics, government, or the relationships of countries. I only knew my own pain, which shadowed any desire to know about external conflicts. The news anchor confirmed that it was a terrorist attack, and Kip and Keith looked scared. Why didn't I feel anything? Why couldn't any authentic emotion break through the high? I wanted to feel something and watched them, sitting close together, with Keys on their laps. Was I witnessing their love for the first time as the World Trade Center towers collapsed to the ground? The unfolding horror was bringing them closer together, while I just wanted to inject more heroin to dull the news. What would happen after this? Would New York ever be the same? I didn't know how to handle the rest of the day, so I went to my dealer. I knew she could comfort me and make me feel safe again.

When I arrived at Kimi's apartment she was drunk, with swollen eyes, and told me in a raspy growl to come in. She launched into a tirade about the injustice of the world and how we must stay high to protect ourselves. I agreed. Panic replaced the air we breathed, and all the comfortable thoughts of being safe as Americans were under threat. The city came unhinged for the next few days, and everything felt surreal. Ghastly looks of horror replaced the city's smiles. Hundreds of deaths were being reported, and it was impossible to escape the images on TV. The news was full of fear, giving the sense that another attack could happen at any moment. So I continued to use, since the only safety I felt I could count on was inside a syringe.

In the following weeks I was in a coma of opiate sensations, and I don't remember the details. Matt and I walked as far as we were allowed to go toward the site now being called Ground Zero. Posters of missing people were everywhere, and crowds gathered around them, with people crying and arguing. It was chaos. Those were images I had seen on TV from other countries, but never my own. My chest heaved as I saw a woman holding a picture of a man who had been missing since the towers fell. She stood there, almost shaking, her skin stained with tears, hair matted, and eyes wild with desperation. I wanted to do something, anything, but couldn't. I couldn't even stop using for more than two days in a row. How could I possibly help?

That night I saw a documentary that claimed using and buying street drugs had enabled terrorists to thrive in their countries. If my addiction had contributed to terrorist attacks, did that make me an enemy too? I felt even worse than before. I would never understand the full extent of what had happened that day. Almost 3,000 people died while I slowly but steadily worked on killing myself. I don't think it was possible to hate myself more than I did for who I was and for what I had become.

We were suddenly thrown into an uncertain world, and my relationship with Matt grew as we clung to each other in fear. He lived on Thirty-seventh Street near the Empire State Building, which received bomb threats on an almost daily basis. New York's legendary dynamic energy was in tatters; the whole nation's central nervous system was stressed to capacity, and everyone walked around in a state of disbelief and unease. The city's body and all its inhabitants seemed to mimic my everyday junkie state: jittery, anxious, and terrified.

I was using more heroin than usual, which made work unbearable. A black pay phone next to the bathroom at work was constantly calling out to me, urging me to call my dealer. I walked to it, touched it, held it, hung it up, left it, and came back to it, again and again, like an insane person. I focused on that damn phone over my tables, standing next to it but forcing my hands to my sides to keep myself from calling Kimi. I'd never felt that demented before, and knew I had to stop. I found a midnight twelve-step meeting, which was perfect since that was usually when I would go to Kimi's apartment. If I could manage not to pick up that phone, I could make it to the meeting and have a night of abstinence.

In meetings I would hear healthy people speak, people who were dealing with the tragedy of losing family and friends. The event changed everyone in the city and the outer boroughs, bringing people closer together. A strength emerged from underneath their fears, and people began to function again. While I was exempt from feeling that extraordinary strength, witnessing it in the people around me gave me a tiny seed of hope.

I finally got a sponsor, which helped a lot, and he got me to the midnight meetings. But I decided that because he hadn't done heroin himself, he wouldn't understand what I was *really* going through. I lied to him about my time in recovery because I was ashamed of constantly relapsing. I was trying to stay abstinent, but I was always seconds and inches away from using again.

Matt was sick of my using and watched me take the opiate blockers every night. On the one hand I loved that I had asked him to watch me take my pill to guard my life, but on the other I despised it because it meant giving up my power of choice. I wanted to be abstinent for him, but the ancient demon was stronger than both of us. I felt like I had taken Matt hostage and was dragging him through the unspeakable life of Joe. He didn't deserve any of that.

And now I was reduced to taking those dreadful pills that removed my power of choice. I tried shooting up on them, but nothing happened. It was like shooting sixty dollars of water into my arm. I was fucking pissed. I called the pharmacist and asked how long naltrexone's effects lasted. The answer: three days. So if I stopped the pill I could use heroin and get high in a couple of days.

What if I got in a terrible accident while on the medication? They wouldn't be able to treat me with painkillers and I would suffer inhumanely, I rationalized. What if I needed emergency surgery? Clearly, I had to stop taking naltrexone. But how could I, with

Matt watching me all the time? I decided to replace the pills in the prescription bottle with Tylenol.

The pain of abstinence was unbearable to me. I knew Matt was tired of my broken promises, of my assuring him I would quit using for the week and then walking into his apartment high as a kite. I saw his joy of being with me fade away. Did I take away his happiness? Did my disease steal his sunshine? Was I feeding off those who cared for me like a parasite? I tried pretending everything was okay, but I had taught Matt every trick in the book to spot when I was using: itching, tiny pinpoint pupils, deepened voice, euphoria. He could now see through all my junkie lies.

I became a human yo-yo, spun alternately downward and upward by the momentum of using on and off, loving and hating heroin, its bliss and madness, warmed and burned by its fire. Matt did his best to help me through that dark period, and I ended up moving in with him. I was going to show him that I could stay abstinent and be a real human being.

Neither of us was prepared for the nightmare of me. I thought I was being sneaky when I used, hiding my syringe in the bathroom by the Q-Tip holder. He knew it was there, but said nothing about it, knowing it would kill me if he threw it out. He knew I would be more tolerable to be around if I was high rather than dope sick. One day we had a big fight because I had used the night before and he knew I was high, but of course I swore I wasn't.

The only way of patching the hole in our relationship was for me to go back on naltrexone, proving to him that I hadn't used, since you needed at least fourteen days of abstinence before resuming the pill. He knew I was lying about my using and my time of abstinence, but I decided to fix our fight by disregarding the doctor's dire warnings about the serious side effects of taking the opiate blocker too soon after using. Since I didn't feel high from the previous night's shot, I was convinced the heroin was gone from my system.

In the cab on my way to work, I took half a naltrexone. Limiting the pill to half the dosage would eliminate the possibility of any side effects in case I was incorrect in my assumptions. I was so proud of my decision and knew that Matt would be proud of me too, and that way I could prove to him that I wasn't lying. It felt so good to do the right thing.

I got to work in a great mood and started setting up the dining room for the dinner shift. The restaurant always sparkled at that time of day, as daylight turned to dusk and cast a delicate glow onto the candlelit tables. In that quaint and immaculate scene, I started folding the soft green napkins. As I put the polished silverware down, I suddenly found it very warm in the restaurant. I asked the other waitress if she thought the building was hot, and she agreed it was a little warm. A gust of heat shot through my body and sweat seeped through my pores. Then, instantly, my wet skin froze and I felt a rush of ice-cold chills, immediately followed by another heart-stopping heat wave. I pulled up my white sleeves and saw my drenched arms covered with goose bumps. I was freezing cold and burning hot at the same time, and it hit me like a car crash.

At first I thought I was having a seizure or a heart attack. Oh my god, what was happening to me? I asked the waitress again if she was hot. She replied with an annoyed smile, "Nope, I'm okay." Pain darted through my shivering body, and my bones felt like barbed wire was growing around them. I had to sit down, but even sitting hurt—that fucking pill! The doctors had warned me. Once again I was bringing pain on myself. How long would this last?

My head told me I had to go to the hospital immediately, but I couldn't justify walking out on another shift. Constantly ill with odd things, I would have to explain again to my manager that I was sick. The room spun around me, and I stumbled over to the woman at the register by the bakery and told her I needed to borrow twenty dollars for a cab home. I got the cash and ran out of the restaurant, coatless and in my work clothes, sweating profusely in the freezing New York winter air as I hailed a cab. The fare to Matt's apartment was twenty-four dollars. I saw him walking home from the gym and called him over for the rest of the fare to put an abrupt end to my argument with the driver. I told him something was terribly wrong with me, and we went upstairs.

"What's wrong?"

"I don't know. I feel horrible, like I'm dying. Look at my skin; I'm sweating and freezing cold."

"Did you eat something weird?"

"No, nothing . . . what should I do?"

"I don't know." He looked suspicious. I got in bed and soaked the sheets with my sweat. It was pouring from my body. Matt looked at me and put the pieces together. "So, you did use last night, and you took your pill today, didn't you?"

"No, I swear I didn't use."

"Joe, I'm not stupid. This is exactly what the doctors said would happen."

"I was trying to do the right thing."

"I know you were. I just don't know why you can't tell me the truth . . . for once."

I didn't respond. I was too sick to speak, and I lay in bed for hours, sweating out the lies and humiliation. Work called, and I told them I was dreadfully sick. I would go in tomorrow and make something up to save my ass. I was walking on eggshells with everyone, and I started going back to meetings.

I knew one thing was true: to stay abstinent I had to leave my job. I knew if I went to work I would use, and for the first time I thought I was doing something recovery-oriented by listening to my body. I was ecstatic that I would never have to see that restaurant again. Not having money gave me the assurance that I wouldn't use, and I put myself through a slow, two-week methadone detox. I had become a pro at detoxing.

But after a few days at home, and looking for work, the itch came back. I was going to meetings, but the voice kept taunting me. I began feeling so empty and betrayed by everyone that I desired, no, *needed* the Devil back in my life. Matt was at work and I began to freak out, convinced that if I didn't get high I would kill myself. I felt I was facing an impossible choice: get high or commit suicide. The high had been so far away, after almost two and a half weeks of not using, and I needed to feel it searing through my veins. I longed for the needle to pierce my skin, to poke me with its bliss.

I called Kimi and told her I wanted two bags. I didn't have any money, and searched Matt's apartment for something I could pawn. I loved him and didn't want to steal from him, but my addiction was bigger than love. It was bigger than anything I'd ever known, and it had me in its grip.

After a few weeks of relapsing and job searching, I landed an opportunity that would forever change my life—an interview for a clerk's position at the *New York Times*. Matt was upset because he knew I wasn't abstinent and didn't want me working there while on drugs. He made me swear that if I got the job I would stay in recovery and treat that job with the utmost respect, that I would never be late and that I would work hard. I was overjoyed and felt certain that working for a company like that would change my life and cure my addiction. Matt eventually agreed, and started to share my enthusiasm, believing the job might kick-start my recovery and give me a chance at finding some peace in my life. I was deeply grateful, and resolved to not mess up my new God-given opportunity.

32

UMBILICAL CORD

THE UMBILICAL CORD LINKS THE FETUS AND PLACENTA,
SERVING AS THE LIFELINE BETWEEN THE TWO. IT FORMS
BY THE FIFTH WEEK OF A WOMAN'S PREGNANCY AND
SHIELDS THE BLOOD VESSELS TRAVELING WITHIN THIS
TUBE. COMPROMISED FETAL BLOOD IN THE UMBILICAL
CORD VESSELS CAN RESULT IN HARMFUL EFFECTS
ON THE WELL-BEING OF THE FETUS.

The heroin was brown and thick, a Louisiana swamp in a plastic syringe. With God waiting for me on the other side, all I had to do was give an offering—my blood—a voodoo ritual granting entrance to the void between life and death, between my states of being. But the chilling, pain-filled memories began to crack through the promised warmth. Past demons pulled me closer and more frequently to the Devil, turning my original, perfectly high world of sweet bliss into a nightmare.

Drops of sweat on my forehead, a pounding heart, and dry lungs jostled me awake from my now-macabre opiate nods. God's highs once guaranteed safe transport to the divine, but the Devil now stood by my unconscious body, stealing my breath and choking my life from me. The Devil's cradling blocked the peaceful dreams of my enchanted forests and replaced them with disturbing memories of gymnastics. I had started this love affair to divorce myself from the sport, but now, like entering an added level of hell, I was thrust back into the gym, with chalked hands bound to my leather grips, as old routines burned into my mind like an endless reel of regret.

I had been able to repress those thoughts to where tragedies belong, but now, as I slumped over and fell asleep, they were freed, and I found myself on the pommel horse, heard my hands clasp the hard, wooden handles, felt the leather tear my flesh each time my body skimmed the horse. Was this my bitter irony? To have my old and new religions and loves fighting for my body and soul?

I was a nervous mess as I walked along Forty-third Street for my first day of work. White globe lights that had *Times* printed on them lined the street leading up to the famed building's overhang bearing the same iconic font and title. Journalists paced the sidewalks, smoking, either late for a deadline or rewarding themselves for meeting one. The *New York Times* was a symbol of the city: with its namesake Times Square, it was a source of news worldwide, and had the power to shape public opinion in everything from politics to the arts. I never actually read the paper, but knew it equaled the voice of God and final judgment to many. By stealing glances at its headlines, I could inject substance into my conversations. "The *New York Times* said . . ." was my favorite way to start a conversation. But now I had to get my act in order as I entered that place of high prestige, en route to my first job that did not include reading the specials of the day to customers.

My anxiety exploded once I passed through the revolving doors, and I wanted to stay within the circle and head right back into the street to shoot up, but somehow I kept moving forward to the elevator. Hired as a clerk in the Style department, which covered design, fashion, house and home, and dining, I had no idea what my job would entail. Diego, an energetic man and everyone's best friend, provided the introductions to my coworkers.

My job was to arrive every morning fifteen minutes before the editors and reporters to deliver the latest edition of the paper to their desks. Later editions had fewer stars printed on the front top corner, and even though Diego repeatedly explained the star system, I always misread the constellations. The rest of the day was spent filling mailboxes, answering phones, running errands, and doing general clerical work.

Miller was my supervisor, and his annoying, know-it-all attitude garnered my immediate contempt. Years of shuttling sheaves of black-and-white newsprint between departments and sorting endless stacks of mail slowly drove clerks insane. I diagnosed Miller with "*Times* clerical anemia." His character had faded into a hazy smudge, his hands forever newsprint-stained, and he incessantly besieged me with facts from yesterday's news. As the new guy, I had to respect, listen, and try to not contract his disease; but an hour with him sparked every personal mental issue I had and whetted my heroin appetite.

Eventually I fell into a work groove, making my daily rounds to the writers and editors of that Holy Grail, passionately enslaved to the dull glow of their computer screens. The syncopated clicking of keyboards, the drone of background chatter, and the flickering of the fluorescent lights became a mundane annoyance that made me want to use again.

However, I did love seeing people work hard, as a team, and create something. I wanted to be more than a junkie. I was going to fight for change by not using, paying attention, and respecting the honor of my new job. At night, I looked at my plastic *New York Times* ID card and smiled. In Manhattan, jobs define who we are, and this job finally turned me into someone with a noteworthy identification. I now had the badge by which to look down on others, as they had on me; to be the annoying guy in the bar, name-dropping, wearing expensive clothes, and talking about my perfect life. I was a *New York Times* employee, with access to the news before everyone else in the general public.

After a few weeks my sweet work romance wore off. Really, what did I expect? All that I had held sacred and with such high regard came tumbling down. I never wanted to see another newspaper. The tireless writers and editors, whom at first I extolled as purveyors of important articles, now exhausted me. They were so busy and focused that many of them never even took the time to introduce themselves to me. Miller hounded me throughout the building, filling my days with meaningless tasks, wielding his unique capacity to dismantle a perfect day with a single word. It seemed like Miller and his phone had the ability to startle me out of every free moment I had to sit in my cubicle and drink a coffee. His very presence made me want to use faster than being with my parents; there was no way I could stay abstinent. I shot up after receiving my first paycheck.

Matt was crushed. He had witnessed my many attempts to change my life only to be swallowed by the disease that corroded everything and everyone around me. I tried to refrain from getting high at work, but I always failed. I would take my backpack into the fourth-floor bathroom near the Style department, sit in the stall, and then remove my kit with its used spoon, cotton swab, rubbing alcohol, and syringe. I would return to work in a vigorous state—heroin convinced me that I loved working for such a well-respected corporation.

My work high cultivated an attachment to the illusions and grandeur of the department—labels, vanity, money, objects, and clothes, along with an obsession for binge cleaning and chain-smoking. I would clean and organize my workspace to obsessive neatness and then go outside and smoke cigarette after cigarette, denying myself even a second of fresh air. The heroin blocked any lung or asthma pain, and I loved watching the smoke pour out of my mouth as though from a car's exhaust pipe. As the high faded and lung pain resurfaced, I would chain-pump my inhaler to recapture my breath. A large part of my workday was spent outdoors among the smoking journalists as I scheduled my next high, leaving me little time to sit still and actually perform my job.

Every other Thursday, our checks were ready upstairs on the eighth floor at 2:00 p.m. The secret society of addicts were always first in line, usually late for work, but early to secure their spot, nervously waiting to receive, run, cash, and use. The anticipation and anxiety of our group while waiting those fifteen minutes before the floodgates opened were palpable.

I scheduled my lunch break on payday to coincide with paycheck time, trying to crunch two hours into one. With check in hand, I ran to Thirty-eighth Street and Sixth Avenue, cashed it at my bank, sprinted all the way up to Kimi's apartment on Forty-ninth and Eleventh, cooked my heroin, shot it, and returned to work on Forty-third and

Eighth a new man. In my delusion, I always won that emergency death race, arriving back to work in time, but the reality of Miller's beady eyes and clogged-sinus breaths met my triumph with a menial assignment. Despite his attempts to bring me down, I now had the power—I had my high.

Matt tried to keep me through gifts, clothes, and nice meals—anything to distract me from using. I wanted to stay clean for his sake, but I couldn't do it. I refused to surrender, and he got sucked into the vortex of my addiction. Matt came to hate that I spent more time with Kimi than with him, as well as the unusual bond and secret codes she and I had created for contacting each other. A single ring and prompt hang-up on his apartment phone meant either her guys were dropping off the heroin soon or it was ready for pickup. Either way, I knew Christmas was around the corner. Matt quickly caught on to our system and tried to confront her, but never got a word in until I owed her money. Then she called the apartment continuously and got in a huge phone fight with Matt, who in turn lent me the money to pay her back to get her off his line.

Years of running to Kimi's home to heal my pain through shooting up, crashing on her couch, and chain smoking cigarettes forged a deep bond between us. Listening to my laments like a bartender at closing time, she comforted me with "Oh, Chico, it's gonna be all right. You and I are the same and nobody understands us. We need this stuff to live."

Kimi was my lifeline when I needed to talk about life, when I needed my sustenance, and when I needed nurturing—when I needed mothering. We talked for hours and fought like mother and son over money, relationships, and the strength of my heroin—all the normal things families talk about. Drugs wove our lives together—blood is thicker than water, but heroin is thicker than blood. Kimi wanted my money and I wanted her high; we would never cut the cord that connected us. During heavy binges, she would reprimand me for using too much heroin and insist that I slow down, mirroring the humiliation and shame I experienced during my childhood. When her dysfunctional love became too much for me to handle, I escaped to the place I initially ran away from by making small detox trips to Boston. The old neighborhood, which had always triggered my disease, became a place of refuge where I could be when I was too ill to be anywhere else. I would sleep for two days straight at my mother's house, taking bitter sips of methadone sandwiched between even more bitter dreams.

For years, I told my parents that I was in recovery and attending twelve-step meetings, but those desperate trips home made the truth clear. My mother never asked what was wrong with me, consciously or subconsciously knowing, and too afraid of losing me again—aware I might never come back if pushed too far. I ran from the mother who gave me life to a mother who offered me death. My birth mother was afraid of me, and I was afraid of my death mother. I created the same tarnished relations inside my family and outside it, among strangers I called friends and drug friends I called family.

When my mother's house failed to detox me I would switch to my father's home, and I would walk the beach, searching for the gymnast's strength and superhuman power I once knew. I believed the ocean could pacify the most depressed person, and that this place would heal me through the casting of prayers into the deep blue.

I climbed the rocky cliff overlooking Boston harbor where a memorial to someone who had jumped to his death was written in once-wet cement, now hardened with time. *Did he fall to the hand of my demon, and would I be next on the list?* The ocean's black mirror below flashed visions of my youthful entry into this world of darkness. That vibrant, naive raver with every desired chemical in hand, that drug boy in baggy pants following LSD trails into the moonlight, that freedom child jumping from transcendent trip to trip now belonged to the Devil. He was now one more link in strengthening the demonic chain, one more unheeded warning passed down from user to user, one more soulless junkie. All the discipline, dedication, and talent that had once characterized me drained into the sea, and no amount of once-held talent in the world could change that.

After fourteen days of not using I would leave my mother's house, strong and confident, but as the bus entered Port Authority, the

Chrysler Building greeted me like a giant syringe piercing the night sky. The city lights of Manhattan would deflate all my gained recovery. My skin would change as I walked through Times Square and, with temptation swelling up inside, I always found myself running back to Kimi, having left mother for mother, imparting the travails of recovery. Only Kimi understood my ailment, only she had the cure, only she could agree with me and identify with the rawness of our beings. I sold the unconditional love of my own mother for the synthetic love of a fictitious one.

Months passed and my recovery ebbed and flowed, occasionally gripping an edge of grass from within my grave, but never making it out. I led my relationship with Matt down my now seemingly destined path of destruction. We both tried to make it work, but living with me was like having an avalanche in the apartment. Matt took me on a vacation with his friends to a beach in Florida, and I ended up stealing his friend's pills. The guy had fibromyalgia and had hundreds of OxyContin, Valium, and Percocet in his suitcase. I decided he wouldn't miss a few. Matt saw this behavior as sinking to a new low. But to my way of thinking, the only difference was that his friend could easily have his prescription refilled, but I had to fill prescriptions myself. I justified my thievery as normal addict behavior—we cling to the sick, stealing painkillers from dying loved ones. There was no end to my betrayal, and it became painfully clear that Matt and I had to break up. He deserved better. My love affair with heroin was destroying us, and I had shoved a kind and generous man into the shredder. After two years together, during which I had brought only death, disease, deceit, rage, and sadness to our relationship, we broke up.

"but I want to tell them
that all of this shit
is just debris
leftover when we finally decide to smash all the things we thought
we used to be
and if you can't see anything beautiful about yourself

get a better mirror
look a little closer
stare a little longer
because there's something inside you
that made you keep trying

despite everyone who told you to quit
you built a cast around your broken heart
and signed it yourself
you signed it
"they were wrong"
because maybe you didn't belong to a group or a click
maybe they decided to pick you last for basketball or everything
maybe you used to bring bruises and broken teeth
to show and tell but never told
because how can you hold your ground
if everyone around you wants to bury you beneath it
you have to believe that they were wrong

they have to be wrong

why else would we still be here?
we grew up learning to cheer on the underdog

because we see ourselves in them

we stem from a root planted in the belief
that we are not what we were called we are not abandoned cars
stalled out and sitting empty on a highway
and if in some way we are

don't worry

we only got out to walk and get gas
we are graduating members from the class of
fuck off we made it

not the faded echoes of voices crying out

names will never hurt me

of course

they did

but our lives will only ever always
continue to be

a balancing act

that has less to do with pain
and more to do with beauty."

An excerpt of the poem *To This Day* by Shane Koyczan.
From the book *Our Deathbeds Will Be Thirsty*.

REVERSE PLANCHE

33

THE MIND

SIGMUND FREUD'S ID, EGO, AND SUPEREGO CONSTITUTE
THE THREE-PART STRUCTURAL MODEL OF THE PSYCHE WITH
WHICH HE DESCRIBED AND DEFINED THE ACTIVITIES AND
INTERACTIONS OF A PERSON'S MENTAL LIFE. THE ID CONSISTS
OF UNCOORDINATED INSTINCTUAL TRENDS, THE EGO COMPRISES
THE ORGANIZED, REALISTIC ASPECTS OF A PERSON, AND THE
SUPEREGO PLAYS THE CRITICAL MORALIZING ROLE. EVEN
THOUGH THE MODEL IS "STRUCTURAL," THIS PSYCHIATRIC
TRIPTYCH IS A FUNCTION OF THE MIND RATHER THAN THE
BRAIN, WITH NO ACTUAL DIRECT, SOMATIC, STRUCTURAL
RELATION INVOLVING NEUROSCIENCE.

It was midsummer in Manhattan and the heat bounced off the
concrete and the trash, suffocating all who walked the streets. The
name *Hell's Kitchen* was appropriate for my part of the city—it felt
like we were living inside a microwave oven. After Matt and I broke
up, I had moved back in with Keith and Kip.

I missed Matt and wished I could have quit using to save our
relationship, but I was happy to have escaped one of my biggest
fears while we were living together: Matt coming home to find my
cold and lifeless corpse on his bathroom floor, with my syringe as
the murder weapon. Now single, I could use as much as I wanted
without thinking about inflicting images of my overdose upon my
relationship hostages.

Living in New York meant being trapped in a nonstop fashion show of sex, pride, prestige, and power. Gorgeous people, too busy to appreciate each other's beauty, dominated the avenues, desperately trying to see their own reflections in the storefronts, cabs, and each other's dark glasses: the black holes of vanity. Everybody had something someone else wanted, and it pervaded the perfect-bodied dancers, actors, and singers living in my Theater District neighborhood. New York provides a tough competition for beauty and youth, magnified exponentially in the gay world where human qualities are overlooked for flesh, muscles, and flawless skin. If we don't end up hating ourselves because our families told us we were wrong, we hate ourselves by creating a social grouping in which aging is considered worse than death. It's so much better to die young than to wake up to a wrinkle. Fellow gays can be crueler than the society we protest against. Internally we react and defend ourselves through a modern mummification of antiaging lotions, sex, drugs, and dance music that makes our fountain of youth bubble up in the club scene.

If I was to survive in New York, I needed to get on the same playing field. Even though I was a junkie, I worked hard in the gym and could reshape my body from the skinny waif I had become to my gymnast form. The problem was that it's difficult to lift weights after shooting up. I would go to the New York Sports Club and nod off with dumbbell in hand, then wake up with my eyes half open, sedated and high, watching the weight drop to the floor in slow motion. While others shot steroids in the locker room, I shot heroin and laughed at the absurdity as I continued to weight-train while high. I was now a professional addict, more or less functioning in life, and wanting to better myself while living in my self-constructed hell.

I checked my email on Kip and Keith's computer every day. They had recently introduced me to a social networking site that felt like a jealousy breeding ground. I clicked through the site, looking at perfect profile pictures and picking the ones I wanted to be. The TV droned in the background, and a story caught my ear about a fashion designer in Manhattan with a triumphant life full of enthusiasm and creativity. I wanted to meet him. Being high brought on an arrogance

I would have never had sober. I searched his name on the Web and he came up. I sent him an email and he quickly answered back. In my confident, delusional drug state I asked him on a date. He said yes, and we made plans to go to the movies. I couldn't believe I had made a date with someone I had just seen on TV, and someone who wasn't a drug dealer, junkie, or crackhead. While I was awful in social situations, I did develop the finely honed skill of exposing my good attributes and selling what I wanted seen, showing off the saturated colors and highlights of my life while concealing my dark truth.

His dark, slicked-back hair; small, sharp eyes; bigger-than-life personality; and a smile that welcomed everyone made Alejandro much nicer than I imagined a famous person could be. He dressed in an old, eighties punk style that I had abandoned in order to find work in the city, and I could barely convince him I was once pierced from head to toe. As we talked in the coffee shop before the movie, strangers interrupted us to tell him how much they loved his clothes. Rather than being a bitchy queen, he was extremely carefree and kind, speaking to them as if he'd known them all his life. While I didn't want a relationship, I liked being around him.

The Devil and the drugs had taken all I had and all I once was, and I saw an opportunity here to be someone by proxy. My ego took over and I thought, *Since he is somebody and I know him, I could be somebody too*. I had been determined to fill the emptiness inside me with external labels and to define myself through things, and now sitting in front of me was a man with a label and things! I was not going to let this guy go.

After the movie we continued our date at a club downtown. Alejandro walked up to the front of the line stretching down the block and the doorman unlatched the velvet rope for us. I felt bad for the people waiting, but it felt good to be treated like someone special. Free drinks arrived from the bartenders all night long, which was good since I had no money to buy him a drink even if I'd wanted to—paychecks went to Kimi and then into my veins. Inside the club's dark lighting everyone seemed to know Alejandro. He was intriguing, artistic, and a big drinker. I kept up with the drinks, even though I would have preferred the sedating effects of my true love; but, not one to turn away a mistress, the first drink turned into a drowning.

The night faded into blackout, and I woke up hung over in his apartment. I was still drunk and had to get home and get to work. I stumbled out, terrified that I had done something stupid and would never hear from him again, but before I reached my apartment he sent a text inviting me to meet him for coffee before my shift. With a short shot of hot, brown liquid dope in my veins, I cured my hangover and met him with the expectation of *the* question: "Do you remember what you did last night?" But he never asked. He just smiled, sitting close to me, with one arm slightly touching my wrist. I wanted to be one of those guys good at cuddling, holding hands, or sharing emotions in public, but I was never good at intimacy, fearing the monster inside me would infect another human being with my darkness. I did my best to let him in.

He invited me to a movie premiere the following night—a world away from the usual evening spent in my drug dealer's dirty bathroom. I was excited and nervous. I had to conceal my habit and hoped my odd high behavior might fit in well among the eccentric company he kept. I had to keep the fresh track marks covered, and did my best to conceal the bruises over my veins using women's cover-up: Thank you, CoverGirl, for helping junkies all over the world fit in like normal people, because "if you don't look good, we don't look good."

Guards released the rope sectioning off civilians from the special, and I entered the after-party with my charming date, who introduced me to Macaulay Culkin, Paris Hilton, and other celebrities. Starstruck, with a smile frozen on my face, I couldn't move. I had lived in New York for years and had never met anyone famous, and now, on my second date, I was in a social circle of celebrities. Everyone was drinking, and a few drugs were being passed around like hors d'oeuvres, but I was terrified of embarrassing Alejandro, so I refrained. Besides, the heroin in my blood, mixed with this new feeling of being part of the people being watched, gave New York a rich patina.

We went back to his place after the party, and, while he was showing me pieces for the upcoming fashion week, Pamela Anderson called wanting a dress for an upcoming event. Just a short week ago my life had centered around Kimi's hellhole in Hell's Kitchen, and now I was sleeping with fame. I would never leave him.

I took Matt to Alejandro's fashion show. It was a dramatic mix of freaky people drenched in expensive and bizarre costume versions of their own personalities, wanting to be seen, admired, and written about. I felt nauseous from everyone's clothes screaming, "Here I am! I'm interesting, deep, and trendy! Love me!" but I had done the same thing with piercing. I hated them because I hated me.

The watchful eyes of massive security guards maintained the boundaries of plastic chairs separating New York's famous socialites from the club-kid mundane. Surprisingly, the usher sat us among the privileged in the second row, an arm's length away from the catwalk. The room's attention shifted as a glittery, aged butterfly of a woman swept in and landed in her seat directly in front of us: Liza Minnelli. Madonna was more my speed as a gay icon. As she left her seat to flit about the room, we checked to see if her gift bag outdid ours, but it just had the same fancy face cream samples and CDs. The evening was gorgeously presented and a big joke: fashion overshadowed by a party catering to the pseudocreative and the ego-driven, set to a soundtrack of jealousy and envy.

The top of the show immediately brought my self-esteem down as flawless-bodied models stampeded down the runway. They were perfect, unobtainable specimens. But Alejandro's hard work and talent blew me away, his stories flowing past before my eyes, woven into each piece. My lasting contribution to the world would be flawless vein explorations. Perhaps we could join forces and create a ghastly haute couture collection in bloodletting: emaciated models armed with beautiful crimson holes, tracks marking their limbs, accessorized with syringes and blood. But my dream line would never happen—Alejandro despised drugs after he had lost several close friends to overdoses. Would I be next on his list? His disapproval didn't stop him from being a hard drinker, which always confused me, since it's just a liquid form of the same disease.

Alejandro and I continued dating through fancy fashion events and pretentious social scenes, but my addiction was starting to show its envy. Sloppy drunkenness led me to forget syringes in places, say the wrong things to the wrong people, and embarrass everyone around me. One night at a club while Alejandro was talking to people and doing his "public relations," I pulled my own PR as a guy asked in my ear if I wanted coke. This was like asking a landlocked fish if he was thirsty. Bored of hearing the extolling of Alejandro, we went into the bathroom, did a few lines, and bought some for later. I stashed the coke next to my spoon, syringe, and heroin in the Dolce & Gabbana bag Alejandro let me use. Drug use and the illusory qualities of clothes, money, and prestige go hand in hand and create wonderful false sensations of identity.

Alcohol balanced out the coke high and provided a cloak of normalcy, so I drank deeply into the night, ending up at Alejandro's apartment with a few of his friends and his assistant, whom I started hitting on. After hours of my sneaking into the bathroom to do more lines, his friends left and Alejandro confronted me: "Are you on drugs?"

The innocence in his eyes was killing me. "No, man, I'm just drunk."

"Okay, you seem a little more than drunk, but I believe you."

Then, in my drunkenness, I got honest and started telling the truth, feeling him out to see how much I could reveal. His face turned angry when I mentioned drugs, so I swerved into lies, baiting him with sympathy on a hook, but that fish wasn't biting, so I had to change my approach and paint myself as the victim. I had to mold his anger into pity, as if addiction had been forced upon me. I grew up in a terrible ghetto of drugs, paving an inescapable destiny, fueled by a fabricated father who taught me how to shoot heroin when I was fifteen. My manipulative and drunken acting, complete with tears, landed him right on my hook.

We cried ourselves to sleep. I woke up late for work, hoping a blackout would erase his mind and my after-school-special bedtime story—the details of which I couldn't remember. I ran out the door to catch a cab for work. I was already late, so I decided to make a quick stop at Kimi's for a bag to cure my hangover when I realized

I had left all my "works" inside Alejandro's D&G bag. I wanted to throw up. Just as I was about to send a text saying "Don't open the bag," he beat me to it.

"I found your stuff. It's over!"

283

Just like that. I was devastated, but more upset that he would trash my coke, heroin, and precious spoon that was bent to junkie perfection. I would never again have access to that world, forever shunned from the fake land of cool.

∞∞∞∞∞∞∞∞

Heroin alone wasn't working as well as it used to, so I went on a strong bender over the next few weeks. I did coke to wake me up, Xanax to calm my nerves, alcohol to get me thirsty, and a shot of heroin to seal the deal. I knew that mixture was deadly, but it felt good. I missed work frequently and my boss questioned my behavior, but I couldn't break that gorgeous cycle of using. Once the money and the drugs ran out, the pain became unbearable and shot me back into a suicidal, sober state of depression and despair. Without methadone to ease the ensuing dope sickness, I braced myself for a hurricane of withdrawal.

I shook, cried, pleaded, threw up, and hallucinated for three days in bed, drenched in a puddle of sweat. Even if I had the money to use, I didn't have the strength to get it. My stomach wrenched and my guts were imploding. Where was the Devil's warm cradling now? Was this him inside me, ripping my organs apart? I grasped for grace as I hit a new bottom. If I survived this detox I would be forever scarred and deranged. When I could get out of bed, I searched the room endlessly for drugs—scraping, scratching, and clawing for old cotton swabs that once drowned in an overflowing pool of heroin—but they were all gone. The only thing left was a small weed roach lodged between the wall and my bed. Instead of numbing my pain, pot made me think too much. I wanted to be absent from me, but I smoked it anyway since it was better than being abstinent.

I turned on the TV. A rerun of *ER* was playing, with snow falling on a terminally ill priest who spoke of accepting his death and mortality and his declination of medical care. I thought he was talking to me, and as I watched the snow fall I thought of my mother. Nature always transported me to her, and in that moment, with her child almost dead, what would she think? The priest showed me my two choices: kill myself or get into recovery. Was I worth fighting for? If I made it my life's work, could I quit using?

I saw a blank piece of paper near my bed and wrote, "God, please help me!" I put it on my dresser, the highest place in my room, thinking the closer to the sky, the closer to heaven, the closer to God. Stuck again in a state of demoralizing pain, I held myself tight and fell asleep to the hum of the television.

A seed of hope appeared the next day. Like a flower fighting for life, I had to compete against the desire to die. Without health insurance I couldn't go to rehab, and I could never stay abstinent long enough for the spiritual aspect of twelve-step meetings to work. Early recovery's excruciating physical withdrawals always led me to failure, and I had to heal my body first so my mind could follow. I came to believe physical sickness was the normal state after I existed for so long with constant back pain, a chronic runny nose, and profuse sweating.

I went to the employee-assistance program at the *New York Times*. I walked into the office of a young, pretty woman, closed the door, and said, "I've been shooting heroin in your company since I started working here. I can't stop. I'm desperate."

Unfazed, she appeared pleased that I came for help and asked if I would consider rehab. Part of me wanted to back out, but I pushed forward and said, "Yes," as the wraith inside me fought back. After I told her I didn't have any health insurance, she made a phone call and said, "I have great news, and this doesn't happen often, so you are in luck . . . if you want it. A rehab in Connecticut is willing to give you a scholarship for fourteen days, but you have to go this Monday or it will go to someone else." It was Friday, and I began to question what I was doing. Would I make it through the weekend? I asked how I could miss two weeks of work, and she replied, "We will cover you, your job is protected. You're doing the right thing, and it sounds like you a need a rest from your life." A rest. Yes, I needed a rest. I accepted the offer.

Knowing rehab was around the corner, I wanted to get loaded; but with the goal of getting back on naltrexone before leaving rehab I needed two weeks clean, so using wasn't an option. If I shot up now, I'd be dope sick upon arrival, and for the first time I wanted recovery to work. Still, I couldn't go to rehab sober, could I? Everyone gets high before they go—it's like an initiation. But I really needed this to work and I would be wasting precious time in rehab lying in bed, trying to recover from dope sickness during my first few days. Naltrexone worked; it wasn't the total solution, but it would buy me some drug-free time and allow my mind to heal. Not using over the weekend ensured I would be on naltrexone before leaving rehab and reduced the chance for relapse upon return to the city. But then, would my last high be my best high? If I knew that would be my last, could I make it better? Once I started to obsess about using, the desire overwhelmed me. Yes, I had to use again.

But I didn't. For the first time in a long time, I stayed abstinent that weekend through TV reruns, tears, and pint after pint of Ben & Jerry's. Monday morning I got in a van bound for St. Mary's rehab in Connecticut. I told my roommates I was going home to visit my family in Boston, and left with little hope in my heart. I was defeated and broken.

While not a five-star hotel, the rehab was nicer than my first one years before, and far better than past mental hospitals and institutions. It was set on a hill surrounded by a dense forest; and I saw two deer in the grass on my first day. We weren't allowed any music, books, or anything non-recovery related for entertainment or distraction. My roommate was a giant steroidal bodyguard at a strip club and talked incessantly about all the strippers he'd banged. He couldn't believe he'd ended up in this place, alone and womanless. Where were all his beautiful strippers now?

Seeing others find recovery through the doled-out twelve-step materials, I scoured their contents searching for answers and trying to decipher the secrets locked inside the same words I'd read countless times before with no result. What was *my* problem? I needed to believe those words and feel them inside what little humanity I had left. I would eat the pages, one by one, and ingest them into my soul, if that were the solution. I cried and clung tightly to the possibility of recovery.

My roommate and I finally spoke late one sleepless night—person to person, human to human, his tough exterior stripped down, connecting on a level of shared suffering. People say the universal language is love, but I say it's pain. Our stories were different but familiar, and I felt a deep sense of peace as we identified our honesty together. In that horrid room where countless sick addicts before us had detoxed, crying and screaming in agony and resentment, we tried to surrender, and the hushed sobs of my He-Man roommate lulled me to sleep: the addict's lullaby.

On my fourth day I was assigned to Kara, a strong Latin-American New Yorker who had battled her own addiction in the 1980s' coke euphoria days, and was now a therapist. Her sharp eyes cut me to pieces, and a foreign glow emanated from within her. This wondrous light only shines from those who have earned it, those whose beaten souls and bodies somehow escaped hell. Her gut-wrenching honesty scared me at first, but, already broken and exposed, I no longer cared if she saw who I really was.

Over the next few days I became accustomed to the long, strict days starting at 6:00 a.m. Outside of rehab my only reason for getting up that early would have been to buy a truckload of heroin. But here, before my day started, I would go into a large stone room overlooking the forest and sip my coffee, which was decaf even though they said otherwise. In those quiet moments as the day broke, I searched myself for strength. Could I summon it again? Could I call out to the warrior I had vanquished to the bottom of the ocean, submerged under years of drugs? Would he even listen or recognize me?

I tried remembering that athletic power, forcing myself to feel the sparkle of muscle memory. I could feel that power lying dormant in my bones and caught glimpses of myself on the high bar, freely swinging against the chalk-stained steel. Those memories gave me a sense of life and happiness, and a dim feeling of hope. That small spark rekindled who I had once been, and, just as my soul had demanded so many years ago from an eight-year-old boy, it gave me direct orders to work out and regain my physical strength and flexibility. With a decade lost it wouldn't be easy. How could I return to that kind of form? *I'm too old and too broken*, I thought. But the answer resonated throughout my body: "Do it." I went up to my room and started doing push-ups, sit-ups, and handstands. To strictly concentrate on recovery, exercise wasn't allowed in rehab, but I had direct orders from the sun, bypassing all man-made laws, to guide me out of despair.

I snuck into my room between group therapy and counseling and worked out. I was light years away from where I had been ten years ago. I was weak, stiff, and out of shape. I didn't exactly know why I was doing it, but if felt good to slowly restore my body's natural opiates and give my mind tiny periods of relief. It was a huge mountain to climb, but I knew not to concentrate on reaching the peak. I had to take single steps, not thinking about the past or the future, only about securing a present moment without clinging to an anticipated outcome.

I continued working with Kara, and while her power was intoxicating, her honesty frightened me. One day she shut the door and said, "Sit down. I'm going to tell you something I've never told another human being." I was nervous that she was about to drop a bomb on me or reveal a secret I could not handle. She continued with conviction, "Joe, you are special. There is something powerful about you. I don't say this to anybody, and as everyone knows, I'm very honest, but you are unique. You have something to give the world. I'm not saying this for your recovery. I'm saying this for your soul—and you need to know it. You're special."

Instead of rejecting and casting aside the compliment as I would have done in the past, I sat quietly and listened. She wasn't fueling my ego, but feeding my spirit, with purpose behind each word, a direction, a responsibility, and a belief. I started crying, sobbing through countless layers and years of destruction. They were dormant tears of an unheeded truth: "Stop killing the magnificence within, stop hiding, inspire people to be more than they are. Better yourself and humanity." I swallowed her words and held that moment close.

I completed the fourteen days, fighting negativity and secretly training, but fear of relapsing in the outside world set in when it was time to leave. I had achieved my rehab naltrexone goal, and immediately went to a twelve-step meeting once back in New York. Instead of sitting in the back hating everyone, I sat near the speaker. I needed to reveal my addiction, talk to others with the same affliction, and identify with their sense of hope. Living near Kimi made a run-in with the Grim Reaper and her disability stick inevitable. Would I have the strength to turn away from her seduction?

I returned to work at the *Times* a new person—on time, alert, efficient, happy, and amicable. My boss was proud of me, and one day, as I walked the long hallways, a woman stopped me and asked if I had recently had my braces removed. She said she'd never seen me smile before, and I should do it more often—of course, I never had braces. I kept the same daily routine to make sure I had an order to follow: wake up, have coffee, make my bed. I had never made my bed before, but now those small acts learned in rehab made me feel good. I cleaned my room and got rid of a pharmacy of syringes, bent and burnt spoons, and alcohol swabs. I exorcised the demons, closing my eyes as I threw away my past.

A few weeks passed, and my roommates noticed something different about me; I told them I had had a very healing trip to Boston. Keith mentioned a Broadway audition casting gymnasts for the show *Jumpers*. In response, I felt fear radiating throughout my body; but something inside said, "Go and see." After wrestling with the idea, I decided to watch the audition and, if I felt comfortable, put my foot in the ring. At rehab they'd said to treat myself as if I were the only survivor of a devastating train wreck, and, while I should have taken a year off heavy exercise to let my body recover from years of intense heroin use, I was inspired to try. I went to Central Park and started flipping. I could only perform a few flips safely, and my body hated the idea, but I kept at it, the same way I did as an eight-year-old boy in the basement. It felt like I was excavating the remains of my past, brushing the dirt off my bones—it didn't come back easily. Little dizzy stars flashed from the corners of my eyes as my body reacclimated to working against gravity. My inabilities became humiliating, and I wanted to give up and go use, ashamed that I was so out of shape. A few overrotated twisting flips landed me on my back, rolling in the dirt. With sore ankles and a deflated spirit, I had had enough and went home.

My roommates tried preparing me for the audition: Kip took a decent picture of me and said, "Joe, this is your headshot"; Keith handed me a piece of typed paper and said, "This is your resume." I wanted to cry, never having noticed how loving and caring they had been this whole time. Like proud, protective parents they were nudging me out of my nest, telling me to fly. But, fresh out of rehab, I was in no condition to audition. How would I handle personal judgment after all that time? Didn't I go to drugs to escape having to cope with rejection, jealously, and competition? Still unsure, I trusted them, my recovery, and the very small signs the universe seemed to be carefully placing before me—so exquisitely crafted that there was no denying they were there for me to follow.

After a sleepless night I walked to the audition a few blocks from our apartment, arriving an hour early. In my brief period of recovery I showed up to places much earlier than needed, trying to take control, thinking extra time would allow for a clearer understanding of the situation. I started stretching and warming up, focusing on my body and walking through my fears, trying not to obsess over the outcome. The other gymnasts started coming in, some I knew from the past, and I was embarrassed that my once-muscular champion body was now emaciated while theirs had remained strong. I wanted to run and hide, but I stayed put, breathing deeply. Then the dancers began flowing in—superhumans beautifully trained in the art of movement, seemingly able to do anything through space. I sat in the corner.

The choreographer came in, making us run from one side of the stage to the other, zigzagging amongst each other. It was fun, and the feeling of playing a game made me feel less awkward. Then came the tumbling audition. While I wasn't the best, I wasn't the worst. The casting was for a specific look and most of us didn't have it, myself included, but surprisingly, I wasn't that disappointed being let go. It felt like a huge personal advance to garner the strength to audition in front of strangers, while in the daily life of recovery I still had trouble ordering coffee, opening mail, or going to the bank.

As I left the audition, a tall, attractive dancer with muscular legs like a horse approached me. His name was Jason and he stood out by being big yet moving with ease and grace in both his dancing and tumbling. Without an ounce of fat on his body, he was well trained and familiar with the industry. We exchanged phone numbers, and even though I didn't want another boyfriend, we hung out a few times and I saw him dance with the company Momix—making difficult skills look easy through his artistic passion, strength, and flexibility.

I continued training hard at the gym, going to twelve-step meetings and working at the *Times*. I had my sights set on a future at the paper, but Jason continually told me to keep auditioning and to take classes. While it felt good to move around again, I believed that without dance training I couldn't compete in New York, where everybody seemed to be a world-class somebody. He took me to Manhattan Gym one day to train in the gymnastics space—the same place I had come to years before, high on heroin, for the Disney audition. But now, somehow, his enthusiasm and talent inspired me to train more seriously and regain my body and fire.

Three months passed, and even if I didn't want to be in a relationship, I had settled into one. Everything was perfect—until he came to me with the news that he had been offered a job with Cirque du Soleil's *Zumanity* and would have to quickly leave for Canada, and then Las Vegas. I was thrilled for him, but devastated that he was leaving me. I had never been in recovery this long, and I had never been in recovery this long with someone else in my life, almost five months. It was unusual, new, and special for me to remember every moment with someone, and I didn't want to part with that.

34

SPINAL COLUMN

In human anatomy, the vertebral column (backbone or spine) usually consists of thirty-three vertebrae, the sacrum, the intervertebral discs, and the coccyx situated at the bottom of the torso. The spinal column houses and protects the spinal cord in the spinal canal.

I had five months of recovery when I picked up heroin again. I had stopped taking my opiate blocker and didn't tell anyone. Once again I chose death instead of life. I was searching for a feeling; I wanted to rebel and destroy. I didn't care about the consequences. I didn't understand why I would do that, because things had been so good. I hadn't missed a day at the gym. I had gone to my old gymnastics gym in Boston and made amends to my coach Antonio.

Maybe I missed Jason out there in Vegas, or maybe I just felt sorry for myself. I was brokenhearted and I hated it. I was scared and I didn't know how to stop again. I would stop for two or three days, but physically couldn't get beyond that. I hadn't gone to a meeting because I was afraid that everyone would be mad at me. I was angry, confused, guilty, remorseful, and anxious, and I just needed more heroin to forget all about it.

I had gotten two gigs outside of the *Times,* working with a group of acrobats and doing some modeling. Why would I go out and use? I prayed to God, asking him to unlock my willingness, to give me hope and faith to take on my disease one hour at a time. I begged him to give me the strength to sit through the withdrawals.

One day in the spring I woke up from a two-month run. My last use had been an overdose. Balancing heavy weight lifting and heavy heroin use finally resulted in injury—the opiate pain-numbing effects blocked my awareness of how hard I was working out. I torqued my bones and tore the muscles in my back. I went to the ER with a well-rehearsed act guaranteed to coax out something stronger than the usual Vicodin remedy and got a small prescription for Ativan and OxyContin to loosen the back muscles surrounding my spinal column.

I filled my prescription, went home, shot up, and took a handful of pills. I felt incredible, and, as I sat cross-legged on the floor, my sweat-laden forehead slumped forward. I slowly fell facedown to the ground, alternating between sleep and vomiting. The urge to vomit again woke me and raised me from the floor, and I ran at full speed toward the bathroom but miscalculated the location of the door. Running with the speed of an Olympic sprinter, I hit my bedroom wall with a force that rebounded me flat on my back. I burst out laughing, rolled on the ground, stared at the ceiling, and turned my head to vomit all over the floor. I didn't wipe the contents of my stomach off the side of my face—my arms were too heavy to move. My eyes rolled back into unconsciousness, and I woke the next morning to a room full of puke. I needed to stop using . . . again. That day I went back to my meetings, admitting failure and begging for help. They welcomed me back and were glad that I was still alive and safe.

The beginning of summer brought my fortieth magical drug-free day. Jason and I were trying to make our long-distance relationship work, and he invited me to see his show in Las Vegas. He knew I had relapsed, but wasn't sure how bad it was. He only knew me in recovery so had never had the opportunity to observe my decadent dance in death. I didn't have any money for the ticket, so he bought my flight to Vegas. The city was shocking to me. I had never seen anything so false. Old men walking the Strip with their breast-inflated, liposuctioned, plump-lipped Kewpie dolls, arm in arm, painted with the color of money and arrogance.

Two months apart had created a noticeable distance between us, and despite our being together again, Jason felt far away. Seeing him perform his passion in *Zumanity* made me proud, and I realized I wasn't as removed from the world on stage as I had thought—I could still do many of the skills that they were showing up there. The production transported me back to watching my first Cirque show on HBO, enthralled by the athleticism and grace. Jason embodied those qualities and belonged there, and maybe I did too. I vowed to try again, even though I had just come out of another major relapse.

The circus seeded a new idea, spurred by jealousy and a desire to keep Jason emotionally nearby after my return to New York. Like most of my drug-induced ideas, it was completely fantastical. I would train harder than ever, get hired by Cirque du Soleil, and make him want me. I believed keeping him would keep me in recovery, and, though the distance might dismantle our emotions and the Strip's vices might lure him from my grasp, he would fall prey to my desire to love and be loved. He admired the circus artists of his new reality, and, through my hard work, he would admire me too. I put this sharp sword of inspiration in its case, said goodbye, and carried it back to New York with my new mission for love and recovery.

The relapse filled my spirit with shame and anger, but my new motivation thrust me forward to do everything in my power to get back in shape and stay in recovery. I auditioned and was hired to perform with an acrobatic group for Broadway Bares, a fundraising show by the theater community raising money for Broadway Cares/Equity Fights AIDS. The show was for one night, and it would be my first New York performance.

While I was bigger, stronger, and back in great shape from lifting, arriving at the huge event space full of half-naked dancers with impeccable bodies brewed more jealousy and envy inside me. Unable to see my own assets, I only focused on others' attributes, pushing me to get to their level. There were no drugs going around, which was a relief, but there was a lot of drinking. I managed to stay abstinent, focused on our number, and found joy in flipping again with a group. As a competing gymnast I had had no idea this performing world existed, and wished my coaches or parents had shown me this athletic option. I should have been doing this with my life all along. Our performance and the evening were a huge success, and I connected with a wide range of people in the performance industry. The night was a tiny reward for staying in recovery, and I continued to commit my time to training, working out, and stretching.

My enthusiasm paid off. I was hired as an acrobat in Puccini's *Turandot* at the Metropolitan Opera House. My roommates couldn't believe my luck in getting to work at such a prestigious venue. I was ecstatic. That would be my first paid performance. Rehearsals would start in a few months and I had to stay abstinent, or else I would lose it and again destroy all I had been working toward.

During a long, slow day at work I started searching the Web for different forms of acrobatics. Images of contortionists filled the screen and pulled me in; there were women able to arch their backs practically in half, to the point where their spinal cords seemed ready to snap. Having never seen a man do that, I searched for male contortionists, and Jonathan Nosan appeared. He was extremely flexible and had made a huge career from dedication to his art form. I was very flexible as a young gymnast, almost to the point of contortionism, but an older gymnast had made fun of my flexibility at the Olympic Training Center by saying, "Only girls should be able to bend like that." Humiliated, I stopped working on it and let my flexibility deteriorate.

I had just turned twenty-seven and wondered if it was possible to regain my past flexibility. If I stretched all day long, could I get back to the range I had when I was younger? Unsure of the answer, but sure of my desire, I started my quest into the world of extreme physical pain. Instead of taking a lunch break, I went into the copy room where I mindlessly made hundreds of copies for editors and reporters, and stacked up large boxes filled with blank white copying paper. I put my foot up on top and began my training. Most people don't stretch, because it's slow and painful. Nobody wants to be in pain—especially a heroin addict. I didn't know where this would lead, but I knew that to achieve my goal I needed to stretch all day long, and since I was at work I had to do it there. Regardless, it was a better in-between-tasks hobby than shooting heroin.

I took every opportunity I could find to stretch: under my desk, in the copy closet, at home, on the street. My body resisted the pain and gravity resisted my pushing, but I continued lengthening my body and muscles. I was extremely tight, and the smallest, simplest stretch shot nerve pains throughout my body. The path in front of me seemed impossible, but I was determined to make this dream a reality.

After a month of deep stretching on my own, I asked an acrobat I worked with at Broadway Bares if she knew Jonathan and if he ever taught classes. She sent me to his website, I sent him an email, and then I arranged to attend a class he taught at a yoga studio in Chelsea. I was terrified of meeting Jonathan and ashamed that I needed to relearn how to stretch after having once been flexible. He was tall, very attractive, and lean and muscular, with a magnetic quality and a boyish smile. We walked into the studio and started; he was very serious and ready to work. Leg flexibility was my major weakness, but I had great strength and stamina for holding handstands. Everything in nature stretches to unrealized degrees of plasticity, and within that movement, as we release, connect, and dissolve our ego of physicality, stretching can take on a spiritual dimension.

As I stood with my back against the wall, Jonathan would lift my leg to its limit and then beyond, telling me to breathe deeply. Breath is our primal connection to movement; it is our first bodily expression out of the womb, and will be our last. Raising my leg beyond my extreme, Jonathan kept repeating, "Breathe," though my body resisted the rigorous pain.

He said, "You're not breathing; you're in pain and holding your breath, not exhaling, not letting it out." He was right, and it wasn't just in that training. I could never breathe. I was always fighting to get air inside my lungs, and when I was introduced to some sort of pain or crisis I held my breath, denying my body life and air. I found relief through drugs, which eased me into breathing more naturally. Who or what was constricting my breath?

After class, I opened up to Jonathan and told him about my past. The deep stretching and breathing of the class brought forth the truth, and that poor guy listened patiently as I vomited my story all over him. I imagined that happened to him often after a session, as we become vulnerable in pain. When pushed to our physical limits, there is a moment when we have to let go and surrender to the agony. I told him I was a heroin addict, with almost four months of recovery, and was trying to reclaim my life. He was honored I told him the truth. He opened up a little about his own story and about how and why he became a contortionist.

I saw him again for another class, and we talked about the art of contortion versus the sport of gymnastics. Many people viewed contortionism as a freak-show skill, but Jonathan was preserving the traditional artistry of strength and flexibility. To him it was a beautiful, moving mosaic pattern, following the connections of breath and body. When someone can feel that internally, then they can transport their emotions and experiences outward into their performance and practice.

We began talking privately, and emailing and texting. I was cautious because of my failed track record of making relationships work with Matt, Alejandro, and Jason. I needed to focus on recovery, but nature had other plans, and we started seeing each other. At first we were just having sex, but our relationship developed into genuine, caring feelings for each other. I was in recovery, with no agenda other than to enjoy spending time with him. I wanted nothing back from him and stopped taking classes—I was too stubborn and wanted to stretch my own way. I could feel myself moving in a more positive direction.

Rehearsals for the opera started up in a small dance room underneath the giant complex of the Met with stories circulating of the vastness and history of the yet unseen stage. The other gymnasts and I were extremely honored to have this job, and we took it very seriously. The choreographer ran us through the dance with the corps de ballet, and then we practiced the acrobatic stage combat—a small fight scene with armed guards, flipping, jumping, and battling our way off stage. It was a good time, and I could see why people wanted this as a full-time career. My boss at the *Times* gave me time off for rehearsals and performances.

With two jobs I was making more money than ever, and that made me nervous. Money never lasted long in my life. I sometimes believed my drug problem was purely financial and the problem was never having enough money to use as much as I desired. My addict's reasoning was more money meant more drugs. But I couldn't use now, could I? About to do my first paid performance in front of 3,800 people, how could I manage to do that high? The more energy I put into those thoughts, the stronger the overwhelming desire to use became. I tried finding loopholes in my recovery life, places I could slip off to without anyone noticing, and then began creating alibi scenarios in my head to cover myself if I were caught or suspected. I was already too deep in the thought process and knew using was inevitable— my disease of addiction was stronger than the recent successes I was experiencing in life. Without thinking of the consequences, I relapsed back into my familiar warm highs.

Jonathan only knew me in recovery, and I would now have to act sober around him while high. We had only been dating for two months, and I was working so much I thought I could easily hide my heroin use from him. He lived five blocks away, and Kimi's street was between the two of us, making for another bizarre love triangle. If I shot up I would just avoid Jonathan and try seeing him the next day. He would call me early in the morning to meet for coffee, and I always answered the phone as if I had just woken up from a coma, then met him downstairs at the newest cafe. I wanted to show up with the light of morning in my eyes, but instead consistently crawled out from my crypt, slightly detoxing, cold, sniffing, and sitting uncomfortably on the hard chair. I felt horrible that I was never fully present, but I couldn't pull it together in the morning. He would sit there, somehow tolerating an hour of my negativity as I cursed my existence into a coffee cup.

The next month I was in and out of recovery as we continued rehearsing the show. At first I was fearful to show up high, but quickly got over that after no one seemed to notice. In a way it helped—I could no longer feel the impact of the hard floor in my ankles. Opening night was approaching, and I had to decide whether to get clean now or do the show high. It would take a few days to detox and I couldn't perform while dope sick, but could probably perform while high; it was one thing to be on stage numb, but sweating, throwing up, and shivering would be impossible. With a month until opening, the window of opportunity was closing—get clean or stay high.

My repeated relapse reignited my self-hatred. After all my hard work, I so easily lost my recovery. Yet I continued going to twelve-step meetings, attempting to combat my addiction. It was such a simple concept—surrender to win—but I was stuck in a dark cycle of having a few days clean off dope and then going back out. Between rehearsals, the newspaper, and my needles and spoons I trained extremely hard, trying to become a contortionist. Some days I stretched while detoxing, which I don't recommend to anyone. My spine would burn from the lack of opiates in my system and I would push myself in backbends, trying to rip my muscles apart and lengthen them. I was so driven to transform and become this other thing that even though I was dope sick, I still tried to stretch with aching bones, fighting through pain and addiction with my desire to get clean.

I was back again, running out of options for a cure. I tried self-help books, veganism, organic teas, Dr. Phil, voodoo, the South Beach Diet, Oprah, twelve-step meetings, vitamins, witchcraft, contortionism, and anything else that seemed like it could help me. I was desperate for answers, and a friend recommended a psychic and said maybe she could give me some direction. I always had a thing for psychics because of my deep love for the supernatural, and thought maybe she could provide some insight. In desperation, I went to see if my life would soon end in a grave of my own digging.

I expected to meet a one-eyed woman covered in organic corn husks and crystals with a circle of light around her head, but instead I met Amie, a petite woman from Washington. She had a big smile and welcomed me into the place where she was doing her readings. I wasn't high, but detoxing on my methadone cocktail. She asked before we met to think of three questions I wanted answered. I didn't care about wealth, success, love, or happiness—I just wanted to know if I would ever get into recovery. That question was written on my face. She took one look at me and said, "People think you are someone with good looks, and you are, but you're something much greater. They don't see what's behind the vehicle; they don't see into your soul. You don't see what's in your own soul. I know you're a gymnast, but that isn't your quest, that isn't what you were sent here to do. You're a writer. That's your job, and you have something to tell the world." She said, "Let me see your hands," and I flipped them over. "Yes, I was right; this is what you will do someday." Hearing that news was inspiring and invigorating, yet I didn't care. All I wanted to know was when my next battle with a syringe would take place and if it would bring a peaceful conclusion either through life or death.

I said urgently, "I'm a drug addict and I can't stay drug-free. Will I die or will I make it?"

She said, "You have two roads to take. If you keep going on this road it's going to get much worse. I know you've already camped out in hell, but what lies ahead for you is going to make your skin crawl, and you won't return from it. If you keep using you are going to be permanently damaged. You know, the Devil has a thing for you because you have such a strong light. He wants to devour that light and hold you forever."

"What is the other path?"

"If you go back to twelve-step meetings and don't give up, and keep trying, the spirits tell me that you will find a life of recovery by the time you are thirty."

Those words sent rivers of hope into my blackened heart, but I didn't think I could endure recovery. I didn't think after all this time I could ever find myself again and carry on with the rest of humanity—I wanted to die.

35

TIBIA

IN THE HUMAN BODY, THE INNER, LARGER OF THE TWO BONES
OF THE LEG IS COMMONLY KNOWN AS THE SHINBONE, OR TIBIA,
WHICH HAS ITS ROOTS IN A SIMILAR LATIN WORD. OVER TIME,
THE TIBIA ALSO CAME TO REFER TO A PIPE OR FLUTE DUE TO ITS
RESEMBLANCE IN SHAPE TO THOSE MUSICAL INSTRUMENTS.

Sigmund Freud believed that every person has an unconscious desire
to be satisfied, still, and quiet, to have no needs or problems, and to
be at peace. He called this state a death instinct, or having a wish
to die. I was living life only to experience death. I was trying to find
transcendence, peace, and silence, not knowing that those things
defined the death instinct. The great promise of death is to release us
from the struggles and burdens of our lives. I once believed nirvana
meant a pure heavenly state, but its actual meaning is "to blow out";
attaining this goal is to extinguish the candle of our lives.

My own death instinct, expressed through my drug use, had created
deep trauma in my life. But I was trying to escape trauma by using
drugs, creating more trauma with my escape, and so it became a
never-ending cycle. I had been using for so long, living in a constant
state of extreme highs and lows, disappointment and depression, that
my mind began to disconnect from reality by creating its own fantasy
land. I believe that is the moment in an addict's life when the line
between sanity and insanity dissolves, when mental illness develops,
forever engulfing us. The more times I traveled to that illusionary
world, the less I was able to come back to the reality in which I was
actually living. Even though externally it looked like I was going to

the same places and doing the same things, my inner life began to take on an Alice in Wonderland feel. I didn't realize I was slowly going crazy, and that I was giving myself permission to do so by thinking, *If I'm this strung out all the time, I may as well surrender to the illusions of my mind.* I began to watch the world around me change.

My using was getting out of hand again, and it was reflected in my work. I would often shoot too much heroin and nod out at my desk. The worst part about shooting too much heroin was the nausea. I considered myself a "functioning" addict (an oxymoron, I know), which meant I usually knew how much to take. But sometimes I paid the consequences for misjudging the amount I needed in order to go out in public and be a good citizen of the world. The heroin would make me sick to my stomach without any warning, and the bathroom wasn't near my desk, which meant I often didn't make it. I would have literally two seconds to make it to the toilet, and it wasn't close enough. I never got caught throwing up in the hallways, which I did on more than one occasion. I would just go back and tell my boss that someone got sick on the floor, commenting on how "wicked nasty" that was.

I had recently moved to another department, a new and rewarding move for me. I had more responsibilities now, and I desperately wanted to prove myself as an employee and as a human being who was capable of this job. I wanted my colleagues to like me, but, more importantly, I wanted to someday stay clean and have a future at that company.

My new department was on the news desk, located on the third floor. It was the hub of the newspaper, full of intelligent and hardworking editors and writers. They put out the first page of the newspaper every day, recreating several different editions as the news changed before the deadline, which it often did. I felt like I was working in a shark tank, with time's sharp teeth constantly circling us, waiting to attack.

I was the least educated person at the news desk, with everyone else having graduate degrees from universities such as Harvard, Yale, and

Columbia. All I had ever done was switch my major from cocaine to heroin. I can't even begin to describe how unworthy I felt, and I was always terrified that someone was going to ask me for information about some current event or political policy—there were no politics in my world. There was only the decision to shoot heroin or not to shoot heroin. The only thing I'd ever gotten a diploma for was as a patient at a mental institution; I had graduated from living on the streets to having a bed in the homeless shelter. What could I possibly have to offer?

My job was to rewrite the tiny weather blurbs or "ears" that appeared at the top right of the front page each day, which would say something like "Cloudy, little rain, windy," etc. I had around twenty different weather blurbs to do per day, which covered the entire country. I received the initial weather report from Penn State's meteorology department and then revised it to fit into the little square of space.

When I was finished with my rewrite, I would send the blurb over to one of the editors, Anna, to check for errors. At first I was terrified that she would make fun of me when I handed her my work, but even though she always found mistakes, she never belittled me. She was professional and kind, and I wanted to be able to thank her for that. In fact, I came to love her; she reminded me of my own mother when I was younger. Her approach was loving and nurturing even though my palpable distress must have been obvious to her.

This was serious work, so I couldn't have my usual three-course heroin lunch. I had to be alert and clear-headed. At almost every shift I would freak out in fear that I wouldn't be able to meet the deadline; I was afraid I would be humiliated in front of all the influential people at the newspaper. The more overwrought I became, the more I needed heroin to function. In my torn and dirty backpack, I had my bent spoon, syringe, lighter, rubbing alcohol patch, and brown powder in a wax paper bag, with its marketing brand like "undead" or "nightwalker" printed on the outside. I had to use or else I couldn't concentrate on the work.

Like most addicts who try to hide their using, I tried not to bring my backpack with me into the bathroom. It's the same thing as alcoholics hiding their bottles by wrapping them in newspapers to prevent a clanging sound in the trash. I was paranoid someone would be watching and question me as to why I always brought my backpack with me. Instead, I took a large manila envelope printed with the *New York Times* stamp, opened my backpack, and prepared my mobile pharmacy kit.

With my large, drug-filled envelope in hand, I walked past all the high-ranking people on my way to the bathroom, feeling like I was getting away with something. I don't know why I found great pleasure in doing that, but I did.

"Heroin . . . brought to you by the *New York Times*." The slogan I made up in my head always made me silently laugh, and in a way it was like saying "Fuck you; fuck you!" to the corporation that was basically giving me a chance in life. Addicts will always turn the rope that saved them into a noose to hang themselves. I would go in the stall, with coworkers right next to me; get rip-roaring high; return to the news desk; and get back to work.

Now that I was good and wrecked, I would be able to concentrate. When I was loaded, I had no barriers between myself and reality, no boundaries between right and wrong, and I would try to write those simple weather forecasts, as poetically and creatively as possible. However, the weather ears didn't need my creativity; they just needed accuracy with perfect grammar, and I was far away from being able to do that.

Now that I worked at night, my lunchtime break changed, and while most employees went out to eat their dinner, I escaped as fast as possible to Forty-ninth Street. Even though I had done this hundreds of times, each time still held its own mystery and enchantment. I would get to Forty-ninth Street and Eleventh Avenue and stand before the parallel rows of apartments. In my delirium, reality and make-believe began to blend. Many addicts still lived on this street and it mimicked the destruction in their lives, as any good junkie street does. There's a bridge that goes over the train tracks, full of broken glass and usually some homeless people camped out by the spray-painted, cracked wall. I knew I was crossing into the darkness. Passing by the homeless man, I saw another version of me—a broken bike and his trash were simply other versions of my things—as I entered Kimi's apartment, a place I imagined to be engulfed by flames.

I imagined her place to be a castle of sand sitting up high on a cloud, with this mystical dimension visible only to those who knew of its secret and power, for those foolish enough to drink the bottles that say "POISON: Do Not Ingest." It gave me such relief that Kimi was always there for me, the only ravishing woman who helped me dig my own grave, rusty shovel and syringes in hand, with a large, sweaty smile, forever challenging my dignity. I had been in her apartment more than in my own, and I always stood in the kitchen, afraid to touch anything for fear that I would become like the thing touched, dusty, sticky, and dirty. It was an odd reassurance that the apartment never changed and always looked like an old flea market, smelling like old vodka, stale cigarettes, sweat, rubbing alcohol, and regret—years and years of regret.

Once the demon handed me my bags, I would run into the bathroom, tear open the wax paper, and put the heroin onto the bent spoon. I hated this part, because it took too long and I wanted my shot ready at that moment, even though it only took about two minutes in real time to prepare. My addiction was urgent, and I was constantly fearful that I was going to have a moment of regret. I didn't want to have time to think about "right and wrong"; I just wanted to get high and eliminate any lucid thoughts that still lingered in my mind. Each new high meant that I was hurting someone in my life, and the new person now was Jonathan. However, those people didn't understand that this was the only way for me to continue to exist. I needed this, and nobody besides other junkies could understand my fate.

After mainlining, it was six seconds to oblivion. I reached my destination, then watched my pupils shrink from big to small, and the bliss washed over me like an internal fleece blanket.

I returned to work as quickly as possible, repeating that sacrament daily. Year after year, Kimi answered the door, waiting for my money, and I believed she loved me, that she cared for me, and that she understood the true pain that I bore. Everyone else, including my coworkers at the *Times* and the Metropolitan Opera House, could not reach me, though they could hear my cries, see the pain splattered on my face, the look in my eyes that I was screaming inside my body like a tortured prisoner.

I started my performances for *Turandot* and my *Times* coworkers were glad for me, honoring my new schedule restraints. I never stopped using for opening night, which meant I couldn't stop using until we finished the season of shows. It pained me to be performing and using at the same time. I had abandoned gymnastics many years ago, and it was because of recovery that I ever dared to go back. I knew recovery was a gift, and here I was, returning it. I couldn't believe what a hypocrite I had become.

In my heart I wanted to perform drug-free, and I tried many times, but failed because my body was in too much pain from the withdrawals and there was no way I could flip onstage while detoxing. I needed to get high in order not to be sick. Ironically, my life seemed designed for me never to get into recovery again.

Even though I was strung out, I was always on time for my rehearsals and performances, attentive, and courteous and respectful to everyone. I considered the other acrobats in the show my family members. Performing at the Met was one of the good graces in my life, and the stage had an amazing power to it. It was one of the hopeful things I looked forward to, and I always thought that somehow either the music or the applause of 3,800 audience members could cure me.

One day Anna handed me an article from our Arts section featuring Andrea Gruber, who was the soprano in Puccini's *Turandot*. The article spoke of how Andrea used to sing at the Metropolitan Opera House while high on painkillers and how she overcame her addiction. It was an honest story of her triumph over drugs. Some prescription painkillers, in a sense, contain the same substance as heroin; it's the opiate-based chemical that gives one the sense of euphoria. It was an odd coincidence—even before I knew of Andrea's struggle with drugs, her strong presence and amazing voice pulled me in during rehearsals. Her voice carried her past, rising from the depths of the Earth with a rich, strong, and powerful tone, moving everyone. There was definitely some strange irony here with me, the addict, reading an article at work written by my colleague about a woman in the same show in which I was performing who was also an addict.

After I read the article, I wanted to talk to Andrea during rehearsals. She seemed to glisten and shine—I desperately wanted what she had. How could I approach her, and what would I say? Her story portrayed hope, but it made me feel even worse about my actions. Shooting up in order to flip disrespected everyone who had ever helped me train when I was younger—but my body was already too far gone, and I needed the high to perform.

I always arrived early to the Met to warm up and stretch, still aiming for the goal of becoming a contortionist, and just before I put on my costume, the demon would strike. I would shoot up, get dressed in the costume, and wait for the cue to come out flipping in a scene with the other acrobats. Costumed as homeless people, we tumbled through a choreographed fight scene and then rioted with the guards. After that, we did a few random stage moves, giving us the best seats in the house: onstage.

After the tumbling fight scene, I lay onstage as Andrea sang, trying to catch my breath, dressed in my tattered costume as a sick, dying beggar. Between the power of the music, the massive stage space, and my drug-induced euphoria, I came close to believing I was living that scene. It felt as though we were inside a giant box, and although the audience was difficult to see through the darkness, I could feel them watching.

Emanating from Andrea that night was the most beautiful, rich voice I had ever heard; her voice came from a place of pain, sorrow, and redemption, and I knew if any voice could cure me, hers could. Her voice was a powerful instrument that pushed away the darkness within me. At that moment I begged for transformation, as if the sonic shapes could cast the spell that would turn me into a butterfly. It brought tears to my eyes, and I would suffer there onstage in my own silence, listening to her metamorphosis instead of mine. While she was singing for her life, I was listening for my death, and the audience bore witness to that but knew nothing of the truth or the irony of real stories before their eyes, concealed by the darkness, sounds, and stage lighting.

Act Two, Scene Two ends with one of the most famous arias of the opera, the first five notes and three words of which Andrea had tattooed on her lower back. Walking up to the edge of her platform, she began and her breath rose and fell, as if she was slightly unsure of the power of the words, feeling her voice fill the cavernous space. She quickly gained confidence with her striking stare, eyes focused straight ahead. Her voice gained the momentum of a cyclone, ready to tear through stillness and silence, and then rising to the aria's climax—a song to the gods, to all women who have played Turandot before and will play Turandot after this moment, proclaiming her inner meaning and declaring her anthem. She sang with perfection.

Was Andrea singing to her addiction as my addiction sang to me? For me, her voice was a guide of redemption, ringing into the air and crying out for all souls tortured by this disease to break through into a sobering stillness. As the audience took in an amazing performance, I felt only I could hear and take in her true story and the intention behind those words—no great performance can come from a place without experience and compassion. Those words were not for Puccini, the press, or the rich, critical audience in front of her; I was convinced they were for Andrea, and for me.

Andrea graciously took her bow to the audience's standing ovation, and her recovery beamed through her skin. If only I could have touched her robe, maybe I could have stolen a molecule of her strength. I went back to the dressing room, but first stopped in the bathroom to shoot that memory away, because it was too painful. I lived that pattern for a long time and had to use more during future shows, because you can't keep a hungry lion starving for long.

The Met hired me for two more productions. I wasn't sure how I had managed that, but even though I was using, my acrobatics were still solid. Through some innate muscle memory, I could do gymnastics on any drug without falling, and my body was conditioned to flip on its own while my mind went somewhere else. It felt like driving heavy machinery through quicksand, but I always managed to land on my feet, and I was fortunate to not make any mistakes onstage—until later that year in an afternoon performance of Verdi's *Un Ballo in Maschera*.

I did a simple front flip, and was so strung out that I landed short and fell on my ass. I stayed there for a minute onstage, in shock. Again, my addiction infiltrated my art, my God, and everything that I had thought was mine.

Gymnastics, the last thing that made me human and gave me a reason to live, was now pulled out from under me and dragged to the underworld. I didn't see the Devil or hear his laugh, but I felt him. I was his now, in completeness, the two of us, forever and ever in his hell of misery and pain. My disease had won, and I knew it.

I told the other acrobats I slipped on something, which neither they nor I believed. I went home fuming and rueing the day I had invited this destruction into my life. Neither the music, the prayers, nor the wishing could fix the reality of me. Again, as I had always done to battle my addiction, I stood by my window, thinking, pleading, urging God to take physical form and to send a bolt down with some sort of power to remove me from this insanity. And I said, bitterly, "Well . . . all right now . . . just swallow me whole . . . but take me fast." As usual, my prayers were met with silence.

36

PITUITARY GLAND: PART II

NALTREXONE IS AN OPIOID RECEPTOR ANTAGONIST USED PRIMARILY IN THE MANAGEMENT OF ALCOHOL AND OPIATE DEPENDENCE. IT WORKS BY BLOCKING THE "PLEASURE" EFFECTS. THE ORAL FORMULATION MUST BE TAKEN DAILY. ADDICTS WHOSE CRAVINGS BECOME OVERWHELMING CAN OBTAIN THEIR OPIATE EUPHORIA BY SKIPPING A DOSE BEFORE RESUMING ABUSE OF THEIR DRUG OF CHOICE. A NALTREXONE IMPLANT, SURGICALLY INSERTED UNDER THE SKIN, IS AN ALTERNATIVE. THE IMPLANT PROVIDES A SUSTAINED DOSE OF NALTREXONE TO THE PATIENT, PREVENTING THE POSSIBILITY OF SKIPPED DOSES, AND MUST BE REPLACED EVERY THREE MONTHS. CASES HAVE BEEN DOCUMENTED OF HEROIN ADDICTS CARVING OUT THEIR IMPLANTS AS A RESULT OF CRAVINGS.

The psychic's words resonated in my head like a church bell: "If you pick up again, you will suffer a fate worse than death." What was she talking about? I'd already been through the four corners of hell and slept with the Devil, but her words haunted me. I continued using on and off, and kept a steady eye out for anything abnormal approaching in the distance.

I trained exceptionally hard for months and was in my best physical condition since quitting gymnastics. I was becoming more flexible and could perform some of the same skills as Jonathan. I took pictures of him contorting and tried to mimic the postures he created with his body. With stretching and contorting it takes years to achieve excellence, but in my mind I didn't have years. I had to destroy the physical restraints that kept me from my goal. I started a precarious training regimen, unaware of the actual physical effects of what I called "muscle stretching," presuming that tearing muscles would bring results faster.

I complained to Jonathan of how much my body hurt, and he repeatedly told me I was training incorrectly; but, like a mindless idiot, I continued doing the things that pained me and not connecting breath with my body. I would slide into a split with a twenty-five-pound plate on my leg and aggressively bounce, not following Jonathan's recommendations of slow pulses and gradual stretching. Whether training or trying to kick my addiction, I was constantly in a rushed plight of agony, and both left me stuck in the same place: pain. High, abstinent, or in withdrawals, I still trained—tumbling, lifting, doing handstands, and stretching like a crazed maniac.

I was rehired at the Met for *Samson & Delilah*. I was to be practically naked, painted bright orange, and dance onstage in the third act for the bacchanalia. I had to start my junkie preproduction regimen of methadone detox to get through the impending withdrawals and try for recovery. I had done that so many times, it was becoming habitual. Acclimated as I was to pain through my sport, the physical turmoil of detox became just another event I had to endure. Gymnastics had trained me to become a great addict—capable of enduring, surviving, and striving toward the most uncomfortable and painful body moments.

My roommates were doing renovations to the apartment, and I had to stay with Jonathan for a little while. Staying with him was going to be problematic—it would be impossible to keep my secret in a one-bedroom apartment. The first morning I realized I left my "cooking spoon" at my old place, so I lurked into Jonathan's kitchen, snuck a spoon into my pocket, and tiptoed to the toilet. I bent his shiny new IKEA spoon, cooked my breakfast, washed off the bottom burnt by the flame, and incanted, "Out, damn'd spot! Out, I say! One—two—why then 'tis time to do't. Hell is murky." I tweaked it back close to its original position, slipped back into the kitchen, and replaced it with the others. As I learned from my sisters years ago, if nothing changed, then nothing happened. Moments later I saw Jonathan smiling and eating his cereal in the living room. Was he holding my truth in his hand? Unknowingly feeding himself through the same tool that fed my veins? The spoon came back to haunt me that night, as the three of us shared Ben & Jerry's from the carton.

Those situations increasingly complicated my daily existence, as my syringe affair started flaunting itself at the junctures of our "family" life. A few times I cooked up too much and had to save the surplus in an unused syringe for later. With its plunger pulled back, if my needle full of heroin got bumped or pushed, my gold would escape, squeezing out my life force; I somehow had to escape the bathroom and get it into my backpack undetected by Jonathan. I cradled the needle in the pocket of my cargo pants—the ideal wardrobe item for all types of drug using—cautious not to strike the plunger. But during the mission I ran into Jonathan, who approached, wanting to hug me goodbye. I always pulled back from contact, but this time I was terrified to be touched too tightly, fearing he would rub up against the plunger. My addiction became an awkward lover, and the longer I stayed at Jonathan's apartment, the more she showed up.

Unknown to me, Jonathan knew I was using the whole time. Any sane person would know that. It was so obvious—I woke up with one personality, left the bathroom with another, and hours later turned into yet someone else. I was financially defective, vexed, cynical, and always sleeping late. Jonathan knew my history with rehabs and twelve-step meetings, and I promised him I would return to a life of recovery; but I knew this time I needed more help. The up-and-down cycle was obliterating me, and my methadone concoction wouldn't be enough this time around.

I decided to try a new drug: Suboxone. Yet with all my good intentions, I quickly discovered the loopholes in that medication. There was always a back door in addiction, and junkies were notoriously the first to bust it down. It took me a week's trial and error, but I found a dose I could take every day that wouldn't leave me in withdrawal while still feeling the effects of heroin when I shot up. What made this even greater was that when Jonathan would ask me if I was using, I could tell him it was only the effects of the Suboxone—I had it all.

An agent called for me to play a bartender on a popular soap opera. In my mind I thought I would be so exceptional that they would cast me as a new character on the show. What it actually meant was that they needed an extra to serve drinks in the background.

The night before the shoot I laid out everything I would need— organized to control an uncontrollable event. I washed my face twice to magnetize the camera to me; they would be powerless over my good looks and unable to resist hiring me. The next day I showed up at the job and was petrified. What if I was bad and they didn't like the way I looked? They sent me to wardrobe to fit me for a tuxedo, and a woman guided me to a dressing room. I couldn't believe I had my own dressing room. She told me I would hear my call over the intercom, but it could take hours. My room was essentially a closet with a large mirror that I gazed into, making sure my hair was immaculate and trying not to move in fear of messing it up. I waited and waited, but the intercom remained silent.

The more time passed, the more I desired personal obliteration, and, like a good junkie, I had come prepared. I cooked up, shot up, and fell into oblivion, slumped into my own arms as pillows on the little desk, waiting for my call. A violent sound blared repeatedly into my brain, startling me from my bliss. I remembered the woman whose aggravated voice was rumbling through the intercom. I looked in the mirror at my disarrayed hair and drippy skin, wiped the drool from my mouth, and tried to erase the lines in my face made by the sleeves of my tuxedo. I looked like death, and it was time to shoot; I must have missed the first call, and now I was late.

All I had to do was to impersonate a bartender, which was not difficult, but I wanted more. I wanted someone to notice me, give me a line, but nothing happened. I tried getting in front of the camera as much as possible, but in the end I appeared only as a big, black-and-white blur passing through the frame.

My dissatisfaction dumbfounded me. I had everything I wanted—an endless trip into my underworld without physical consequences—and yet I remained wholeheartedly dispirited. Had I suffocated my soul in this overly medicated physical confinement? Was my spirit crying to reunite with my body and experience life as it was intended? Had I taken myself prisoner and become incapable of personal liberation? If only I could live my life without emotions, then I could truly be at peace. For years I had prayed to God to remove my traumatic emotions, and now I was living in a heartless, dreadful paralysis. I had received what I had hungered for, and now I was disconsolate, praying to God to grant me back the ability to feel anything.

Even the rapturous feelings of ecstasy had become anesthetized, and I could no longer experience any form of joy or connection to the natural world. A sunny day might as well have been cloudy, and all laughter might as well have been screams. My fundamental ambition had been to attain the greatest high possible, and there I was, experiencing my dream, and I'd never been so spiritually broken—a godless heaven is no heaven at all. I lived like a solitary and soulless, medicated old man, a breathing cadaver wanting and waiting for the nightmare to end. I prayed for the return of every old delicious feeling I'd ever owned. I reached the point of a terrifying admission: my drugs no longer worked. In a final attempt to preserve my nirvana, I threw cocaine into the mix, but only the vicious side effects emerged—something was clearly malfunctioning within my drug-laden body and soul.

I finally resolved to give Suboxone an opportunity to heal me as professionally prescribed and not as a crutch for withdrawals. I returned to the clinic and told the doctor what I had done, and learned I wasn't the first. He raised the dosage to close the opiate receptors and prevent the heroin from breaking through. I started a new, month-long, honest regime of the bitter orange pills.

The first week of taking the recommended dosage I felt peculiar, not exactly high but not myself. Jonathan thought I was using, but I wasn't. The next week I maintained the same dose, but still my personality was bizarre; I was feeling the raving madness of a deranged entity brewing inside me.

I was becoming a Suboxone lifer, becoming addicted to "the cure." I had unwillingly become shackled like the prisoners in the methadone line, the hopeless army of the damned, the Devil's henchmen. I could handle many atrocious results from heroin, but addiction to Suboxone or methadone would forever destroy me.

I submerged myself in the Suboxone blogosphere, seeking an escape from the impending dependence. People on the treatment were detoxing with promising futures, but quickly fell into the same orange pill nightmare, with similar personality shifts to my own. Hopeless addicts blindly walked into the promised lands of a new solution, believing in the possibility of one month of detox, but many of us remained on the medication for years. Was that my fate? My Prozac generation hooked on a new methadone? In desperation, I tried detoxing from Suboxone, and fell into the same "dope sickness" of chills, vomiting, and excruciating body aches.

I told Jonathan what was happening, and he began to understand how truly ill and messed up I was. He saw me ambitiously train as an athlete, but I lived my life inside a war zone. I knew what I had to do to mend the situation, and told him my plan: return to heroin to get off Suboxone, then detox from heroin with my old-school potion of methadone and Xanax. My plans always involved other people's money, since I rarely had any of my own. I needed to borrow money from Jonathan to shoot up, which seemed bizarre, but I thought my idea for escape was foolproof.

I let a few days pass until I could feel the withdrawal effects from the Suboxone, and then took a big, brown shot, hoping to scour my system of one evil with another. I prayed the heroin would form a raging river, tearing apart the chemical dam from my brain cells and overriding my ingested Agent Orange. I was careful not to do too much and drown myself in heroin—wanting to get clean, not die. Within seconds of shooting it into my vein, I felt it: "Oh yes, there you are." I tried not to fall in love again, but I did. Once again I felt good, whole, and complete, the way life or the afterlife should be. I quickly fell into the sweet, silent euphoria. "Oh god, how I missed you."

I used every day for two weeks and didn't want to separate from the Devil, but the moment came when Jonathan's tolerance ended. We met one afternoon in Bryant Park, surrounded by giant trees dismantling the skyline. He was distant as we ate lunch and finally said, "I can't do this anymore. You've promised for so long that you would get clean, and I know you've tried, but this is too much for me. You keep doing the same thing over and over again."

I had heard many times in twelve-step meetings that insanity is doing the same thing over and over and expecting different results. Yes, I was insane. The sadness in his eyes reflected my own, and I was again faced with the choice: hell or humanity. I saw what I was doing to yet another trusting person, but wasn't ready to disappear from that relationship. This was my last shot, and I was ready to fire my final bullet. I said with complete truth and sincerity, "If you could meet the man I really am, the man I'm supposed to be, I know you would really like him." I wasn't trying to manipulate him. Unsure, he said, "Okay, I'm giving you one last chance." I had to quit using or I would lose him.

I began recounting my fall from grace to identify a recovery time and determine a path toward reclamation. It was like watching old gymnastics routines, repeatedly inspecting and dissecting my mistakes. Twelve-step meetings and naltrexone brought me the most time in recovery, but when the urge to use surfaced, I stopped taking the pill. I needed something that lasted longer than a few days in the system and disabled my power of choice, something to stop me from using for months. I found a doctor who created and was administering a non-FDA-approved method in New Jersey: the naltrexone implant. He would make a small slit in the arm and insert the implant subcutaneously and then staple it back up, and the capsule would slowly dissolve over time, releasing small amounts of medication into the bloodstream for up to three months. While it was a little expensive, it was a new solution I had yet to try. After the first implant wore off, most addicts returned—or, more often, were dragged back by family and loved ones—for another. This seemed like a solution, but I faced the same problem as before. I needed fourteen days off opiates so I wouldn't go into immediate withdrawal.

With no money, I asked Jonathan, promising to pay him back. If I made the appointment and got fourteen days of abstinence, he said I could borrow the money. I mixed up my regular methadone-and-Xanax cocktail, went back to meetings, and started into recovery again. I wanted to use every day, but fought the desire.

After two weeks Jonathan rented a car, and after an hour's drive we arrived at the clinic and were greeted by a waiting room full of fellow junkies. Most of them did not look sober or pleased to be there. I could feel their pain and thirst. We were vampiric entities, possessed by the evil we shot into ourselves, now all in a room praying for some form of salvation.

The doctor was astonished that I had come in of my own accord, as most of his patients were court-mandated for the implant. I told him I was willing to do anything to get into recovery. Before starting, he gave me a shot of naltrexone to test the truth that I was completely opiate-free. He expected to see me go into withdrawals from that "polygraph injection" like most of the other junkies, but I passed. I was clean and ready for the implant. He started the procedure with two shots of Novocain. It was bizarre to have a needle in my arm without a high; it felt like sex without orgasm. He waited until the area was numb, made a one-inch incision behind my left triceps, crammed the implant under the skin, and clamped it shut with three staples. It hurt, but was over quickly. It was trapped inside my body. I had finally surrendered. It was rare for an addict to willingly put himself in pain, with no escape in sight. I stupidly took the two antibiotics afterward on an empty stomach and threw up for our whole drive home to New York.

With my implant I would be safe from heroin no matter what. I feared being in a devastating accident, screaming in terror with agonizing burns in an emergency room and unable to receive painkillers since my implant would block their opiate effects—but I needed this to work. The doctor said some patients try using huge amounts of heroin to override the implant, but they overdose and die. Others cut open their own flesh in desperation, digging out the pellet so they can use. While it seemed unfathomable, I knew it wasn't beneath me, for once the demon wakes, the addict is powerless over its demands.

A month passed, and I was continuing my contortion work relentlessly with Jonathan. I wasn't using and feeling better. Knowing I couldn't get high even if I shot up brought great relief and let me focus on my recovery issues while attending meetings every day. People learn to dance by doing what dancers do, and learn to paint by doing what painters do; to get into recovery, I started doing what people in recovery do. I put my dreams aside and focused on recovery while training like an Olympian. It helped me focus on positive aspects of myself and provided small, achievable goals. Years of mental corrosion slowly began to clear.

Jonathan had recently booked a workshop for a Broadway-bound show choreographed and directed by Twyla Tharp. I had also auditioned for it, but had no recollection of how I did. The show was moving forward, and I received a call from my agent to be seen again. Jonathan loved Twyla, finding her creative and inspiring to be around. I still had almost no dance experience, but the few classes I took made me feel good, moving without restrictions, feeling free, and experiencing a sense of being at home in my body.

I walked into the audition room slightly paralyzed by fear and saw Twyla sitting behind a desk. She had gorgeous silver hair cut short and was eating soup. Her smile was intense, and she looked pleased with the group of men in front of her, gymnasts who dance. I could tumble, but dancing was out of the question. Her assistant taught us the combination, and I couldn't remember a single step. I was a disaster—tripping on the guy beside me and bumping into the guy behind. Then she had us reverse the choreography. If I hadn't learned the first direction, how on Earth could I learn the second? I didn't get called back, but I wasn't distraught; that show was beyond my abilities, and I was simply proud to have auditioned without getting high. A month later they called me in again. I didn't want to embarrass myself once again, but I went in, and it went the same way. I wasn't cut out for that type of movement. The dancers in the room had trained in their art for as many years as I had done gymnastics and drugs combined.

But that audition wouldn't go away. A few weeks later I got called in again; Twyla still hadn't found what she was looking for. I wanted to be the one, but knew I wasn't. She had seen hundreds of dancers, all with incredibly honed skills and God-given talent. Athletically, I had advanced tremendously, training with Jonathan in different circus arts like juggling, aerial work, and unicycle, but I was nowhere near in the same movement dimensions as those other performers. However, my agent said Twyla had specifically requested me, and this time she needed to hear me sing. I laughed. I had trouble just speaking out loud, so singing was out of the question. Jonathan had his role secured for the show, and encouraged me to try. While certain that I wasn't what she was looking for, I had learned that sometimes even those who are casting don't know what they're looking for. And though it seemed ridiculous to audition again, I gave it a try. Jonathan recommended a vocal coach to find an audition song and some confidence.

My first day with the vocal coach was tragic. I stood in front of him, shaking and trembling, and he could barely get a sound out of me. I tried singing so low that it was hardly audible. Then he said, "I don't know why you aren't singing louder. You're strong and have such a nice, high range." I felt as though I'd been hit by a crowbar. Confused, I said, "What?"

"You have such a high range. This is what they're looking for." Though it wasn't what I wanted, I could hit high notes easily, and when I put some air behind the words it sounded decent enough to audition. Still, reaching a few notes didn't mean I could sing in front of strangers. For the next two weeks I sang every day, visualizing shooting the notes out above Twyla's head, but I didn't know how to stand, where to look, or what to do with my arms. Should I mime the song, move to it, rock back and forth? I had no clue.

Every morning I made Jonathan listen to me sing to the point of annoyance; but my perfectionism demanded I get it right. I stretched, lifted, flipped, held handstands, and sang until I was exhausted. I was coming close to ninety days of not using and was thrilled with the implant—enthralled and bewildered that I had gone to such lengths to stay drug-free.

I spent the night before the audition sleeplessly recounting my journey, lying in disbelief at my present place, proud of my uncomfortably hard work. Gymnastics, a gift bestowed on me, was as easy as child's play, but after I had readily exchanged it for a life of drug addiction, nothing had ever come easily again. I was forced to fight for everything, to work harder than anyone I ever knew to reclaim and relearn my life's true love. I faced recovery with the same adamancy, battling emotional crises every day.

I could barely breathe as I entered the audition room in terror—this time not as much of the dancing, and certainly not the acrobatics, but of the singing. The floor was covered with perfect-bodied dancers warming up, people who did this daily and had trained their entire existence for that moment. If they saw my track marks they would have kept their distance, but I was proud of my scars.

Twyla sat confidently next to her assistant and orchestrator. The audition began with strength, flexibility, and handstand endurance tests. I excelled at them all. She then made a first huge cut, and I was still there, still standing. I thought she had made a mistake until she looked directly at me and smiled. I nearly peed my pants. Then she taught the dance portion, and I was disastrous. With only three of us dancing in a large, open space, I managed to smash into both guys. With all my new recovery I still looked like a falling-down drunk. "Joe," Twyla said, "I know you can do this, but it's going to take some time. You go in the back. Stand behind them and do your own thing." I could do that. I wiggled around to my own rhythm. Then we did the acrobatic portion, which I nailed. Twyla was impressed; but the worst was yet to come.

The other remaining guys sang first, and those dancers could sing. As I waited outside, their huge, clear voices filled the space and resonated through the closed door. Their volume destroyed my confidence—there was no way I could continue. I needed to either leave or get high. I texted Jonathan, "I'm still here, but I can't do this. I can't stop shaking. I hate my voice, I'm so embarrassed. Please . . . can't I just leave?" He replied, "No, you can do this. Just do it like you practiced."

The door opened and it was my turn. I handed my sheet music to the musical director and he asked, "Where did you get this song?" I shyly said, "My roommates gave it to me." He looked shocked. "I composed this almost twenty years ago," he said. But at that moment, all I could think about was the paralyzing fear engulfing me.

Jonathan told me to take one deep breath before I sang—one breath, to connect with myself, to stand firmly on the ground and confidently mark my space. Take one breath for my hard work, for my past, and for where I'm going. Take one breath to protect me and remind me that none of those things really mattered. I took my breath and thought of Andrea Gruber at the Met—how she had confidently walked on stage, breathed, and belted out the purest notes I'd ever heard. I thought of her and borrowed her confidence, knowing she wouldn't mind.

Before I sang my first note, I made the decision to sing for my recovery. I had only been singing for two weeks, with no actual idea of what I was doing, but I put truth behind the words and pushed them from my lungs as clearly and passionately as possible. The sound of my voice deafened my ears, and while my brain told me to stop, I didn't. I sang for that college boy, kicked out of school, homeless in a park, and waiting for a miracle. I sang for my first injection and the way the needle broke my skin. I sang for Kimi and her abused girlfriend. I sang for the methadone line, terrified of becoming a part of it. And finally, I sang for the accomplishment of singing against fear, which was something I could never have done before.

I don't know how it sounded or what they thought, but Twyla thanked me for the audition and said I would hear something either way. That was commonly said in the industry, and I didn't expect to hear anything. Two hours later, Jonathan and I met for lunch and I told him about the audition. I was proud of doing my best, and my phone rang midstory. It was my agent: "You got the job!"

37

DNA

DEOXYRIBONUCLEIC ACID IS A NUCLEIC ACID THAT
CONTAINS THE GENETIC INSTRUCTIONS USED IN THE
DEVELOPMENT AND FUNCTIONING OF ALL KNOWN LIVING
ORGANISMS. THE MAIN ROLE OF DNA MOLECULES IS
THE LONG-TERM STORAGE OF INFORMATION. IT IS OFTEN
COMPARED TO A SET OF BLUEPRINTS, LIKE A RECIPE
OR A CODE, SINCE IT CONTAINS ALL THE INSTRUCTIONS
NEEDED TO CONSTRUCT OTHER COMPONENTS OF CELLS.

After having seen hundreds of dancers in countless auditions—she picked me. Did she make a mistake? I did not question the outcome; it was a good grace for me and my recovery. But the real work would start soon and, regardless of the pressures, I couldn't use. The desire to get high was ever present, but a new phenomenon presented itself—my addiction was hushed, slowly getting pushed from the front of my thoughts.

I was cast as Jonathan's understudy, being one of few men who could cover his contortion scene. The character's name was Stilts and his role encompassed twenty years of acquired circus and music skills—I had a lot to learn in a limited time.

I couldn't remember the last time I felt I was in the right place. Years ago, during one of my many detoxes, I heard a popular daytime TV host say, "Luck is what happens when preparation meets opportunity." If that were true, then I was lucky. In two months we would leave for San Diego to work and open the show before Broadway.

Before leaving for the West Coast, we worked the show in New York at City Center. The McDonald's where Nick and I had met Asten for heroin was on the way, and I passed it daily going to rehearsals. I lowered my eyes for fear of seeing Asten. I had heard he moved back to the neighborhood and was using again. Once in the rehearsal space I was safe and could switch mind-sets into the hardworking environment. The other dancers were breathtaking. Many had previously worked with Twyla and they clearly adored her, dancing with a velocity that was passed down through her vital force. I quickly perceived a kindred spirit: an unbreakable, working perfectionist who never gives up, pushes her body beyond human limitations, and guides others to do the same. I found Twyla to be an elegant, fearless leader and, having made that connection, swore to die in her army. It was no coincidence I ended up there.

The next two weeks were spent hovering behind the real dancers, mimicking their movements and bending my body in odd ways so that I could create their compelling lines. I wished I had been dancing my whole life. When our legs could no longer move, we worked the songs, the music of Bob Dylan. In the past, I would get blind, stinking stoned while singing Dylan. Now in recovery, I was dancing and singing his music in a Broadway-bound show, and I wished Tara were here beside me. The first week of rehearsals I tore the bottoms off my feet, making walking excruciating, but I just kept marching forward through the pain.

The cast was extraordinary—some of the most talented, hardworking people I'd ever met, readily helping me when I couldn't follow a step or staging. One day Twyla kept me after rehearsal. *Uh-oh . . . this is it*, I thought. *She realized she made a mistake and is letting me go.* She asked about my gymnastics history and had me demonstrate every acrobatic skill doable on a dance floor. Afterward, when I was thoroughly exhausted, she asked if I would be willing to teach acrobatics to the dancers who didn't tumble well, in addition to being Jonathan's understudy. I was honored and accepted the responsibility, wanting to help in any way possible. Being part of that project was a privilege, and helping others helped to keep me steady on the complex path of recovery. I wanted to tell Twyla the story behind the large scar on my triceps and that I had just recently achieved ninety days of recovery, but I didn't. I gave a little bow as I said, "Thank you."

Jonathan strived to instruct me in all he knew, and I battled him every step of the way. I continually hit my head juggling clubs and fell off the unicycle, but I found comfort training on the slack rope—a long, braided rope that was popular in old circuses, walked across in a similar way as a tightrope but swinging back and forth from the slack. My first few attempts at standing on the rope shot me to the ground, but gradually, after emptying my mind and concentrating on the quiet balance of the rope, I could stand without falling.

During difficult days my recovery friend always told me, "Move a muscle and it will change the thought": do something, anything, and you'll find a different result. His words became my mantra for whenever I was about to fall off the rope—I moved a muscle and found my balance to continue a natural movement. The slack rope became a meditation and indicator of my level of recovery—the two were almost inseparable. Standing on wobbling rope, I cleared my mind and remembered who and what I was: a heroin addict attempting to stand on a rope, finding his balance and place in the world. If I didn't move, I would fall. I had to trust myself and not allow my fear of falling to stop my forward movement, accepting the possibility that I might not stay on the rope. If I fell, I'd get back up and do it again and again. I fell in love with standing on that silly hemp rope, my simple speechless guru, showing me how to remain in recovery while handling life's uncertainties. Increased recovery time increased the time I could stay on the rope, walking forward and backward. I would balance like a bird swaying on an electrical wire in a storm, remaining solid and unaffected.

The other skills I had to learn brought me difficulty, and I didn't find the same meditation as with the slack rope. It was a completely new lesson of understanding, and I tried the same technique riding the unicycle as I had walking the slack rope. I'd let go, search for the balance, and . . . crash! I was constantly smashed onto the pavement like a child thrown from a bike, skinning my knees. The patient master I had become on the rope was absent on that single-wheeled beast, and, like an uncoordinated fool, I found myself repeatedly tossed to the ground in deep humiliation and pain. At first I blamed the seat, accusing it of being too high or too low, but the real reason I fell was because I didn't have trust. I tried to control the outcome and remained held back by my fear. Every day I practiced on that damned unicycle in the park near the Hudson River, and every day I continued to fall.

Along with training in contortion, stilt walking, singing, dancing, juggling, riding a unicycle, playing a trumpet, and slack rope with Jonathan, I tumbled and lifted weights—trying to reclaim my former gymnast's shape. My track marks and bruises were fading, and I could wear tank tops again without advertising a history of drug abuse.

I moved out of my apartment before leaving for San Diego, planning to stay with Jonathan until I found a place of my own after returning to New York. Excited about my first trip to San Diego, as part of the preparations I had a second implant inserted into my arm, assuring my continued abstinence.

The calmness and serenity of sunshine and palm trees after everything I had been through was refreshing, transporting me back to a trip my family and I once took to Florida. I believed I would be happy in San Diego. A tall, blonde woman met us at the airport and drove us to our apartments. She radiated a warm light and, with a smile, mentioned parties and drinking, to which I replied, "I don't drink anymore. I'm in recovery," as newly sober people love to say.

"Oh, I've been in recovery for a very long time," she told me, promptly handing me a meeting list. With that interaction I knew I was safe in California, and she would become a wonderful source of support as I learned to perform.

The intimacy of the show brought a new challenge for me. I was accustomed to working at the Met and never actually interacting with the audience—we entered the stage, did a few flips, and left. The Met stage and productions allowed one to easily hide behind lights, set pieces, and costumes when in doubt of what to do; but smaller

Broadway houses demand an immenseness to come from the hearts of the artists. Did I have that quality of heart to give? With nothing to shield me, I would be forced to become a strong performer.

Everyone worked diligently with Twyla, drilling with the choreography, score, and acting while pushing our bodies beyond their boundaries. We tirelessly rehearsed to the degree of injury, and ultimately her vision began to materialize. Everyone was gratified, and after just a few weeks our creation became a strong ensemble performance as we approached opening night. I, however, was not ready for that, as my body and mind became frozen with overwhelming performance trepidation. I adored Twyla, but was petrified of making a mistake in front of her, publicly showing her my flaws and inadequacies. I was determined to convince her through perfection that she had made the right choice in picking me.

Yet another difficult aspect of the project was understudying my boyfriend and having to act like him on stage. Jonathan was trained by some of the best teachers in the world: Philippe Gaulier, Lu Yi, and Katsura Kan. My acting techniques were self-taught and refined in emergency rooms to win pity prescriptions—a desperate addict is a hell of an actor. But my boyfriend's energy on stage was commanding, unpredictable, and wild—he was a born performer—while I was restrained with apprehension over the possibility of humiliating myself. How could I leap into the unknown spectrum of conveying emotions onstage when I couldn't recognize emotions as a human being in daily life?

Twyla brought a pastiche of artistic elements into her show, *The Times They Are A-Changin'*, a story set in the timeless state between reality and dreams, told through characters in a traveling circus. During a rehearsal, a couple came in after the lights went down and sat in the back of the theater. I assumed they were producers or Twyla's friends. When the show finished, the man and woman walked up to the stage and Twyla said, "Cast, this is Bob . . . Bob, this is the cast." I couldn't believe it: the legendary Bob Dylan! I wished Tara were there to witness this with me, or Nick, who had loved Dylan. The reality that my life was changing finally started to set in.

The show opened to favorable reviews and great audiences. Artists camped outside the Old Globe Theater, painting pictures of Dylan, selling T-shirts and memorabilia, and listening to his music. I kept studying Jonathan's stage presence, attempting to siphon it into my own performance. The understudies hadn't been onstage yet and I practiced every move backstage as the show ran, like the janitor knowing every actor's cue as he continues sweeping the floors. I watched the dancers' confidence and grace, praying to obtain even a fraction of it for myself.

My time finally came to perform in front of an audience, and, despite having seen Jonathan perform the show countless times, I was a nervous wreck. My skills weren't entirely ready for the public, but I had to suppress my fear and allow my vulnerable heart to be placed before judgment. The minutes waiting for the curtain to open brought on the familiar emotions of competing in gymnastics, the gut-wrenching time waiting for the judge's nod before beginning my routine. In those moments I wanted to quit, questioning why I or any human would willingly place himself in such a situation.

I heard my cue, "God said to Abraham, 'Kill me a son,'" and entered the stage on three-foot stilts, my vision distorted by a giant headpiece with a mop beard covering my face and wearing a long, white robe that wrapped tightly around the bottoms of the stilts, almost inviting me to fall. I tried to embody Jonathan's character while giving my own energy to the audience. After a grueling two hours it was over, and I remembered why I did this: for the feeling and the overwhelming sense of pride that participating in a production can bring to one's soul. This was a new high, and I wanted more.

As the show finished in San Diego, I knew the transition back to New York would be difficult. After nearly a year of recovery, my opiate blocker had worn off and I toiled daily with my broken strands of character, attempting to reassemble myself as an individual while aware that temptation pulsed though the soul of New York City. Would the towering, sky-lit silhouette reanimate my demons? After just barely scratching the surface of who I could become, and discovering whether I was made more from love or hate, I wasn't ready to return to hell. I wanted to experience life without the anchor of drugs sinking me down. I was experiencing a basic level of knowing myself, my likes and dislikes, and realizing I had the power to make positive choices.

I had blamed everyone and everything for my addiction, but all my life horrors were consequences of my own poor and ignorant choices. I was not the victim. I was the creator. My parents and friends did their best, and in their way shared pieces of their souls to encourage a better world for me. No one forced me to use drugs. I made that choice, and, were I given the opportunity to make the decision again, I would choose the same path. I was grateful to know hell, heaven, and all the rest in between. The pain I walked through formed a blessing, transforming my suffering into a deep compassion for and identification with others. Upon setting foot in New York, I continued my meetings in order to form a network with others in recovery.

The show would move forward and open in the fall at the Brooks Atkinson Theatre on Forty-sixth and Eighth—a one-block walking commute from our apartment. We trained relentlessly through the summer at a space in Harlem, working with new cast members and changing many show elements. Getting off the subway uptown was a familiar walk to rehearsals, full of junkies who were calling me—my sleepless sirens reaching up through the sidewalk cracks, trying to pull me back into their nothingness. Nobody else felt their presence, but I wanted to dive in and devour their pleasure. Though my brain wanted to stop, I forced my body forward; the process of creating the show had strengthened my recovery, and I was too proud of both to lose what I had gained. Arriving safely to work, I thanked the heavens for my protection.

Finally, we moved onto Broadway, did tireless technical rehearsals, and were ready for our opening night. Twyla's revered status in the dance world generated huge anticipation around the show; but strangely, there was also an undercurrent of buzz desiring or predicting its demise. I've been on that other side, fueled by jealousy, ignorance, ego, and envy, hoping for a new show to close with no knowledge of the production.

We received mixed reviews, and one of the least admiring came from my old employer, the *New York Times*. I didn't know the writer personally, but remembered delivering his mail regularly in a heroin daze. The reviews seemed to miss the entire point of the show. I thought Twyla a genius at submerging political symbolism within her choreography and storytelling, but the reviews attacked and dissected the dance without seeing the poetry of the production. I was hurt, and I knew the voice of the *Times* had power behind it—bad reviews stop ticket sales. My love and respect for the work and the dedication of each individual in the show had me emotionally too involved to recognize any validity in the reviews. The project had thoroughly challenged everyone involved and provided an eternal satisfaction from simply seeing it through to completion. But the reviews were not what we had hoped for.

The fragility of the show kept Twyla from allowing any understudy to perform; every element needed to remain solid and strong in an attempt to boost ticket sales and gain a public following. My father and stepmother came to a matinee. He beamed with pride as we took a picture under the marquee, next to the poster with my name printed in the middle: Joseph David Putignano. I couldn't imagine what that moment was like for my father—my name on Broadway and not on a prescription bottle, warrant, or hospital bill—standing together with me in my success, so far away from finding the limp body of his son on a bloodstained bedroom floor. The autumn light cast a new memory to replace the nightmares of my past, and I saw a never-before-seen joy on his face as he looked at me, and I thought, "So this is what happiness in recovery feels like."

After one night's performance the entire company was called to the stage and the producers entered; our show would soon be closing, unable to survive the reviews. New York didn't value our creation of artistry, dance, circus, and song, and the announcement demolished me, a heartless blow to my ego, strength, and hard work. It was an absolute miracle that I had achieved almost two years of recovery during *The Times They Are A-Changin'*. I wrote a letter to Twyla, explaining the truth and details of my past and how privileged I had felt to have been given the opportunity to work with her.

The show and my recovery were deeply connected, and the desire to use came over me fast, planting a small, quick question in my brain: *If I used just once, to numb my pain, would anyone notice?* Was I about to throw away almost two years of recovery? Jonathan knew I was distressed, and thought I would snap out of it. I thought I would snap out of it, too. But I didn't. The show's closing, in addition to extreme dental pain from another botched root canal, brought on the urgent need to feel held and protected from the next thing trying to bring me down. What could I do after this? I wouldn't audition for another show; I was through with being judged. Ultimately, the battle against my addiction was lost. I called my dealer, who seemed to be waiting by the phone, having expected my call for the last two years. I went to Duane Read and stood in a long line at the pharmacy, terrified of running into someone from my meetings, armed with my shopping list, ten 1/2 cc insulin syringes.

I entered the stage door, went to the understudies' dressing room, and waited for the show to start and for Jonathan to finish his more dangerous elements. If he got injured, I didn't want to go on stage high during a hard part. I went down to the second-floor bathroom outside Jonathan's dressing room, cooked up, and shot up. It was so smooth, so wonderful, and the wash of euphoria cleaned all the recovery off my bones. The hot fire burned again brightly under my skin. As I sat on the toilet with my head slumped forward, the low-laughing Devil gently caressed my pale flesh. I no longer cared. He could have me all to himself. I fell into my old place in hell, kept exactly as I had left it, and softly woke to the sounds of "Knockin' on Heaven's Door" coming out from the monitors.

There are those odd moments in life when the music we hear actually accompanies our situation—and that was one of those times. It was the Wednesday of our last week of shows, and I was sitting on a toilet, high on heroin, wondering what I would do next. How could I tell Jonathan I had relapsed again, after all this time? How could I tell my friends at my meetings what I had just done? I wouldn't. I would pretend it never happened. I would feign being drug-free until I figured out my next steps. I would use a few more times, then throw this shit away and return to where I had left off in recovery.

How could I do this so soon after handing Twyla my letter declaring her importance in my life as a role model and cornerstone of my recovery? Here I was, backstage of her baby, digging holes in my arm and inviting darkness back in to my soul. Would she understand? Would anybody understand? I didn't even understand . . . how would anyone else? And there I sat, reprising the role I knew best and hated the most—the needle-marked heroin addict, surrounded by opportunity and love, and incapable of stopping. What had I done?

That night I went home and tried to avoid Jonathan, not wanting him to figure out what he probably already knew. After a few hours he asked if I was high. I told him I got a migraine during the show and took the medicine that makes me feel sick and spacey. I tried using sparingly for the next few days and concealed my high to appear somewhat sober.

Our final performance was on a Sunday night. I couldn't believe we were closing. I shot up all week and, despite wanting to experience that day sober, I had to stay high or risk feeling shitty and performing poorly. My decided last use was always the worst. I went down to the same bathroom and, as I brought the golden-brown liquid up to a boil in my spoon, the lyrics of "Desolation Row" drifted through the monitors.

I raised my syringe in honor of our last Broadway performance and prayed this would be my last time shooting up. I pushed the needle into my thick vein, dismantling the painful and sorrowful reality surrounding me. I collapsed into the wall in slow motion, eyes closed to heaven, waking up sometime later to "Rainy Day Woman." I burst out laughing. I decided to watch the end of the show from the balcony, high as a midnight kite, seeking a moment of joy in my self-made prison.

Then the unexpected happened. After the finale, the lead actor called the entire cast onstage to bow together. *No way!* I thought. *I'm obliterated and can barely walk a straight line. I'm not standing onstage with those good people who became my family in this state of disrespect.* But a dancer grabbed me, forcing me down with the others to accept the audience's unending standing ovation. I had performed the show in San Diego, but never on Broadway. And there I was, freshly shot up with my relapse on full display, making my first public appearance on a Broadway stage. The audience silhouettes created a cavern of dark shadows, and from the second-floor center Twyla extended her arms out over the crowd, like a ship's figurehead, bowing to us. Her limbs broke through the powerful stage lights as the applause and adulation resonated through the cast's years of hard work; and I stood among them, left with only a drugged-out feeling of emptiness. All that applause and hard work for that one single moment, and I felt nothing but shame. I was nothing.

38

THE HUMAN BEING

It's hard to walk a tightwire by looking behind you; to go forward one needs to focus and put energy toward what lies ahead, not what remains behind. The connection, presence, and awareness of the bottom of the foot on the wire allow the body to appear suspended by a force from above. This is a Human Be-ing: present in the moment, in a state of oneness, allowing his or her stillness to advance toward greater goodness as an individual and to lighten the way for others.

"Now I do not know whether I was then a man dreaming I was a butterfly, or whether I am now a butterfly dreaming I am a man."
—*Zhuangzi*

Sitting in the back row, traumatized and beaten, I restarted my recovery day count with the predictable mumbling, "One day back." Why was I always the guy with this problem? I was never the man in the meeting who came and surrendered completely, never touching another substance again.

I thought back to the time before doing my first snort of heroin, standing together with my friends, peering into the brimming well of enchanted water. This captivating liquid had the potential to alleviate all our sufferings, and once we tasted it, satiating our curiosity, I soon became terrified it would leave us eternally thirsty. I never foresaw drinking the well dry, falling to the bottom, and interminably trying to claw my way out. For years I had battled my way up to the edge, only to have my brittle fingers slip between the damp bricks, sending me plummeting back into the underbelly. Now, my skeleton lay bone-dry at the bottom of the well, the solitary remains of countless shared blissful memories and highs. Was it all worth it? Was there anything to show for it?

Jonathan, dismayed and bewildered by my relapse, began to comprehend the disease of addiction. The part he couldn't understand was why I would choose drugs when my life was traveling in a positive direction; but addicts will relapse for no apparent reason, frustrating and infuriating those who love them. The aftermath of a relapse is always unique, but this one brought a shocking discovery—I liked being in recovery more than being high!

A pleasant intensity and vibrancy filled the still-awkward feeling of recovery, which I had only started to recognize over the previous two years. The world inside an addict's high is false, factual only to the user. If others cannot witness our experiences, does that make them less real? Recovery allowed me to live without guilt and shame. I only came to truly hate myself due to my inability to stop using drugs, but without drugs my self-hatred evaporated. My moment of realization: on drugs, this would be the best it would ever get; but by staying in recovery I could go beyond the best, consciously choosing and creating a continuously better life.

The relapse was short-lived. And, while I fortunately didn't become physically dependent on heroin this time, I still suffered an entire month of feeling terminally ill. All my previous recovery time disappeared, and I started the process from scratch, exactly where I had dropped my needle. I heard addicts recount the same experience, but it seemed scientifically preposterous. If I had two years of recovery under my belt, wouldn't it take years to fall back into my depth of addiction? Had I gained no merit for time served in abstinence?

The hard truth is that no matter how long I stayed clean, one relapse and I would lose the title of recovering addict. My disease was dormant like the trees in a winter forest while I was substance-free, but it would spring back in full bloom with the slightest hint of encouragement. My compassion had grown for all addicts with the realization that we ailed from the same chronic, progressive, incurable, and life-threatening disease.

I returned to training and auditioning quickly, thinking if I physically kept improving I could escape that poisoned well forever. Auditioning and preparation were arduous, but there was no other way. If I hoped to emerge a butterfly, I needed to create within the cocoon.

Bouncing back from the relapse and remaining abstinent, I realigned my life to the path I was on: training, writing, contorting, auditioning, and attending twelve-step meetings. I performed on various projects with Jonathan's performance design firm Acroback and returned to the Met stage with *Turandot*.

Backstage, the Met posted a casting call for acrobats and aerialists for a new production of *La Damnation de Faust*. The audition called for me to transform from a man into a devil—a story I'd lived, but trying to act it in front of strangers was mortifying to my ego. But I let go of self-criticism as I tried to physically express my descent from a sober man into a heroin addict, finding great irony in the situation: a boy pretending to be a man, pretending to be an actor, pretending to be a devil.

Although I felt it wasn't the greatest audition, I booked the job. We immediately started rehearsals, learning how to safely maneuver aerially in a harness suspended high over the stage. The straps hurt our legs and tore the flesh around our abdomens, but after a few days we toughened up. The project generated huge excitement because it was directed by Robert Lepage. Lost in my addiction, I had never heard of him, but people around me described him as a genius, one of the great theatrical minds of our time.

My prior experience in theatre had taught me that directors only interact with principal performers; acrobats and other background performers are left to the devices of choreographers and production assistants. But as a director, Robert proved to be the exception. He spoke with us as if we were on the same level as the opera singers, erasing the usual performer hierarchy. His approach with the entire cast was kind, respectful, and collaborative, rather than that of a dictator. We connected through the creative process. I believe our shared internal dissatisfactions solidified the friendship. We were both searching for something through our work, feeling unsatisfied and restless until its discovery.

La Damnation de Faust received great reviews. After opening night, Robert left for another project, but we stayed in contact through email. One day he sent me a message asking if I would be interested in joining a new Cirque du Soleil show he was creating, as a featured character. As I read his invitation, I had to laugh. My whole master plan had been to get into recovery and get hired by Cirque du Soleil in order to get Jason back. Life had now come full circle, though this time with me standing firmly on the other side of the Gates of Hell.

The tour schedule for Cirque du Soleil's production of *Totem* included parts of Europe, Canada, and the United States. I hadn't traveled much in my life, having been primarily imprisoned on the island of Manhattan by heroin. I had to take that opportunity. The contract would take me away from Jonathan, but we agreed taking the job would expand my growth as a performer. Though I felt flexible and strong, I was hesitant—Cirque's legendary performers and acrobats were top-notch, whereas I was no longer performing daredevil skills. There comes a time in every gymnast's career when he or she stops performing risk-ridden skills, and I had reached that point. But Robert kindly eased my anxiety by saying, "You're plenty good enough. You will be my guest and it will be a good time." I took the job, and was excited and honored to be a part of the company.

I had acquired over two years of recovery again—the longest I'd achieved to date—when I signed the massive contract and went to Canada in November, moving into the Cirque du Soleil Artists Residence in Montreal. I wanted to make friends and needed to move out of my comfort zone, but instead of talking to people I isolated in my room—the way I did when using drugs. I didn't have the desire to get high, but I also didn't have the self-esteem to talk to others. How would I survive in Canada? How could I perform in front of thousands of people every night when I was still crippled by my *dis-ease*?

The day after arriving, I walked into the kingdom and artistry of Cirque du Soleil. It was a world beyond anything I'd ever known. A kind young woman with a thick Quebecois accent gave me a tour of the facility. I tried to hide my fear behind a false smile, but I grew breathless whenever I made eye contact with another human being.

That first day of training involved integrating me into the opening act of four highly skilled, muscle-bound gymnasts swinging on high bars. I met the two acrobatic coaches and sat on a blue crash mat, visualizing where I could athletically fit in, and becoming increasingly nervous about the consequences of my fourteen-year sabbatical from competitive life.

The performance structure resembled the decaying bones of a turtle, with the two steel high bars rigged over a long trampoline. Two large speakers surrounded the turtle shell, blaring music from an iPod shuffle ironically playing songs I'd listened to as an active addict, songs I still loved but had promised myself never to play again.

The speakers poured out haunting melodies from Radiohead and Pink Floyd. The addict's dying fire in my soul bubbled up reminders of the sparkling, sharp syringe and the lingering astringent scent of rubbing alcohol—my entrance to heaven and my gateway to hell—all glistening before my eyes. Those songs had made me, created me, molded me, and in that powerless moment I looked up and searched the ceiling for a hint of God. Where were the angels now who had carried me to that point? I didn't want the music or the memories to stop, but I knew I couldn't stay with them either.

I was assigned to portray a character called Crystal Man—symbolizing the spark of Darwin's theories on the origin of species, the theme of the show. I was to descend from the thirty-foot grid to join the opening number. When the coach asked me to perform a few simple skills on the high bar, a small part of me wanted to climb back on and grab my lost love, but a bigger part didn't; the other acrobats in front of me were too incredible. I wasn't prepared to embarrass myself or to ruin their act, but in the end I did as I was asked.

I hadn't touched a high bar for almost fifteen years, but I chalked up and started to swing, as I had for so many years before my addiction.

My palms, no longer those of an athlete, tore against the friction of the steel, and while my muscles remembered what to do, my body was slow to respond. When blood leaked out from underneath my leather grips, the coach told me to go and wash my hands. The smallest drop of water on raw, bloody flesh feels like hydrochloric acid, and rinsing my fresh wounds was agonizing. But the only way to toughen one's skin is to keep going, rip off the old skin, and create a stronger, more protective layer of calluses. The smallest swinging movement felt like razors were digging into my hands, but I grasped the bar and continued.

High-bar rehearsals resumed the next morning as Nirvana, Hole, and rave music played to my old mental and new physical pain. Tiny Ziploc bags, straws, and CD cases reminded me of using, but the greatest trigger of all was the music.

Weeks of training and development went by from morning into night; I endured some of the hardest physical work I'd ever known. After rehearsals I felt like a shadow on the wall, searching for solace, stubborn to remain secure in my recovery. The circus challenged every level of my addiction, and I often found myself running to my room in fits of anger for no discernible reason. Part of my disease included the inability to express feelings and emotions normally, and I didn't want to tell Robert what was plaguing me. I felt that he had given me a chance and, in return, I could offer only my weaknesses, which would make him look bad.

Everyone worked relentlessly, and after four months there was finally light at the end of the tunnel. The creation period was over and we started running the show, perfecting and fine-tuning it for opening night. But I still didn't feel prepared to perform in public, and my overwhelming performance fear made me desperately want to quit. On top of that, I was the show's first image, solo and spotlit, radiating light and traveling down to Earth. What if I screwed up and ruined the whole show? The first performer of a show must bring shatterproof confidence to set the tone for the other performers; I felt the heavy burden of this obligation. I couldn't open the show as a figure from heaven bringing the concept of evolution in complete terror—what kind of Earth would be created through such fear?

It was opening night, and I was unable to stop thinking about every terrible thing that could happen and every repercussion that would transpire after I would destroy the show. I had an hour to warm up and prepare my body for the fight. I said my prayers and quietly tried pushing the anxieties away. The hour sped by, and it was time to board the unstoppable train. I chalked my hands and slowly began climbing the thirty-foot ladder to the top of the grid.

As I climbed, I prayed for all those who kill themselves in their striving for perfection. I prayed for specific skills I wanted to perform without mistakes. Then my foot slipped off a rung of the ladder, breaking my compulsive thought process. It woke me up to the "cure" I had been seeking, which had been in front of me the whole time: though the solution was spiritual, I realized I was praying in the wrong direction. The answer was within me, based on teachings passed from person to person, from the people in my twelve-step meetings, from Jonathan and Robert, from the other artists, from the crazy and the damned. My epiphany was love. If I was going to bring anything down from the grid, it had to be love.

That revelation changed my entire system, the same way a good meeting changes one's desire to use, and my self-centered fear dissolved into humility. It didn't matter if I did a good job or a bad job; what mattered was my intention behind the performance. In that moment, I changed my prayer. I no longer prayed for perfection, but for the ability to share my hope, strength, and story with the one person, or the many others, suffering among the audience. I decided to perform for them an act of resilience against pain, creating an allegiance against our self-centered fears. I remembered why I was there, and why I was putting myself through this. I was doing this for them. I was doing this for all the addicts who wanted to be more but couldn't because of their addiction. This was for that person sitting in a bar right now who knows he could be more, but can't put down that drink. It was for the person in that long methadone line who sees no end in sight. This was for my friends, and for all the people I'd never met who died of addiction, for those who could not climb out of hell against the unyielding forces of our disease.

I was doing this for all of them. With each step up the ladder I gained confidence, climbing right to the top, feeling each soul standing behind me like an army of angels. It didn't matter if I messed up and got fired the next day; I had to honor this challenge in recovery—no longer for myself, but for others. I wouldn't allow myself a drink or a pill, to sniff a line, or to open a vein, because this had to be the most honest of performances God intended it to be. By my committing to that belief, the courage of light overcame the darkness of fear. Humbled by my new awareness, I wanted my character to represent strength to reflect to everyone below. I said one last prayer, and then the show announcements were made and it was time to clip into my harness for suspension.

I came down from the grid and felt powerful, safe, and connected. I had heard in countless twelve-step meetings a teaching that now, on opening night, I finally understood: to remove unwanted negative emotions from within ourselves, we must first help remove those emotions from others. I took it on as my job not to perform, but to help. I had to find someone else in fear and learn to comfort them in order to withdraw my own angst; often the darkest of men carry the brightest of lights.

It was a smooth show, and in a blur of exhilaration we took our final bows to the overpowering waves of applause and screams from the audience. I stepped forward, took my bow in the whirlwind of sound, and felt nothing except broken and numb. All that strenuous work, nervous energy, and time spent building up to this monumental moment, and the payback was nothing compared to the high off a twenty-dollar bag of heroin. This empty feeling shocked me to my core; I had expected the rewards of accomplishment to catapult me into the stratosphere. Instead I felt robbed and devastated that there was nothing more to this feeling of victory.

Where was my happy, Hallmark-card ending after entering recovery and getting this great job? In my naiveté, I'd harnessed myself to the belief that achievements would somehow mimic my past wondrous highs—I felt a great loss in the absence of heroin and alcohol.

There was a beautiful champagne toast with the entire company after the show, and I slowly walked back to my *loge d'artiste*, as I'd come to call my dressing room, trying to conceal my inner turmoil. I changed, grabbed my recovery coin, and sneaked out. There was a huge after-party, but I wasn't ready to watch others in their drunken victories as I soberly stood by. Walking past the thin, tented walls, I could hear everyone sounding happy and laughing.

As I continued my walk with the river by my side, alone, I cried for every pain I had endured. I cried for my recovery and for my heroin addiction. I cried for my inability to socialize in large crowds and for punishing myself over it. I cried for my loneliness and pain that still lingered in the shadows. I walked home under the same damned moon I'd always known and cried myself to sleep to, as I had done so many nights back in my bunk bed at my parents' house.

I woke up to a sunny, beautiful morning and could not pinpoint where last night's sadness had come from. I was grateful not to have a hangover, not to be scrounging for change to shoot up "just one more time." I was determined to find a way to celebrate achievements in recovery. Although I wasn't blissed out of my bones from our victory the night before, it was better than what I had experienced before—a day in recovery is better than the agony of addiction. I gave up my highest highs, but I also rid myself of my lowest lows, and now I would live balancing between the two. I was thankful for my life in recovery and for the ability to now experience life as I believed it was intended to be lived.

The company ran on the absolute dedication of everyone involved, not just the acrobats and artists, but wardrobe, riggers, technicians, creative teams, and office workers, all of whom committed their entire body and soul to their work. Seeing this kind of discipline on every level of the operation was deeply inspiring, and without that job I might have lost gymnastics to my addiction forever. There was a refinement to every inch of the creation and production, which hugely influenced my new recovery perspective on life.

The circus lifestyle required extraordinary human drive to survive its extreme physical challenges and demands. Our bodies were sore to the bones every day; walking, getting out of bed, and even sitting at times could hurt. Most of us wanted to stay in bed, but as the sun rose, we walked through the pain to the big top and began again, and unconsciously we passed the torch to those seeking a dream. Hearing Cirque du Soleil fans tell me, "You're so lucky; it was always a dream of mine to be in a show," ignited an energy and healing amidst the exhaustion and pain, adding great power and passion to my performance.

The show, in many ways, was a metaphor and microcosm of my life in recovery. Upon waking in the morning, I was still tired from yesterday's show, afraid of the unknown, and wanting to hide behind my familiar mask of drugs and alcohol to feel safe and separated from the world. I didn't want anyone to see me. But the show started every day at the same time, and I had to cast away all fears, insecurities, and negativities. I would climb to the grid ten minutes before the performance started, and the show would begin on time whether I was mentally prepared or not. I got into my harness, got checked by my riggers, and, after the preshow announcements began, spun myself into a tight ball.

Spotlights drenched me in a warm glow, and in that illumination I could no longer hide from the world—any insecurities I may have had were exposed before our audience of thousands. I followed my breath, in and out of my body, and slowly unrolled myself. *Evolutio* in Latin means "unrolling"—the theme of the show being evolution of the universe. Through my recovery, I realized that I had been evolving too.

I opened up my limbs and slowly started contorting my body, pushing the limits of my flexibility to create hieroglyphic shapes, tapping into the origins of my first cells. The audience remained unaware of the story I retold inside myself each night, of how I would reconnect to each chapter of myself. I connected with the boy who was endlessly ridiculed for his sexuality. I connected to the young man trapped in his Sisyphean nightmare, waking up on a sidewalk, freezing cold, shivering and broke, dope sick and desolate, trying to figure out how he was going to eat next with no money. I breathed in the man fighting to change and struggling against his progressive and fatal disease of addiction, forever relapsing and falling further into hell. I stretched my bones and honored the man who was suffering from heavy drug withdrawal, but attempting to train and become better out of sheer desperation and inspiration.

As I began to contort even further, I would think of Jonathan, who had trained me for this very moment, teaching me to let go and be with my breath. I thought of him by my side, throughout the time when I carelessly killed my own human spirit, and I attached myself to the endless hours we trained together, trying to transform a beat-up, withering, drug-addicted junkie into a powerful body of strength, flexibility, grace, and humility. The music intensified and I opened to my last pose, extending my arms and feet out to the universe: north, south, east, and west. The band shot out a big bang and I jetted my limbs out, physicalizing the creation of the universe.

At the final crescendo I got wrapped up in a timeless state, traveling back to my origin. I returned to my parents' basement and the moment I met my God, who bestowed the gift of movement to me. I remembered the look in my parents' eyes and now realized that it hadn't been surprise, but wonder, and I gained strength from the support and undying love from my entire family.

Before tumbling, I thought of Dan, remembering his instructions in execution and fearlessness. The lights exploded, the music howled, and I flipped backward and traveled to that beautiful, eternal place of my soul. In that moment I had no physical body, no time, just pure energy rushing through my veins, overpowering and transcending any blissful heroin high I could have ever produced. This was an absolute union—with my body, mind, spirit, God, and the universe.

39

THE SOUL

IN 1907 DR. DUNCAN MACDOUGALL MEASURED PATIENTS
AS THEY DIED. HE CLAIMED THERE WAS A LOSS OF WEIGHT IN
THE BODY OF VARYING DEGREES AFTER DEATH, BUT HIS RESULTS
HAVE NEVER BEEN REPRODUCED AND HAVE RECEIVED LITTLE
SCIENTIFIC MERIT. HIS RESULTS STATED THAT THE AVERAGE
WEIGHT OF THE HUMAN SOUL IS TWENTY-ONE GRAMS.

THE SOUL IS PERCEIVED DIFFERENTLY IN DIFFERENT
RELIGIONS AND BELIEF SYSTEMS.

ANCIENT EGYPTIAN RELIGION HELD THAT AN
INDIVIDUAL IS COMPOSED OF VARIOUS PHYSICAL AND
SPIRITUAL ELEMENTS, A BELIEF ALSO SHARED BY ANCIENT
ASSYRIAN AND BABYLONIAN RELIGIONS.

THE BAHA'I FAITH STATES THAT "THE SOUL IS A
SIGN OF GOD" AND BELIEVES THE SOUL IS IMMORTAL,
CONTINUING TO LIVE AFTER PHYSICAL DEATH.

BRAHMA KUMARIS BELIEVES SOULS ARE INFINITESIMAL
POINTS OF SPIRITUAL LIGHT EXISTING IN THE
FOREHEADS OF THE BODIES THEY RESIDE IN.

BUDDHISM BELIEVES THERE IS NO SOUL AND NO SELF, AS
EVERYTHING IS IN A CONSTANT STATE OF CHANGE AND FLUX.

IN JUDAISM, THE WORDS *nephesh* (LIFE/SOUL), *ruach* (WIND), AND *neshama* (BREATH) TOGETHER DESCRIBE THE SOUL. IT IS BELIEVED THAT GOD BESTOWS THE SOUL ONTO THE BODY UPON THE FIRST BREATH.

THE CHRISTIAN BELIEF, BASED ON THE OLD AND NEW TESTAMENTS, STATES, "THEN SHALL THE DUST RETURN TO THE EARTH AS IT WAS: AND THE SPIRIT SHALL RETURN UNTO GOD WHO GAVE IT."

ROMAN CATHOLICS EXPRESS THE SOUL AS "THE INNERMOST ASPECT OF HUMANS, THAT WHICH IS OF GREATEST VALUE IN THEM, THAT BY WHICH THEY ARE MOST ESPECIALLY IN GOD'S IMAGE. SOUL SIGNIFIES THE SPIRITUAL PRINCIPLE IN MAN."

ORIENTAL ORTHODOX AND EASTERN ORTHODOX CHURCHES SIMILARLY BELIEVE THAT THE SOUL IS INDIVIDUALLY JUDGED BY GOD AFTER DEATH AND, DEPENDING ON THE OUTCOME, THE SOUL IS EITHER SENT TO ABRAHAM'S BOSOM (TEMPORARY PARADISE) OR HADES/HELL (TEMPORARY TORTURE).

PROTESTANTS HAVE TWO DIFFERENT BELIEFS ABOUT THE SOUL'S COURSE AFTER DEATH: THE FIRST HOLDS THAT THE SOUL FALLS INTO AN UNCONSCIOUS SLEEP UNTIL RESURRECTION, AND THE SECOND HOLDS THAT THE SOUL EXISTS IMMORTALLY.

SEVENTH-DAY ADVENTISTS BELIEVE THAT THE SOUL IS A MIX OF BODY AND SPIRIT (BREATH OF LIFE), WHILE JEHOVAH'S WITNESSES USE THE HEBREW WORD *nephesh*, REFERRING TO THE LIFE FORCE OF ALL ANIMATE LIVING THINGS.

LATTER-DAY SAINTS BELIEVE THAT THE SOUL IS THE UNION OF THE SPIRIT, PREVIOUSLY CREATED BY GOD, AND THE BODY AS A PHYSICAL FORM CONCEIVED ON EARTH. AFTER DEATH, THE SOUL RETURNS TO THE SPIRIT.

HINDUISM USES THE SANSKRIT WORDS *Jeeva* (IMMORTAL
ESSENCE OF A LIVING ORGANISM), *Atman* (TRUE SELF), AND
Purusha (COSMIC MAN) TO DENOTE THE INDIVIDUAL SELF.

ISLAM BELIEVES THAT THE SOUL IS PUT INTO THE
HUMAN EMBRYO FORTY DAYS AFTER FERTILIZATION.

SIKHISM BELIEVES THAT THE SOUL IS A PART OF GOD.

TAOISM BELIEVES THAT EVERY PERSON HAS TWO TYPES OF
SOULS CALLED *hun* AND *po*, OR WHAT WE CALL *yang* AND *yin*.

VOODOO BELIEVES THAT THERE ARE TWO PARTS
TO THE SOUL, *ti-bon-ange* (LITTLE GOOD ANGEL)
AND *gros-bon-ange* (GREAT GOOD ANGEL).

DOES THE WEIGHT OF A SOUL GIVE ANY
INDICATION AS TO THE LIFE IT HAS LIVED?

I had four years in recovery, and my soul was growing restless. How many performances would I have to do before I could move on to something new? How long does it take before the love and passion for the same performance melt into the politics and reality of the business, before Astraea's scales are tipped out of balance?

A year had passed, and I had fallen into a deep depression. The tour brought us to San Francisco, and my sadness rolled alongside the fog that tumbled over the Golden Gate Bridge—not too golden from where I stood. My ongoing dilemma began to weigh heavily on me as I kept asking myself what was wrong with me, and how much more of this could I endure. I faced every one of my demons head-on, but I was crippled by loneliness and began to isolate again, as I had during the creation of the show. I longed for a close friend on tour, but had avoided most social situations to protect my recovery, as many events revolved around alcohol. I knew what I was seeking from life could no longer be found at the bottom of a beer bottle or the tip of a syringe. Between my own busy demands and going back to school, I believed I was missing out on many experiences.

In an attempt to find rejuvenation, Jonathan and I went on a much-needed vacation to Hawaii. While there we traveled to the Palace of Refuge ("Pu'uhonua o Honaunau") where a broken warrior could be forgiven for his sins, failures, and defeats. I felt it was a place of power and a place where I could find some divine healing. Jonathan and I walked to the end of the lava rock that jetted out into a deep-turquoise ocean. The jet-black rock glistened and sparkled with minerals. Together we sat in front of a small tide pool that captured the reflection of the sky above. We watched the sun fall beneath the horizon line into the sea as the waves splashed up against the rock. We both closed our eyes and meditated until a dark sky shifted over our heads. In my silence, in perfect solitude and somber desperation, I prayed to God with every fiber of my being for restoration; for freedom from myself, my ego, my hatred, my pain; and for the ability to continue on.

When I returned to the tour, the memory remained, but the powerful cleansing emotions quickly evaporated. I knew if I was to survive this tour, stay in recovery, and remain sane, I needed to develop a stronger social structure. I needed to reevaluate what I wanted out of life, and what type of person I was becoming. Out of pure curiosity, desire for entertainment, and need for an outside point of view, I made an appointment with a well-known psychic in the Bay Area.

I always expected to cross over a mystical veil upon entering the home of a psychic, and was saddened to remember they lived like everyone else—no floating clouds, secret doorways, or magic potions, just happy, ordinary human beings with the capacity for sight in a place where I was blind.

I walked into his room, sat on the couch, and waited for him to begin. I imagined that for one who really did possess the gift, my past would be easy to see, given how destructive, shattered, and colorful it had been. He looked at me, studying something around me, and said, "This has only ever happened one other time in my life—when I gave a reading to someone who had already crossed over to the other side." Checkmate! My death card returned, and I grew pale. "The reason why you have so much pain in your life is because you know what home feels like, and your soul craves to go back. You know heaven, and now you suffer on Earth because life is full of pain."

I knew that feeling all too well. It described what it was like to enter recovery again and again, knowing what a powerful feeling it was to be fully drowning in heroin bliss, then falling back to Earth's sober state, into the body's daily aches, pains, and constant emotion.

He continued, "You crossed over twice, actually, but within the same time frame, and it happened quite tragically. I am going to say it was drugs." Inside, deep inside, of course I knew this to be true, but I had not heard anyone articulate this back to me since the doctor right after it happened, and his words grabbed my heart: "Joe, it's okay, it's going to be okay." But was it? What if I was going to live out the rest of my life as an incomplete puzzle, forever searching for the last piece that did not exist on this plane? How does one make peace with that? He then said something that echoed the first psychic I'd seen years ago: "You have something to tell the world. You can't give up on yourself."

I had many questions I wanted to ask, curious about my future, what I was supposed to do in life, and how I could cure the chronic pain erupting in the center of my heart. He said, softly and quietly, "You are so lucky." I wanted to punch him square in the face, just to show him how lucky I was.

He continued, "You're lucky because you feel so much, almost the same way I do. If you are around people in pain, you pick it up like a sponge, but if you are around happiness, you also pick it up. You have the ability to absorb everything, the good, the bad, the joy, the pain, the ecstasy, and the darkness, and in this way you are truly a being who has experienced all the ebbs and flows of life. You have already lived a very full life."

The truth was that I didn't want to live life like this, and on dark days preferred to be hidden under a thick brown layer of heroin. I wanted to leave our session hopeful and happy, knowing I would never experience another painful moment for as long as I lived—but that was not going to happen. I left feeling . . . afraid.

The tour was beginning to feel endless—country after country, city after city. I hadn't planned on staying this long, but the longer I stayed on the road, the more I adapted to this lifestyle, even though I knew it wasn't the healthiest existence for me. Like a tree, I needed to have roots embedded in the Earth. Even birds that fly wherever they want always return back home to where they came from. Many people I knew loved touring, and I admired that quality in them, always wondering how they did it. In my perception, it seemed like many people fell into the illusion of what a tour offers, an escape from themselves. It was no coincidence that many musicians drank and drugged in this kind of traveling existence. It was a miracle I hadn't picked up heroin again, and I wasn't sure how long I could hold on.

For the first few years of recovery I had clung to it, fighting off the urge to use from moment to moment. Once the desire to use had lifted, life began. After that I had learned how to become employable, showing up on time and working like the rest of the world. Now I found myself at the stage where my emotions came back, and I began to understand the reason why I ever used drugs in the first place. Emotions were the most difficult thing for me to handle because they are the body's reaction to thoughts, and we humans think constantly. Thoughts are invisible and impossible to catch, and in the past I had used a butterfly net made of substances to catch and contain those thoughts. I couldn't use that net anymore and so my thoughts ran free, and I was powerless over them. I wanted to use again. I wanted those fuckers to slow down, but they didn't.

I realized I had been using the same coping mechanisms since I was a child, and they no longer worked in my adult life. I was a fighter standing in a wide-open field, shield and sword ready for battle, armor fastened, prepared for war. But there was no more battle to fight, and the only thing I was warring against was me. If I was my own worst enemy, and the only voice I could hear was my own, what were my options?

We traveled from San Jose to San Diego. I went back to the Old Globe Theatre, where we had performed *The Times They Are A-Changin'*, and felt old memories of hard work and sweat wash over me. The show poster still stood tall among the giant palm trees, and I thought of Jonathan. After seven beautiful years our relationship came to an end, and I was remembering all the amazing times we had had together. I walked through Balboa Park with its perfectly kept foliage, trying to recapture the original spirit of what it felt like when I was newly in recovery.

My housing was in La Jolla, and almost daily I drove down to the La Jolla shore cliffs overlooking an army of sea lions playing and barking. By the cliff on a park bench I meditated, visiting my sanctuary, a place on the inside where no one could touch me, almost like heroin. Meditation helped me cope with a very difficult, arduous, and lonely tour. I used to laugh at all those self-help, New Age gurus, but here I was, walking in their footsteps. Everything I judged in life I later had to walk through.

I was beginning to understand my touring life as a spiritual path, since I was constantly forced to grow, accept, and change. It was a quest I wanted to end, because I still couldn't find where I belonged within the group. How do we find ourselves when we are truly lost? I looked ahead, knowing what city was next, and tried to figure out how I was going to cope with it. We were headed for Boston. While most artists would be excited to go to their hometown, I was terrified. I had escaped for a reason, and had no plans of returning. How could I go back there? If I returned, would I become the same broken boy who had left? Would those old wounds reopen, letting the darkness back in?

Weeks later I found myself standing at the Long Wharf overlooking the harbor in Boston, watching sails slice through a pink sunset blossoming up from the horizon. These were my iconic waters, the waters that had cradled the dead, and not just any dead, but my dead. I had buried my warrior here many years ago. I had wrapped him up in iron chains and sunk him miles down into the Atlantic Ocean, never to return to the surface. I stood watching the sea in a trance as tourists walked behind me.

I returned to my apartment to unpack, the old cobblestone streets of Boston awakening the memories in my bones, biomechanically melting the ice, thawing out what used to be. We can leave our homes to become new people, but what happens when we return? Do we take on our old forms to fulfill our destinies as though we had never left?

I walked all of Boston, carefully examining my territory, and ended up in Kenmore Square. I was slightly oblivious because I was focusing on opening night and the perfection of performance. As I looked up, I noticed I had walked over the bridge on Brookline Avenue and sidestepped onto Lansdowne Street. I'll never forget that place, and though it had changed a lot, I was flooded with images from the past. There I stood in my old, dirty raver clothes, pupils as black as midnight, loaded on benzodiazepines and coke, swaying in a long, crooked line into club Axis, which had been resurrected into the House of Blues. I stood under a giant mechanical parking lot where I had once crashed my mother's car three times trying to get out.

That street was the birthplace of my addiction. My old ghost still stood in line, waiting for something. What was he waiting for, and why couldn't he see me? It killed me to see myself looking like that. He was confused, terrified, desperate for love, but doing the exact thing that would never achieve all that he was after. His anger chained him to that line and he would forever remain there, searching for the key that only existed inside his bones. I left before that ghost could possess my new flesh, and made my way back to the Green Line station. The catacombs of Boston still had the smell of old, rotted iron, heavy, oxygen-stealing soot, and loud, screeching wheels from the subway car sounding like a band of banshees.

Boston had changed tremendously since I had left. Many of the graffitied streets I knew had been repainted. Old, broken neighborhoods were rebuilt, and what I remembered as sad was now a new, exciting, and thriving city, full of enthusiasm and hope. Not only did the landscape change, but the people transformed with it. My brother and sisters had had children who were becoming teenagers, and everyone seemed to shed their old, uncomfortable cocoons, emerging into the beings they were meant to be. I tried to embrace the change, but the powerful energy around my past still filled me with dread.

I walked down to the Seaport, where the Cirque du Soleil tent stood. The pungent smell of the ocean drifted in, and though I had traveled to many shores, no other seawater was this intoxicating to my senses. The scent of salt reminded me of something I wanted to keep forgotten. Was it the rotting corpse I had left on the ocean floor?

My mother, sister, and two nieces were all coming to tonight's dress rehearsal. It was always difficult for me to perform in front of people I knew, even though they tend to be the least likely to judge. We had almost reached our 800th show and I knew my track inside and out, but I was a nervous wreck. I wanted tonight to go perfectly, because I wanted my mother to see how much I had changed. I wanted her to see the boy she once knew—the boy she had held while he overdosed and trembled from seizures—come down from the grid covered in thousands of shiny objects, reflecting all the changes his recovery represented. I wanted my sister, who had sat there in court trying to save my life while I was shackled and handcuffed, see me finally break free of my chains of addiction and move on to something good and pure. I wanted them to finally see the man I had become. I meditated twice before the show, feeling dizzy and nauseous. I wanted to control the situation and have it play out exactly as it did in my head.

Unsurprisingly, I failed. I was so terrified that I could not connect with the music or with my own muscles. To my family it was all right, but that performance did not come from the place it could have come from.

I went home defeated and began thinking about my life story, not just in segments but as a whole—it was an odd cycle of birth, death, rebirth, and all the elements I'd survived. The words from the psychic repeated in my head: "You have two large holes in your heart that you have to heal." I had listened to every self-help book on my iPod, prayed, and meditated, but the truth was that I was falling apart. I had done so much work to surrender, and when I removed my ego's fortress brick by brick with spiritual principles, I discovered a terrified, angry little boy who had run out of options. There was so much deep-seated rage and self-hatred that I didn't know where to begin. I lay perfectly naked, absolutely defenseless to the world.

I knew I had clawed my way through a self-made hell, and I wanted to live a new life where I no longer identified as a victim. I dropped all my defenses and stood where I was—birthmarks, scars, ugliness, jealousy, hatred, despair, grief, and my debilitating lack of self-acceptance. I had no idea that the real work began here, and that my drug use had been part of a huge fortress protecting this naked being. The only way for me to change was to continue walking, bare and exposed.

Every day, my ego tried to come back with a new weapon of defense, a new way to cover my nudity, but I continued to be vulnerable without shame. Every time I went for a weapon, I stopped myself and thought, "I no longer need this; put it down, accept what is happening to you." A few weeks after we opened, my father and twenty other family members were coming to the show. I hadn't seen many of them in over fifteen years and felt a sense of shame because of who I had been in the past. I knew they were coming to see me perform, not shoot drugs, but I didn't want a repeat performance of the dress rehearsal. I knew I couldn't control what would happen, and as my body began to feel anxiety, I did my best at feeling it. I had to perform in the place I stood. It was going to be either good or bad or somewhere in between. I would continue to do my best, but ultimately there wasn't much I could do about it.

I had learned to perform in humility earlier in the tour, but somewhere along the way I had forgotten it. The most powerful spiritual principles that worked were the ones I had to continue to learn over and over, and they seemed to change form. I hated that, and was tired of always thinking, *Haven't I already done this?* But the truth was that I would have to relearn them again and again, for the rest of my life.

It was time I stopped hating myself for what I was not. For a long time my perception had been directed at what I didn't have, but if I looked closely I would see I had everything I needed. There had always been a huge support system in my life, and I had to start listening to those supportive forces instead of the constant insecurities in my own head.

I remembered a few years ago being possessed by the chronic blackness of addiction, unable to stop shooting heroin. I relentlessly prayed, asking God and the universe for one thing: "Please help me stop shooting heroin." In that moment, right then, I was living that prayer, so what was I really depressed about? I had everything I ever asked for. Was this the missing puzzle piece to my soul?

My father texted me a hundred times the day of the show. I knew I had his support and love, and did my best to push the fear back into the realms of my past. Robert was also there in the audience, which helped me relax, knowing I had a true friend witnessing my triumph or defeat. I walked over to climb the ladder and saw my friend backstage, and he whispered, "Stay in your spirit, not in your head." I kept those words close and climbed the ladder to the grid.

My father was in a wheelchair because he had had a series of operations on his ankle that would not heal. The outcome was likely to be amputation, and I would later accompany him to one of his surgeries. On the day of that surgery he had achieved two years in recovery, a miracle I never thought I would see in my lifetime. As he lay on the bed, I remembered a horrible memory of the two of us. I was on a hospital bed as he stood over me; I had just tried to kill myself, completely intoxicated. I had never seen my father look so scared. Now I had the honor of standing next to him on his own two-year anniversary as a son in recovery, and my eyes filled with tears of appreciation. We spoke about the difficulties of being human and of losing a limb, asking ourselves whether we clung to our bones only out of vanity. He looked scared before his surgery, but knew he would be all right.

Before my descent to the stage, I thought of my father. I thought about his fear mixed in with my own. I thought about how proud I was that he had entered recovery, as I had been a witness to his destructive disease. My eyes were welling up, despite the fact that I would frequently say, "I don't cry in recovery, because there is nothing more to cry about." Having had such a tortured history,

I believed I had shed every possible tear. But I was about to cry. The preshow announcements were made, and I took my father's fear, along with my own anxiety, and ate them. Picasso once said, "In art one must kill one's father." I'm not sure I completely understand what he meant, but for me, I absorbed all the incredible parts of my father and used them.

The show was amazing. I tried to give my family a special wave at the end during my bow, but those damn tears kept returning.

Afterward, my family and Robert were going out to dinner at the Seaport. I was nervous to see everyone, but couldn't avoid the gathering. As we walked to the restaurant my brother, who I didn't even know would be at the show, came darting toward me. He was excited to see me perform. I would silently thank my brother every time I saw him, for it was he who had propelled me forward in gymnastics by always creating new objects for me to flip over. We continued to walk, and the fear inside me grew stronger. I felt I had to apologize for who I was, and couldn't figure out why. Why was my family here to see me? I walked into the restaurant, and as we settled into the evening I was blown away by both how much everyone had changed and how much they still looked the same. Yes, all were older, but everyone still had their vital beauty.

Throughout history and in various mythologies we see the role of the father portrayed as that of the protector—his job is to keep the family safe and together. In Norse mythology, father Sigmund's sword is shattered in battle and his son, Sigurd, ends up with a reforged sword with which to finish the task that his father couldn't. Similarly, over time and the course of our lives, my father's sword had been broken and smashed by his own enemies, and the pieces became the scattered lives and broken relationships in our family. Our family, who usually only gathered for funerals, came together for that show; by pursuing this recovery path, I had wielded the broken shards of the sword, piecing them back together to continue where my father had left off.

A giant shield was mounted on the wall at my parents' old restaurant, above the lobby door. On the shield was a unique design: the Putignano family crest. I thought of that crest as we sat at the table, reunited with all our addictions, demons, and ugliness, but together at last under our family's coat of arms. I saw the unusual way in which life strips us down to rebuild us the way we are supposed to be. Over the last year on this tour I had been slowly beaten by depression, fighting an endless battle that pushed me ever closer to the ground. Finally, I had at last admitted defeat and stripped myself of my old weapons and armor, realizing the tools I used no longer worked for me. I found myself naked and vulnerable, and I could finally see why I had gone through this transformation. It was necessary to give up my old weapons in order to receive what truly belonged to me. There I sat, watching my family eat, realizing that I now carried the family crest's shield and sword. Had I not been broken down the way I was, I wouldn't have been ready to accept those weapons, passed down from generation to generation.

I left feeling protected, knowing I had real people who would show up for me and that all my fears were projections from the past. The following day Robert and I walked around Boston, traveling down ancient memory lanes. I was no longer afraid, knowing I had a true friend beside me. Afterward, I took the ferry over to Hull, across my funeral waters, as ferryman Charon brought me to the other side.

I walked down to the beach and was struck instantly by a feeling of power, as if two worlds had collided, as if a circle had just been completed: a beginning and its ending. I stood on the soft sand that pushed through my toes. Those archaic sands had created me, a human sand castle that eventually eroded and washed away to sea. I now stood on my past, my present, and my future. In the distance, I saw the ghost of my youth doing endless backflips in a row, up and down the beach, obsessed with his God-given path and determined to live out his dream. To the left of him, another one of my ghosts ran past me. He was a skinny young man, addicted to Klonopin, trying to outrun his anxiety. He fell to the ground, detoxing and having seizures, writhing in the sand that smeared all over his body. He was alone, terrified, and sick. Then there was the last ghost, whom I had not seen before. He shone like the sun but wasn't painful to look at. I followed that strange image to the end of the beach, where the giant seawall overlooks Boston Harbor. The stench of red tide strangled the air around me. That ghostly figure full of light climbed the wall and walked behind the massive boulders protecting the houses on the cliff. I climbed the rocks covered in dark, slimy seaweed with tiny periwinkles peeking out, tasting the salty, humid air on my lips.

I climbed to the top of the rocks as an expansive feeling of power overcame me. The apparition continued on, out of my vision behind a rock, and then I couldn't see where it went. I walked along the seawall looking for it, stepping over the "Danger: Keep Off Seawall" sign spray-painted on the rock.

I walked past the memorial of a teenage suicide, where I used to sit and contemplate my own, but the words in stone were difficult to see now, having been washed away by rain and wind, reminding me that everything changes. I saw the luminous ghost image of myself out of the corner of my eye, and I ran to the spot as it vanished. That was it. That was the place where I had buried him, my ghost, my warrior.

I stood for a moment and started choking up at the thought of what I had to do, but I knew it was time. Under the sun, I removed my addict, my dark self, whom I had loved so much—the shadow in me who had protected and fought for me. He was everything I had wanted to be, powerful, eternal, and dark, but it was time to let him go. I looked into his hateful eyes, and he looked away, still angry with all that wasn't him. I went in to touch him, and gave him the strongest thrust, pushing him over the giant boulders off the seawall and into the blue ocean. The waves crashed over him, and I watched him fight to stay afloat, but the waves were too powerful and he began to sink.

I raised my sword to the sky, fully intact and forged by the many memories and pieces of my family's history. Its ancient inscription gleamed in the sunlight, depicting the story of our lives. I raised my shield, our family crest, and stood with honor, as a giant glow emanated from under the water. It was an image of me rising out of the depths of the Atlantic. It was pure of heart, an image of heaven, and shining with a powerful light. I knew it was my childhood warrior, who had now grown up. It was strong, sincere, loyal, and honest—everything I wanted to be. The image rose up, dripping from the waters as it reached me, eye to eye. For a moment I felt terrible for having drowned that most important part of myself, but in its gaze I saw it understood. As I let out a smile, the image—my former self, my warrior—merged with my bones and skin, fastening itself to my soul and wrapping around my spine. We had been reunited and become one. The sword and shield vanished from my hands and became fused into my skin. I stood tall, changed, confident, and sure. This battle was over.

EPILOGUE

Behind every fresh and gentle breeze there is a scent of burnt cinnamon and hot ash. The Devil is patient, waiting for me behind every opportunity to slip up and once again claim my former position in hell.

I can't say with complete conviction that I will never drink or use other drugs again. But as I'm writing this, I can say that I won't use just for today. My addiction is a representation of the universal *disease* in this world. Any form of self-hatred and self-sabotage, be it in the form of an eating disorder, sex addiction, gambling addiction, or alcohol or other drug abuse, is fundamentally the same; they just have different symptoms due to the side effects of our particular poisons. I use the word *addiction* to encompass all that ails our spirits as individuals, all that forms obsessions, envies, self-centered fears, self-destruction, traumas, discomfort, pain, and anything else that is the opposite of love, humility, serenity, and genuine peace. I once heard a man say, "Addiction is a death sentence, except that we aren't given the exact date of death."

For many years I was one of those people who could not quit using no matter what I tried. I attempted to stuff everything into the God-sized hole addiction created—relationships, exercise, vacations, self-help books, religion, voodoo, switching drugs—but nothing seemed to work. I couldn't live with heroin and I couldn't live without it, and I compromised everything in my life for my addiction: my friends, my family, my future, my dreams. I saw an opportunity to self-destruct and fell into the romance of oblivion. All manifestations of addiction have a romance or some type of reward at their center; otherwise we wouldn't continue using. I became the exact thing I hungered to become, the abandoned, angry boy on the street, unreachable and crazy, oddly falling in love with the promises of death.

I reached a level where I thought fear alone could keep me abstinent, but it was the opposite. I used in order to forget my past, while only creating more bad experiences to further escape from. One cannot stay abstinent for a lifetime based just on the memories of one's painful past and traumas, because recovery, like life, is a daily reprieve. I'm not going to analyze the Twelve Steps or explain why I believe they worked for me, because the truth is that I really don't know how I quit using in the end. There are many elements I've found that altered my spirit when I consciously made a decision to align myself with them. These concepts and words can be found in many spiritual teachings, books, and affirmations used today.

Even though I had been to hundreds of twelve-step meetings and rehabs, the information alone could not keep me in recovery. I had to experience the knowledge by absorbing it into my own being and my own life. We do not get nutrients by staring at an orange; we must take action and eat it in order to obtain its energizing qualities. Sitting and listening to the messages wasn't enough—I had to become active. In the beginning I was an enraged demon, unaware that my emotional system was detoxing into its natural state of being. Anger is a bizarre emotion because it gives us the opposite of what we are truly seeking. When we are angry it makes people back away from us, resulting in more anger and isolation, which in turn feeds and fuels the emotion. I had to find the root of my anger and allow time to heal my spiritual state. It is not only our body and mind that get damaged by addiction—it is our spiritual being.

Over time I came to accept many things I could not change, and began to detach from my imperfections. This in no way released me from the emotion of anger, and if you saw me on a daily basis you would have been able to see a cloud of rage encircling me. I was no longer angry about the Olympics as I came to realize that many other gymnasts came far closer to that goal. It was only an unfulfilled dream. There were certain times I would get cross that I couldn't do something perfectly, or that the outcome didn't happen the way

I had imagined, but I've come to believe that life will always unfold the way it needs to. I think of this belief as true perfection because, once events happen, they are finished and perfect as designed. There are still days when I wish I wasn't gay, but I do my best to try to function as a human being with a different sexual orientation than what sometimes feels socially acceptable. My sexual preference is not my defining characteristic, and I try to remember that I am Joe the human being before Joe the homosexual. I still hate aspects of myself, like my voice and my asthma in the winter—these things are still a battle, but I have uprooted the rage that allowed them to blossom into something unmanageable. I believe the poison guarding my anger was an absence of faith, humility, and self-love. I couldn't transmit anything but darkness to others because we cannot give what we do not have.

In spiritual jargon, the words *surrender* and *acceptance* are common, but I had no actual knowledge of these words and would always place them in a negative context. My damaged ego in addiction became the controller, and the need to be right triumphed over the desire to be in recovery.

The self-destruction I experienced was a blessing wrapped in thorns. It destroyed, dismantled, and dehumanized my ego through catastrophe and suffering. The hell I experienced brought me to a state of complete and utter defeat, giving me humility once I was able to relinquish control. It was here that I processed my own interpretation of acceptance. Acceptance has a rule—if you truly accept something, you have to comply with the boundaries of that acceptance. If I accept that the speed limit is sixty-five miles per hour, then I don't go seventy miles per hour; I accept that I cannot fly, so I don't attempt to. If we apply this rule of acceptance to the realm of addiction, then we have to obey the definition of those terms, which is to surrender. These terms go hand in hand, because when you truly accept something, you surrender to it. Surrendering does not mean admitting defeat; it means joining the winning team. There is an infinite peace in surrendering. When we fight with something or someone, and agree to let it go, a substantial weight is lifted. Our body subconsciously takes a deep sigh of relief, because it feels good to surrender. When we surrender to sleep, isn't it peaceful and healing? When I live these two concepts completely, I surrender and accept that I will have the willingness to abstain from alcohol and other drugs.

In the beginning of my addiction I thought I was having the time of my life. I believed the only escape I could find was through substances that made me feel good. But in the end this escape became a destructive reality, and the only way out of it was recovery. I didn't realize my drug use was stemming from a deep hunger for a spiritual solution. I remember a rehab exercise where we had to describe in detail what we believed drugs brought us: euphoria, love, happiness, comfort, peace, joy, safety, and confidence. Then we were asked to describe the characteristics of people seeking a spiritual life, and the two lists of words were identical. There is a definite connection between drug use and God, as they both give people hope. Per Eckhart Tolle's definition, meditation is a way of becoming removed from thought, and one could say that alcohol and other drugs do the very same. But while both actions have similar results, the consequences and processes are different. In his book *The Power of Now*, Tolle explains it by saying that if we take drugs we go "under" the thought, and if we meditate we go "above" the thought. Meditation elevates the positive mental and physical being, while alcohol and other drugs do the opposite. It's not about being "right" or "wrong," because that concerns the ethics and morals of an individual, and I'm not the judge of "good" or "bad." I don't have a problem with others using drugs, as they can achieve the very aspects I am speaking of—transformation, escape, and euphoria. I believe it's intelligent for a species to seek different levels of being, but a heavy price is paid for using the path of substances, while the path of spiritual solution pays the practitioner.

For many years I was angry with God, or the creator, for my having to live with this affliction. Would I be searching for an escape from my uncomfortable emotions forever? After knowing "heaven," would I ever love life again on its own terms? Then I heard an amazing spiritual teacher explain that addiction or pain is a call from God. At first this idea seemed ridiculous. How and why would God or the universe "call" us? And if the calling came in the form of anything other than tragedy, would we humans listen or change? The message tells us, "I'm here for you. I will hold you and love you. I'm calling because what you are doing isn't working and you have to change." This beautiful call that ultimately leads to our transformation is spiritual evolution. Those of us with addiction have been given the opportunity to spiritually evolve into better, more realized beings. I needed this evolution even before my addiction grew out of control because I was an arrogant asshole. And now that life has beaten the shit out of me and I have received the calling, I have compassion, understanding, humility, patience, willingness, and love.

But this spiritual evolution comes with a great responsibility for me to be a lighthouse for others who are still lost in the darkness. We must be a beacon of light so they can find their way back home. Our lighthouse isn't built by spiritual arrogance, didactics, or leadership, but on pure humility and experience. I will constantly attempt to shine my light, because doing so gives me the ability to connect with others who are suffering. Every day my own light dims, so I go to twelve-step meetings to identify with others and rekindle the flame to spread it further in the world. I cannot keep the fires burning by myself. The fires of the world are our souls kept in the hearts of our bodies. I've come to believe that enlightenment is nothing but the kindling, keeping, and transferring of this fire.

Through the hell of growing pains I have finally gained the compassion and the recovery I have today. But I don't take it for granted, and I know that I could lose it all in one quick decision, as I've done so many times in the past. I stay abstinent for many different reasons, but this is the main one: I actually feel better. Sometimes I think back to sniffing cocaine and watching the sun rise, or nodding out on a heroin cloud, and I cringe and smile at the same time. I dread those memories and know that it is nostalgia, believing the past was better than it actually was. My recovery is a living amends to all the angels I single-handedly destroyed. I stay in recovery as an example to those who aspire to be more, but who are pulled deeper into the addiction cycle, being taken ever further from their dreams and goals. We are all connected by years of "I could have been," "Someday," and "They don't understand." This book is for the sufferer who says, "Someday, I'm going to enter recovery and write a book." Well, I've done that, and he or she can, too. It was simple—incredibly difficult, but simple. I did it just like the program teaches us: by not using just for today and by writing one word at a time.